SUPERSIMPLE
BIOLOGY

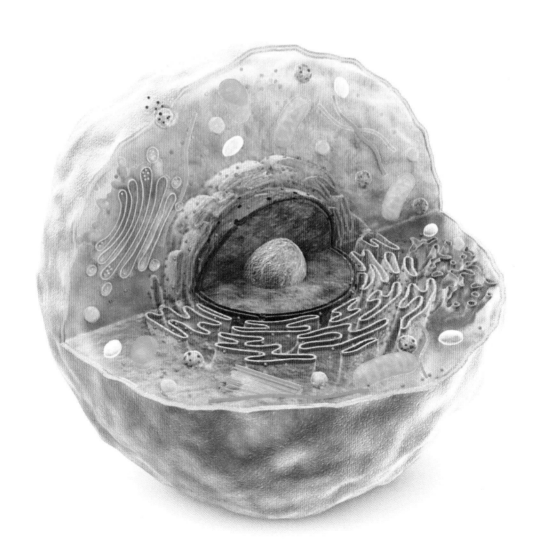

DK Delhi
Senior editor Dharini Ganesh
Senior art editor Shreya Anand
Project editor Bipasha Roy
Project art editors Sanjay Chauhan, Noopur Dalal
Editorial team Sukriti Kapoor, Andrew Korah, Rupa Rao
Assistant art editors Bhavnoor Kaur, Aparajita Sen
Assistant picture researcher Geetika Bhandari
Managing editor Kingshuk Ghoshal
Managing art editor Govind Mittal
Picture research manager Taiyaba Khatoon
Senior DTP designer Vishal Bhatia
DTP designer Nand Kishor Acharya
Pre-production manager Balwant Singh
Production manager Pankaj Sharma

DK London
Senior editors Shaila Brown, Ben Morgan
Senior art editor Samantha Richiardi
US editor Jennette ElNaggar
Illustrators Peter Bull, Arran Lewis
Managing editor Lisa Gillespie
Managing art editor Owen Peyton Jones
Producer, pre-production Kavita Varma, Gillian Reid
Senior producer Meskerem Berhane, Ed Kneafsey
Jacket designer Akiko Kato
Jackets design development manager Sophia MTT
Publisher Andrew Macintyre
Art director Karen Self
Associate publishing director Liz Wheeler
Publishing director Jonathan Metcalf
Authors and consultants Anne Farthing, Susan Kearsey,
Jo Locke, Ben Morgan, Matthew Sison
Special sales & custom publishing manager Michelle Baxter

Smithsonian consultant Darrin Lunde, Supervisory Museum Specialist,
National Museum of Natural History, Smithsonian Institution

This American Edition, 2021
First American Edition, 2020
Published in the United States by DK Publishing
1450 Broadway, Suite 801, New York, NY 10018

A catalog record for this book
is available from the Library of Congress.
ISBN 978-0-7440-4426-3

DK books are available at special discounts when purchased
in bulk for sales promotions, premiums, fund-raising, or educational use.
For details, contact: DK Publishing Special Markets,
1450 Broadway, Suite 801, New York, NY 10018
SpecialSales@dk.com

Printed in China

For the curious
www.dk.com

Smithsonian

Established in 1846, the Smithsonian is the world's largest
museum and research complex, dedicated to public education,
national service, and scholarship in the arts, sciences, and history.
It includes 19 museums and galleries and the National Zoological
Park. The total number of artifacts, works of art, and specimens in
the Smithsonian's collection is estimated at 156 million.

MIX
Paper from
responsible sources
FSC™ C018179

This book was made with Forest Stewardship
Council™ certified paper—one small step in
DK's commitment to a sustainable future.
For more information go to
www.dk.com/our-green-pledge

SUPERSIMPLE
BIOLOGY

THE ULTIMATE BITESIZE STUDY GUIDE

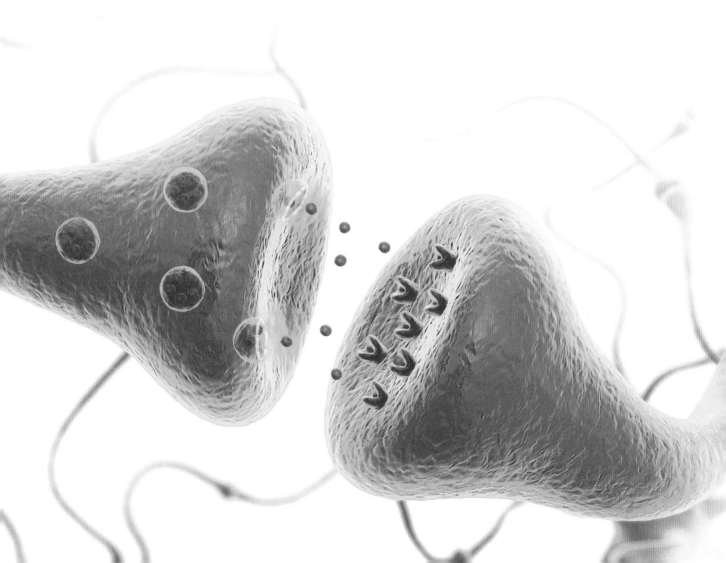

Contents

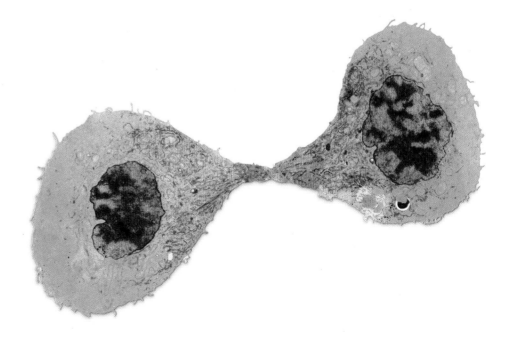

Respiration

Enzymes

Nutrition in Plants

Nutrition in Humans

Transport in Plants

Transport in Animals

Nervous System

Hormones

Reproduction

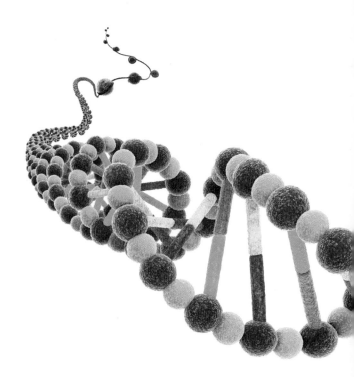

Genetics and Biotechnology

Evolution

Ecology

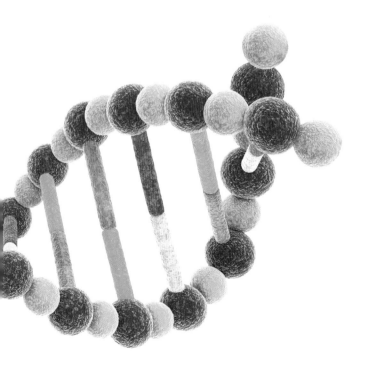

Humans and the Environment

Health

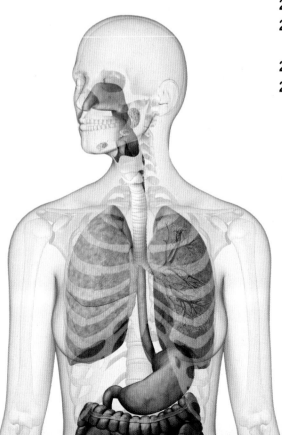

Working Scientifically

How science works

Science is not merely a collection of facts. It is also a way of discovering new facts by having ideas and testing them. Scientists use ideas (hypotheses) to make predictions they can test with experiments. This process of testing ideas with experiments is known as the scientific method.

Key facts

✓ The scientific method involves testing hypotheses with experiments.

✓ An experiment cannot prove a hypothesis is true—it can only support it.

1. Make an observation
The first step in the scientific method is to make an observation. For instance, you might notice that spring bulbs in a garden always flower first at the sunniest end of the garden.

2. Form a hypothesis
The next step is to form a hypothesis—a scientific idea—that might explain the observation. For instance, one possible explanation is that flowers emerge in the sunny spot first because the soil is warmer there.

3. Perform an experiment
You test a hypothesis by carrying out an experiment and collecting evidence. If temperature makes spring bulbs grow faster, you might set up an experiment to grow bulbs of the same plant species in identical soil containers at three different temperatures. To collect reliable evidence, you might grow many bulbs at each temperature. This makes it easier to spot if something has gone wrong, such as a plant not growing normally.

Hyacinth bulb grown at 10°C	**Hyacinth bulb grown at 15°C**	**Hyacinth bulb grown at 20°C**

4. Collect data

Scientists collect results (called data) from an experiment very carefully, often by taking measurements. These may be repeated to make sure they are accurate. The results are often recorded in a table.

	10 °C	15 °C	20 °C
Height in 5 days	0 cm	0 cm	0 cm
Height in 10 days	0 cm	1 cm	2 cm
Height in 15 days	2 cm	5 cm	8 cm
Height in 20 days	5 cm	9 cm	16 cm
Height in 25 days	8 cm	14 cm	20 cm

5. Analyze the results

To make the results easier to analyze, they are often shown on a graph. The graph here shows the average heights of the plants over 25 days. In this case, the results support the hypothesis that warmer temperatures make flowers emerge sooner. The results are considered to be repeatable if the same experiment is carried out several times and similar results are obtained.

6. Repeat the experiment

A single experiment doesn't prove a hypothesis is true—it merely supports it. Scientists usually share their results in scientific journals so that others can repeat the experiment and verify the results. This is known as peer review. After many successful trials, a hypothesis may be accepted as a theory.

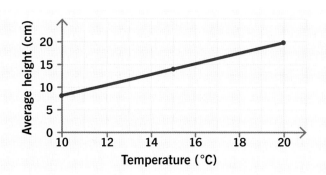

🔍 Fact or theory?

If a scientific theory has been tested many times and has never failed, it might eventually be accepted as a fact. For instance, we now accept the theory that germs spread diseases as a fact. The theory that fossils are the remains of prehistoric organisms is also accepted as a fact. However, no scientific theory or fact can be proven true beyond doubt, as new evidence that a theory can't explain could always come to light.

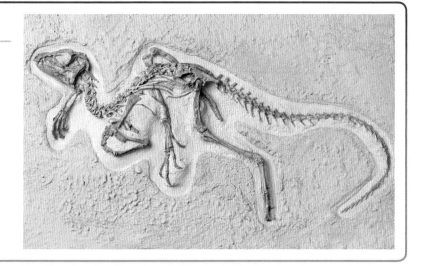

Taking measurements

Many experiments involve taking measurements of physical quantities, such as temperature, volume, and mass. Measurements should be both accurate and precise.

Measuring equipment

Biology experiments often require equipment to measure mass, volume, temperature, time, or length. To ensure a reliable reading when using measuring equipment, it is often wise to repeat a measurement several times and then figure out an average.

A balance is used to measure mass.

Thermometers measure temperature.

A stopwatch measures time.

Measuring cylinders measure volume.

Rulers measure distance.

🔍 Accuracy and precision

The words accurate and precise have slightly different meanings in science. A measurement is accurate if it is very close to the true value being measured. A measurement is precise if repeating the measurement several times produces the same (or a very close) value.

Precise but inaccurate
Imagine you measure the temperature of a beaker of warm water four times with a digital thermometer. All four readings show the same number to two decimal places, but the thermometer is faulty. The readings are precise but inaccurate.

Accurate but not precise
Now imagine you use a different thermometer that isn't faulty, but the readings are all slightly different. Perhaps the tip of the thermometer was in a different patch of water each time. The readings are accurate, but they aren't precise.

Accurate and precise
Finally, you stir the water before taking the temperature, and all four readings are the same and correct. They are accurate and precise. Whenever you take measurements, try to be accurate and precise.

Working with variables

Things that might change during an experiment are called variables. There are three important types of variables: independent variables, dependent variables, and control variables.

Key facts

✓ The three important types of variables in experiments are independent, dependent, and control.

✓ An experiment deliberately changes the independent variable.

✓ The dependent variable is measured to obtain the experiment's results.

Experimental variables

The experiment below measures how quickly an enzyme digests starch in test tubes kept at three different temperatures: hot (60°C), body temperature (37°C), and cold (4°C).

One variable—the independent variable—is deliberately varied in experiments. In this experiment, temperature is the independent variable.

Control variables are variables that are kept constant so they don't affect the dependent variable. In this experiment, the volume and concentration of reactants in each test tube are control variables.

The dependent variable is the variable you measure to get your results. In this experiment, time is the dependent variable because starch is digested at different rates at each temperature.

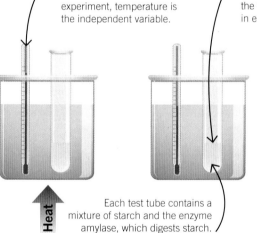

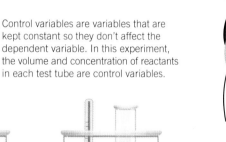

Each test tube contains a mixture of starch and the enzyme amylase, which digests starch.

A water bath maintains a constant temperature in each test tube.

Scientific controls

Some experiments involve what's called a scientific control. This helps rule out the effects of unwanted variables, making the results more reliable. In the example shown here, the control is set up the same as the main test, except the organisms being tested are not included. This reveals whether changes in the dependent variable are caused by the organisms or by other factors.

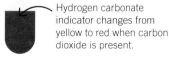

Living organisms

Gauze

Hydrogen carbonate indicator changes from yellow to red when carbon dioxide is present.

This experiment tests for the presence of carbon dioxide produced by respiring organisms. Carbon dioxide changes the indicator solution from yellow to red.

No organisms

Gauze

Hydrogen carbonate indicator

The control is exactly the same but has no living organisms. If the solution in this tube does not change color, any color change in the first test tube must be caused by the organisms.

Scientific models

We often use models to help us understand scientific ideas. Like hypotheses, models can be tested by experiments. There are five main types of scientific models: representational, spatial, descriptive, computational, and mathematical.

Key facts

✓ Models help us understand or describe a scientific idea.

✓ Models can be used to make predictions, which can then be tested by experiments.

✓ The five types of models used in biology are representational, spatial, descriptive, computational, and mathematical.

Representational models
These models use simplified shapes or objects to represent more complex objects in the real world. For instance, a "lock and key" model of an enzyme and the chemicals it acts on helps us understand how enzymes work without using realistic images of the molecules involved.

The substrate molecules fit into an active site on the enzyme molecule.

Enzyme molecule

Spatial models
A spatial model shows the way something is arranged in a three-dimensional space, such as the way carbon, oxygen, and hydrogen atoms are arranged in a molecule.

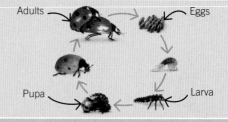

Black spheres represent carbon atoms in a vitamin D molecule.

The red sphere represents an oxygen atom.

White spheres represent hydrogen atoms.

Descriptive models
Descriptive models use words or diagrams to describe something. A diagram explaining the life cycle of a ladybug is an example of a descriptive model.

Adults

Eggs

Pupa

Larva

Computational models
These models use computers to simulate complex processes, such as changes in Earth's climate. This image produced by a NASA climate model predicts maximum summer temperatures in the year 2100. Many places could regularly experience daytime temperatures of more than 45°C (dark red).

Higher temperatures are shown in red.

Cooler areas are shown in blue.

Mathematical models
Mathematical models use math to model processes in the real world. For example, the growth of a population of bacteria in ideal growing conditions can be modeled by a mathematical equation and shown on a graph. The model can be used to predict how many bacteria there will be after a given length of time.

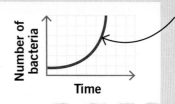

Number of bacteria

Time

The curve shows bacteria numbers doubling with each generation.

Questions in science

Questions are an important part of the scientific process. Good scientific questions are questions that can be tested by experiments or observations. Science sometimes also raises ethical questions. These cannot be answered by experiments and depend on people's opinions.

Key facts

✓ Scientific questions are questions that can be tested.

✓ Some scientific questions cannot be answered yet because not enough evidence is available.

✓ Ethical questions ask whether something is right or wrong and cannot be answered by science. The answer is a matter of opinion.

Intensive farming

Many modern farms use the latest developments in science and technology to maximize how much food they can produce. This practice, known as intensive farming, raises a range of questions. Some are scientific questions that can be answered by collecting evidence— such as when the best time to spray crops is. Others are scientific questions that can't yet be answered or ethical questions that science cannot address.

Tractor spraying fertilizer

Questions raised by intensive farming		
Scientific questions that can be answered	**Scientific questions that can't be answered yet**	**Ethical questions**
What's the best time of year to spray fertilizers on crops?	What effect will climate change have on crop yield?	Should the farm change from intensive farming to organic farming practices?
How might pesticides affect biodiversity?	When will genetic engineering make pesticides unnecessary?	Is growing food more important than protecting the environment?

🔍 Animal welfare

Ethical questions are raised when biologists carry out experiments with animals. In cancer research, for instance, special strains of mice bred to develop cancer automatically are used to study the disease. These mice lead short lives and can suffer. Is it right or wrong to use them? In many countries, strict regulations govern the use of animals in science. Scientists must demonstrate the potential benefit of an experiment to receive a licence, and they must minimize the animals' suffering.

Benefits and risks of science

Developments in science can produce both benefits and risks. For example, low doses of the drug aspirin might protect people from heart attacks, but aspirin can also cause internal bleeding. Is it a good thing to take aspirin or not? To answer such questions, benefits and risks have to be compared.

Key facts

✓ Developments in science and technology can produce benefits and risks.

✓ To answer questions involving risk, it is important to weigh benefits against risks.

Measles vaccine
Measles is a disease that can have serious complications. About one in 1,000–2,000 people with measles suffer a brain infection that can cause permanent harm. The MMR (measles, mumps, rubella) vaccine prevents measles, but it also has risks. One in 10 children develop mild symptoms of measles after vaccination, and about 1 in 24,000 develop a rare complication that requires hospital treatment. However, the risk of harm from an MMR vaccination is much less than from a measles infection.

The MMR vaccine is given by injection.

🔍 Science and society

Scientific developments can have positive as well as negative implications for society. The benefits and risks need to be weighed when decisions are made about how to use science.

Economic implications
Some scientific developments save money but also create problems. For instance, selective breeding has produced fast-growing chickens that make meat cheaper, increasing profits for farmers. But the birds' rapid growth can make them unhealthy or even too heavy to walk.

Environmental implications
Biofuels are fuels made from crops. Growing biofuel crops benefits the environment by reducing emissions from fossil fuels. But it also uses up land that might have been used to grow food, which can lead to food shortages.

Finding the average

Biology experiments often involve collecting data and then figuring out an average to make comparisons. For instance, you might want to compare the average height of plants grown in a greenhouse to plants grown outdoors. There are three types of averages you could use: the mean, median, and mode.

> **Key facts**
>
> ✓ Mean, median, and mode are the three types of averages used in biology.
>
> ✓ The mean is the sum of the values in the data set divided by the number of values.
>
> ✓ The median is the middle value when all values are arranged in order of size.
>
> ✓ The mode is the most frequent value in the data set.

Mean
The most common type of average is the mean. To find the mean, add all the values and divide by the number of values. One disadvantage of the mean is that if some values are unusually large or small, the mean may not represent the midpoint of the data set.

$$\text{Mean} = \frac{15.5 + 20.4 + 10.2 + 15.5 + 18.4 + 16.6 + 8.7}{7} = 15.0 \text{ cm}$$

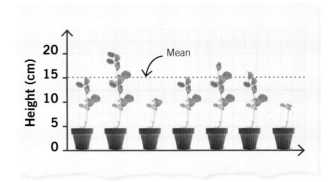

Median
The median is the middle value of a data set when all the values are arranged in order of size. This can give a better idea of the midpoint if there are one or two very low or high values in the set, which would skew the mean.

$$\text{Median} = 15.5 \text{ cm}$$

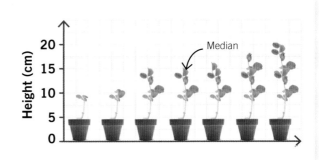

Mode
The mode of a data set is the most common value. The mode is sometimes useful when the mean and median make no sense. For instance, if you wanted to know the average kind of plant grown in a greenhouse, you would use the mode.

$$\text{Mode} = 15.5 \text{ cm}$$

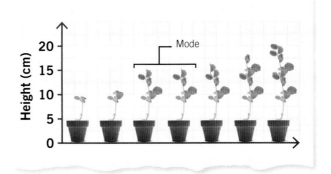

Presenting data

The facts and measurements collected in a science experiment are known as data. Patterns in data are easier to see when the data are displayed in tables or diagrams such as charts and graphs. Choosing which type of chart or graph to use depends on the type of data collected.

⚙ Drawing charts and graphs

Follow these guidelines to help you draw charts and graphs well.

- When drawing a graph, put the independent variable (see page 13) on the x-axis (the horizontal axis) and the dependent variable on the y-axis (the vertical axis).
- Label each axis clearly with the measurement and its unit.

- Use a suitable scale for each measurement so that more than half of each axis is used.
- Use a sharp pencil to mark points clearly and accurately with crosses (x) or circled dots.
- Draw the trend line using a single thin, straight, or curved line that best fits the points.

Pie charts

These charts show percentages in a simple graphic that's easy to understand at a glance. For example, the pie charts here show the percentage of people in a population with different blood groups. Pairs of pie charts make it easy to compare different sets of data quickly.

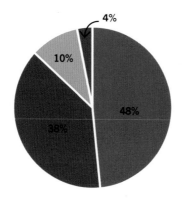

UK blood group distribution

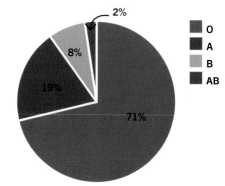

Peru blood group distribution

- O
- A
- B
- AB

Tables

Tables are useful for summarizing data collected in experiments. They can also make it easier to spot errors. For instance, the table on the right, which shows the reaction times of people catching a falling ruler (see page 130), has a possible error.

Age	Measurement on ruler where caught			
	1st try (cm)	2nd try (cm)	3rd try (cm)	Mean (cm)
15	4.7	5.1	4.9	4.9
38	5.5	8.2	5.7	6.5

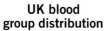

This unusually high value may be an error. The person might not have been ready for the test.

Bar charts

Bar charts are used when the variable on the x-axis is made up of discrete (separate) categories. For example, in this chart, the x-axis shows types of trees. This bar chart is also a frequency chart—a chart in which the y-axis shows the number of times something happened or was counted (in this case, the number of trees with algae growing on them).

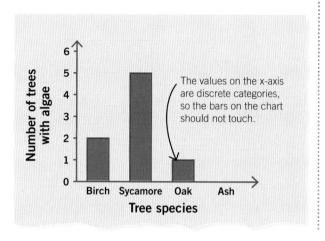

The values on the x-axis are discrete categories, so the bars on the chart should not touch.

Histograms

Histograms are frequency charts in which the variable on the x-axis is continuous (made up of numerical data that can vary across a range). The continuous data is divided into chunks to help reveal patterns. For example, this histogram shows the frequency of different foot lengths in a class of schoolchildren.

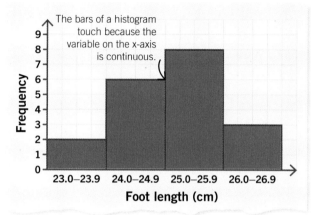

The bars of a histogram touch because the variable on the x-axis is continuous.

Line graphs

A line graph is drawn when the x-axis and y-axis both show numerical values that are continuous rather than discrete. For instance, in the experiment on page 55, a change in the mass of potato pieces is measured after soaking the potato in sugar solutions of varying concentrations. Both variables (potato mass and sugar concentration) are numerical.

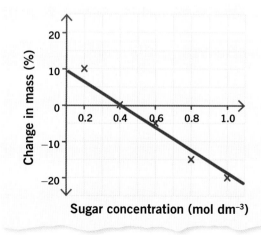

Scatter graphs

Scientists sometimes look for relationships between two independent variables, such as a person's height and the length of their feet. These data are displayed in a scatter graph. A "line of best fit" is then drawn so that about as many points lie above it as below it. The scatter graph here shows a rising trend line (a positive correlation), indicating that as height increases, so does foot length.

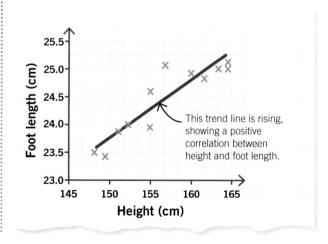

This trend line is rising, showing a positive correlation between height and foot length.

Scientific progress

Scientific methods and theories change over time. For example, the invention of the microscope led to the discovery of microorganisms, which changed the way organisms are classified. As microscopes became more powerful, new discoveries were made, and the classification scheme was changed again.

Key facts

✓ Scientific theories and methods change over time.

✓ The invention of the microscope led to the discovery of cells and microorganisms.

✓ The discoveries led to new theories and new classification systems.

Compound microscope

The compound microscope (a microscope with more than one lens) was invented by placing two magnifying lenses in a tube. A few years later, Italian scientist Francesco Stelluti used one to draw incredibly detailed close-ups of bees.

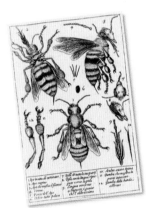

Stelluti's drawings of bees

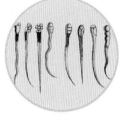

Leeuwenhoek's drawing of sperm cells under a microscope

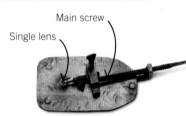

Main screw

Single lens

Replica of Leeuwenhoek's microscope

Discovery of bacteria

Dutch inventor Antonie van Leeuwenhoek learned how to make exceptionally good spherical lenses and improved the magnification of microscopes from 50x to 270x. He discovered many kinds of microorganisms, including bacteria, and he viewed blood and sperm cells.

| 1620 | 1660 | 1665 | 1676 |

Blood capillaries

Using a compound microscope, Italian scientist Marcello Malpighi observed blood coursing through microscopic tubes in the lungs of frogs. He had discovered blood capillaries—vessels that carry blood between arteries and veins. His observation led to the theory that blood circulates through a closed system of vessels.

Early Italian microscope like the one used by Malpighi

The cell

By shining light through very thinly cut slices of plant tissue, English scientist Robert Hooke discovered cells. He published drawings of them in a book, along with drawings of a needle and razor blade, which looked blunt and jagged when viewed through his microscope.

Replica of Hooke's microscope

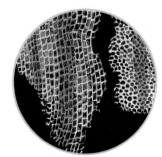

Hooke's drawing of cells

Electron microscopes

Electron microscopes use electron beams rather than light to view specimens. This makes it possible to see objects more than a 1,000 times smaller than can be seen with a light microscope. However, the sample must be free of water, so only dead material can be viewed. There are two main types of electron microscopes.

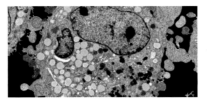

Transmission electron microscopes can magnify images up to 1,000,000 times. The image is made from electrons that pass through the specimen, resulting in a two-dimensional picture of a very thin slice of the specimen.

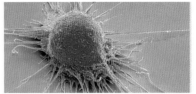

Scanning electron microscopes typically magnify up to 30,000 times. They create images by scattering a beam of electrons off the surface of an object, resulting in a 3-D image. Color may be added artificially

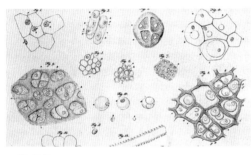

Drawings from Theodor Schwann's 1839 book *Microscopical Investigations*

Ruska with an electron microscope

Cell theory

By the early 19th century, cells had been seen in so many biological specimens that German scientists Theodor Schwann and Matthias Schleiden put forward the theory that the cell is the basic building block of all organisms.

Electron microscope

German scientist Ernst Ruska invented the electron microscope, which uses a beam of electrons instead of light to create images, increasing maximum magnification from 2,000x to 10,000,000x.

1839 **1866** **1931** **1930s**

Illustration of microscopic algae by Ernst Haeckel

Three kingdoms

The discovery of many different kinds of microorganisms inspired German biologist Ernst Haeckel to propose a new way of classifying life. Instead of dividing all organisms into two kingdoms (animals and plants), he created a third kingdom, Protista, for microorganisms.

Eukaryotes and prokaryotes

Using electron microscopes, scientists discovered that bacteria have no nuclei. This led to another new classification system, with all organisms divided into two groups: those with nuclei (eukaryotes) and those without (prokaryotes).

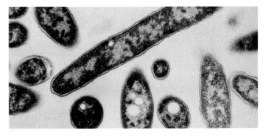

Legionella bacteria seen with a transmission electron microscope

Scientific units

Scientists in most parts of the world use the same system of units for measuring physical quantities such as distance, temperature, mass, and time. The units are known as metric units or SI units (International System of Units).

Standard form

Huge or tiny numbers with lots of zeros are hard to read and so can cause errors. Scientists simplify these numbers by writing them in "standard form," which shows them as small numbers multiplied by powers of ten. For instance, 6,000,000 (6 million) can be written as 6×10^6, and 0.000001 (one millionth) can be written as 1×10^{-6}. To convert to standard form, count how many times the decimal place needs to move right (negative powers) or left (positive powers). In the example below, the decimal place has to move 6 digits right, so the power of ten is 10^{-6}.

$$0.0000012 = 1.2 \times 10^{-6}$$

Measurement	SI unit	Imperial unit
length	meters (m)	feet (ft)
volume	liters (L)	pints (pt)
mass	kilograms (kg)	pounds (lb)
temperature	degrees Celsius (°C)	degrees Fahrenheit (°F)

Base units
The table above shows some of the most common metric units used in biology classes, along with the traditional imperial units they replace.

Using prefixes
Most SI units can be easily changed into larger or smaller units by placing a prefix in front of the unit's name. The prefix stands for a power of ten. For instance, the prefix "kilo" means x 1,000. 1 kilometer = 1,000 meters (1 km = 1 m $\times 10^3$). Using prefixes helps keep the numbers short, which makes calculations easier.

Prefix	Symbol	Multiple of unit	Example	
kilo	k (e.g., km)	x1,000 (x 10^3)		1 kilometer
centi	c (e.g., cm)	x0.01 (x 10^{-2})		1 centimeter
milli	m (e.g., mm)	x0.001 = (x 10^{-3})		1 millimeter
micro	µ (e.g., µm)	x0.000001 (x 10^{-6})		1 micrometer
nano	n (e.g., nm)	x0.000000001 (x 10^{-9})		1 nanometer

Working safely

There are many potential hazards when carrying out science experiments. You need to be aware of these hazards and know how to work safely.

Safety goggles
Always wear safety goggles when working with substances that can harm the eyes, such as liquids that can splash.

Hazardous chemicals
Always check chemicals for hazard warnings and use only as instructed. Use a fume hood when there is a risk of breathing in harmful fumes.

Bunsen burners
When using a Bunsen burner, keep the area around it clear. Tie loose hair back and prevent loose clothing from getting near the flame. Never heat ethanol or other alcohols over an open flame.

Handling glass
Glass equipment can be delicate, so handle it with care and keep it in the center of the workbench. When pushing thin glass tubing into stoppers or rubber hosing, for example, push gently.

Heating water
When using hot water, take care to avoid splashing it on skin. If scalded, run cold water over the skin as soon as possible.

Working with microorganisms
When working with microorganisms, use aseptic techniques (see page 48) to prevent contamination of the culture by microorganisms from the environment. Tape dish lids to their bases, and don't incubate bacteria at temperatures higher than 25°C.

Heating test tubes
If you need to briefly heat material in a test tube, use tongs to hold the test tube. Use a clamp to hold anything that needs heating for longer. Use heat-resistant gloves to handle hot equipment.

Washing hands
Always wash your hands after handling any hazardous chemicals or after working with living organisms or microorganisms.

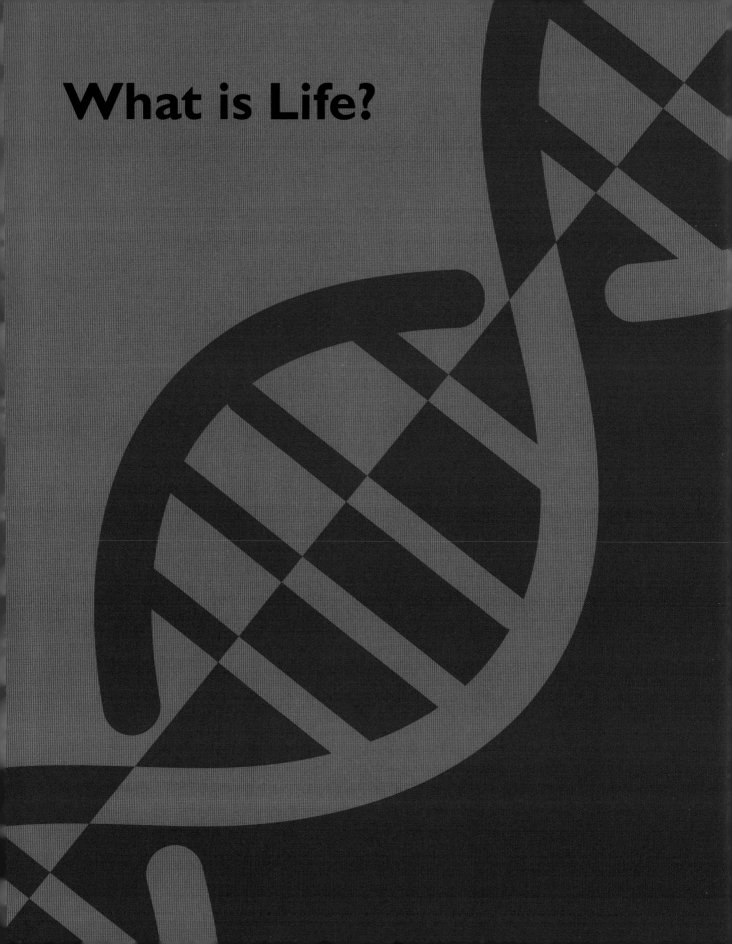

What is Life?

Characteristics of life

Living organisms carry out a set of processes that nonliving things cannot. These processes are the characteristics of life.

Reproduction
Reproduction is the production of offspring. Squash bugs reproduce by laying eggs, but other life forms give birth to live young, or use seeds or spores.

Growth
All organisms can grow, increasing their size permanently—young bugs will shed their skin five times before they are fully grown.

Nutrition
Nutrition is how an organism obtains or makes food. Animals do this by eating food. Plants make their own food from simple chemicals and the energy in sunlight.

Movement
All forms of life can move some or all of their body. Even plants move, often by growth. Squash bugs have jointed legs for walking and wings for flight.

Respiration
All life forms respire, releasing energy from the breakdown of substances to enable all cell processes.

Sensing
All living things can sense changes in their surroundings and respond to them. Many insects use their antennae (feelers) to detect changes around them.

Excretion
All organisms excrete waste substances from their cells. This includes the carbon dioxide that this bug produces during cell respiration.

Life processes
The seven characteristics of life are movement, sensing, nutrition, excretion, respiration, growth, and reproduction.

Viruses

Viruses cannot carry out any of the life process on their own. They can reproduce, but only by invading living cells. Scientists disagree on whether viruses are alive or not.

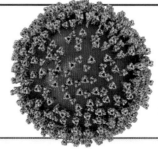

Measles virus

Classification of species

A species is defined as a group of organisms with similar characteristics that can breed with each other to produce fertile offspring. Studies of body structure, body function, and DNA sequences can identify how closely related species are. This is called classification.

Key facts

✓ A species is a group of organisms. Members of the same species can breed to produce fertile offspring.

✓ Classification is the process of putting living organisms into groups.

✓ The binomial name of genus and species is unique for each species.

Linnaean classification

All living things can be classified by placing them into a series of nested categories that fit inside each other, such as species, genus, and family. This is called Linnaean classification because it was devised by the Swedish scientist Carl Linnaeus (1707–1778). Linnaeus divided all living things into only two kingdoms (plants and animals), but today biologists use more.

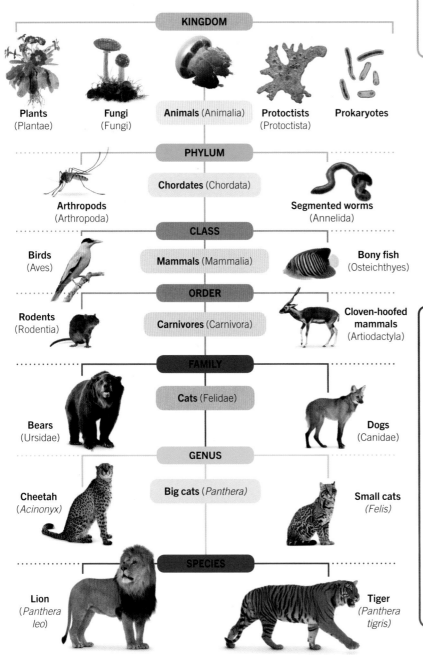

KINGDOM

Plants (Plantae) — Fungi (Fungi) — Animals (Animalia) — Protoctists (Protoctista) — Prokaryotes

PHYLUM

Chordates (Chordata)

Arthropods (Arthropoda) — Segmented worms (Annelida)

CLASS

Mammals (Mammalia)

Birds (Aves) — Bony fish (Osteichthyes)

ORDER

Carnivores (Carnivora)

Rodents (Rodentia) — Cloven-hoofed mammals (Artiodactyla)

FAMILY

Cats (Felidae)

Bears (Ursidae) — Dogs (Canidae)

GENUS

Big cats (*Panthera*)

Cheetah (*Acinonyx*) — Small cats (*Felis*)

SPECIES

Lion (*Panthera leo*) — Tiger (*Panthera tigris*)

Binomial naming

European robin   **American robin**

Every species has a unique scientific name that consists of two parts (binomial)—its genus and species names. For example, the robin that lives in Europe is *Erithacus rubecula*. This distinguishes it from the American robin, *Turdus migratorius*, which is more closely related to European thrushes.

Kingdoms of life

All organisms can be classified into one of several major categories called kingdoms, such as the animal kingdom and the plant kingdom. Biologists have traditionally divided living things into five or six kingdoms.

Key facts

✓ Living things have traditionally been divided into major categories called kingdoms.

✓ Plants make up the plant kingdom, and animals make up the animal kingdom.

✓ In recent years, scientists have devised a new classification scheme based on three groupings called domains.

Kingdoms	Key characteristics	
Plants	● Multicellular organisms ● Cells have a nucleus and cell wall of cellulose ● Chloroplasts allow photosynthesis	
Fungi	● Mostly multicellular organisms ● Cells have a nucleus and cell wall of chitin ● Most species digest plant and animal material and absorb nutrients into their cells	
Animals	● Multicellular organisms ● Cells have a nucleus ● Get nutrients by eating other organisms	
Protoctista	● Mostly single-celled organisms ● Cells have a nucleus ● Some species contain chloroplasts	
Prokaryotes	● Single-celled organisms ● Cells have a simple structure with no nucleus ● Single chromosome; some species have extra DNA in circular plasmids	

🔍 Three domains

DNA studies have allowed scientists to figure out a tree of life showing how the earliest organisms on Earth evolved from a common ancestor, giving rise to the major groups that exist today. This led to a new classification system based on evolutionary relationships. This scheme divides all organisms into three groups called domains. Bacteria and archaeans are prokaryotes. Eukaryotes (such as animals, plants, and fungi) are placed in a domain called Eukarya.

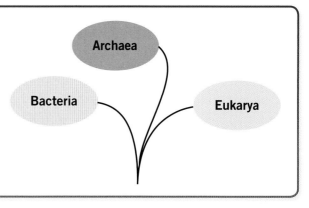

Body organization

The cells that make up a multicellular organism are organized into groups called tissues. Different tissues are joined to form organs, and organs work in groups called organ systems.

Key facts

✓ Bodies have different levels of organization: organ systems, organs, tissues, and cells.

✓ The different levels of organization help multicellular bodies function efficiently.

✓ The main organs of a flowering plant are root, stem, leaf, flower, and fruit.

The digestive system

The human body has several organ systems, including the circulatory system, the nervous system, the respiratory system, and the digestive system. Each system carries out a particular function in the body.

Organ system

Organ systems are made up of a number of organs working together to perform a function. The main function of the digestive system is to break down the complex substances in food so that they are small enough to be absorbed from the intestine into the blood.

Stomach

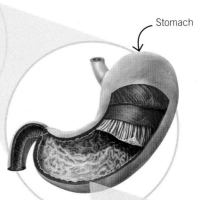

Organ

Each organ in an organ system has a particular function. For example, the stomach helps digest food by releasing enzymes and churning the food to mix it with the enzymes.

🔍 Organization in plants

The structure of a flowering plant is also organized at different levels. The main organs of a plant are the root, stem, leaf, flower, and fruit.

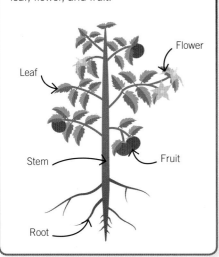

Flower

Leaf

Stem

Fruit

Root

Tissue

Organs are made up of different tissues. A tissue is a group of cells with similar structure and function. For example, the stomach is largely made of muscle tissue that expands and contracts when you eat food.

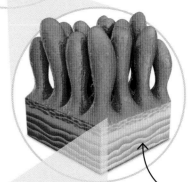

Muscle tissue

Cell

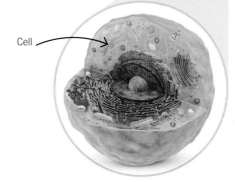

Cell

Cells are the basic structural and functional units of living organisms. Most cells in the body are specialized for one function. For example, some of the epithelial cells in the stomach are specialized to make and release digestive enzymes into the stomach.

Organ systems

Different parts of the human body work together in groups of organs called systems. Each organ system carries out a particular function, such as digestion or transporting substances around the body.

Key facts

✓ Organ systems in the human body are specialized to carry out particular functions.

✓ Each organ system is made up of organs that contribute to the function of that system.

Working parts

Shown here are the organs that make up four different organ systems. Different organ systems work together to make the whole body function.

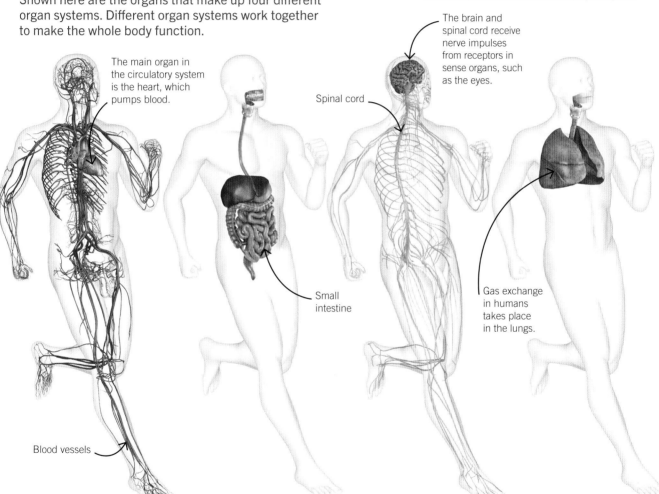

The main organ in the circulatory system is the heart, which pumps blood.

Blood vessels

Small intestine

Spinal cord

The brain and spinal cord receive nerve impulses from receptors in sense organs, such as the eyes.

Gas exchange in humans takes place in the lungs.

Circulatory system
The function of the circulatory system is to transport substances around the body. These substances include oxygen and glucose (needed by cells for respiration) and carbon dioxide and urea (waste products that need to be excreted from the body).

Digestive system
The digestive system breaks down large substances in food, such as fats, carbohydrates, and proteins. The subunits of these substances, such as simple sugars, fatty acids, and amino acids, are then absorbed into the body.

Nervous system
The nervous system is responsible for detecting changes both inside and outside the body. This system then coordinates responses to those changes, such as by causing muscles to move or hormones to be released.

Respiratory system
The respiratory system ensures that every cell in the body receives oxygen and gets rid of the waste product carbon dioxide. Breathing movements, caused by muscles in the rib cage and the diaphragm, move air into and out of the lungs.

Vertebrates

The animal kingdom contains two main subgroups: vertebrates and invertebrates. Vertebrates have backbones and an internal skeleton made of bone or cartilage.

Vertebrate classification

There are seven classes of vertebrates, and each class has certain characteristic features, as shown here.

Mammals

- Give birth to live young
- Feed their young on milk made in mammary glands
- Have hair or fur
- Maintain a constant body temperature

Birds

- Feathers cover body
- Lay hard-shelled eggs
- Maintain a constant body temperature

Reptiles

- Leathery scales cover body
- Lay shelled eggs
- Body temperature usually varies with surroundings

Amphibians

- Lay soft eggs, usually in water
- Young (tadpoles) tend to be a different shape from adults
- Gills, moist skin, or lungs for gas exchange
- Body temperature varies with surroundings

Three classes of fish:

Jawless fish

- Gills for gas exchange
- No bony jaws
- Skeleton of cartilage

Cartilaginous fish

- Gills
- Skeleton of cartilage

Bony fish

- Gills
- Skeleton of bone

🔍 Birds and dinosaurs

Dinosaurs are a group of reptiles that appeared more than 200 million years ago. Evidence from fossils now shows that many dinosaurs had feathers and other characteristics of birds, so birds are believed to have evolved from dinosaurs.

Many dinosaurs had feathers for insulation and display.

Citipati

Invertebrates

More than 95 percent of the animal species on Earth are invertebrates—animals that do not have a backbone. They are usually smaller than vertebrates and have a wide variety of body forms.

Key facts

✓ Invertebrates are animals that do not have a backbone.

✓ Arthropods are invertebrates that have a tough exoskeleton and jointed limbs.

✓ The arthropod group includes myriapods, insects, arachnids, and crustacea.

Arthropod classification

One category (phylum) of invertebrates is the arthropods, which contains several subgroups, as shown here. Arthropods have a tough exoskeleton and jointed limbs and antennae.

Myriapods	**Insects**	**Arachnids**	**Crustacea**
Mostly millipedes and centipedes	Includes bees, wasps, ants, and butterflies	Includes spiders, ticks, and scorpions	Large group including crabs, shrimps, and woodlice

● Body of many similar segments ● Many pairs of legs	● Three main body parts ● Three pairs of jointed legs	● Two main body parts ● Four pairs of jointed legs	● Body consists of head, thorax, and segmented abdomen ● Usually five pairs of legs but may have more

🔍 Insects in the ecosystem

Insects play many important roles in the ecosystem, but one of the most important is pollinating flowering plants. This is a mutualistic relationship—insects get food from the flower (usually nectar), while also helping the plant reproduce by carrying pollen between flowers. This leads to the fertilization of flowers and the formation of seeds.

Butterflies feed on nectar from flowers.

Plants

The plant kingdom is divided into many groups, depending on particular characteristics. Two of the major groups are seed plants and spore plants.

Groups of plants

The type of life cycle helps determine how a plant is classified. Some plants, such as mosses and ferns, grow from tiny structures called spores. Other plants grow from larger, more complex structures called seeds. Some seed plants produce their seeds inside cones, but most produce them in flowers.

Key facts

✓ Two major groups of the plant kingdom are seed plants and spore plants.

✓ Monocots are a group of flowering plants that have parallel veins in their leaves and fibrous roots.

✓ Dicots are a group of flowering plants that have netlike veins and a taproot structure.

✓ Ferns produce spores instead of seeds, and the leaves of ferns are called fronds.

Coniferous plants

Coniferous plants produce their seeds in cones. These plants usually have needlelike leaves. They include some of the tallest trees on the planet.

Needlelike leaves

Cone

Flowering plants

Flowering plants produce seeds in flowers. Some flowering plants are called monocots. These usually have narrow straplike leaves, like grasses and palms. Others are dicots with broader leaves that have a network of veins.

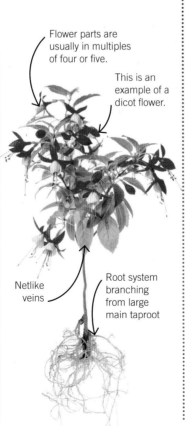

Flower parts are usually in multiples of four or five.

This is an example of a dicot flower.

Netlike veins

Root system branching from large main taproot

Spore plants

Ferns produce their spores in tiny capsules that grow on the underside of their leaves, which are sometimes called fronds.

Spore capsules

Fronds growing straight from the ground

Simple fibrous root system

Evolutionary trees

Different types of organisms were once classified by comparing their physical characteristics, but today we classify species by studying their evolutionary history. This can be shown in an evolutionary tree, which shows how closely related different species are in terms of their characteristics or their DNA.

Key facts

✓ Evolutionary trees show how closely related species are.

✓ Organisms grouped closely together on the tree share more characteristics than those that are farther apart.

✓ Evolutionary trees may be based on DNA, other biochemical molecules, or the physical characteristics of organisms.

Evolutionary tree of mammals

Closely related species are grouped on the same branch in an evolutionary tree, with each fork in a branch representing the common ancestor of two or more groups. This tree shows how some different types of mammals are related to each other.

The farther left a branching point is, the further back in time the common ancestor lived.

Armadillos

Elephants

Hyraxes

Sea cows

Apes, monkeys

Rabbits

Rodents

Others

Armadillos are very different from other mammals, which shows they have no close relatives. The common ancestor they share with other mammals lived a long time ago.

Although they look very different, elephants, hyraxes, and sea cows are grouped together because they have similar DNA, which shows that they share a recent common ancestor.

Rabbits share many features with rodents, such as front teeth specialized for gnawing. There are also many similarities in their DNA. This shows that they share a more recent common ancestor with rodents than with apes and monkeys.

🔍 Evolutionary tree

Evolutionary trees may also be drawn like this, with an approximate time for each of the last common ancestors. This evolutionary tree shows that the common ancestor of all the great apes lived about 13 million years ago.

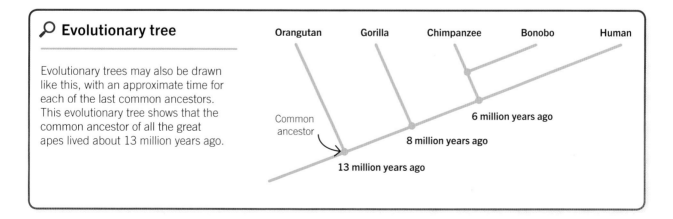

Orangutan Gorilla Chimpanzee Bonobo Human

Common ancestor

6 million years ago

8 million years ago

13 million years ago

Identification keys

Identification keys are used by scientists to identify organisms. Each level of the key asks a question to which the answer is either yes or no, splitting the group of organisms in two. This is called a dichotomous key—dichotomous means to split into two.

📌 **Key facts**

✓ Dichotomous keys can be used to help identify organisms by their features.

✓ At each step of a key, a question is asked that splits the group in two.

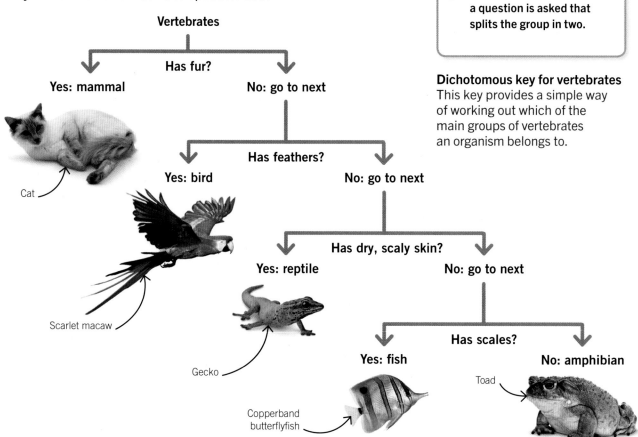

Vertebrates

Has fur?

Yes: mammal

No: go to next

Cat

Has feathers?

Yes: bird

No: go to next

Scarlet macaw

Has dry, scaly skin?

Yes: reptile

No: go to next

Gecko

Has scales?

Yes: fish

No: amphibian

Copperband butterflyfish

Toad

Dichotomous key for vertebrates
This key provides a simple way of working out which of the main groups of vertebrates an organism belongs to.

🔍 Creating a dichotomous key

To create a dichotomous key, list the main features of the organisms you want to identify. Choose features that the organisms always have (for example, number of legs) rather than features that vary with environment (for example, size). Try to find groups that can be separated by yes/no questions. You could start a dichotomous key for these flying organisms using the number of wings or the width of abdomen compared with length (for example, thick or thin).

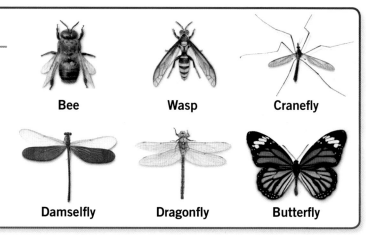

Bee   **Wasp**   **Cranefly**

Damselfly   **Dragonfly**   **Butterfly**

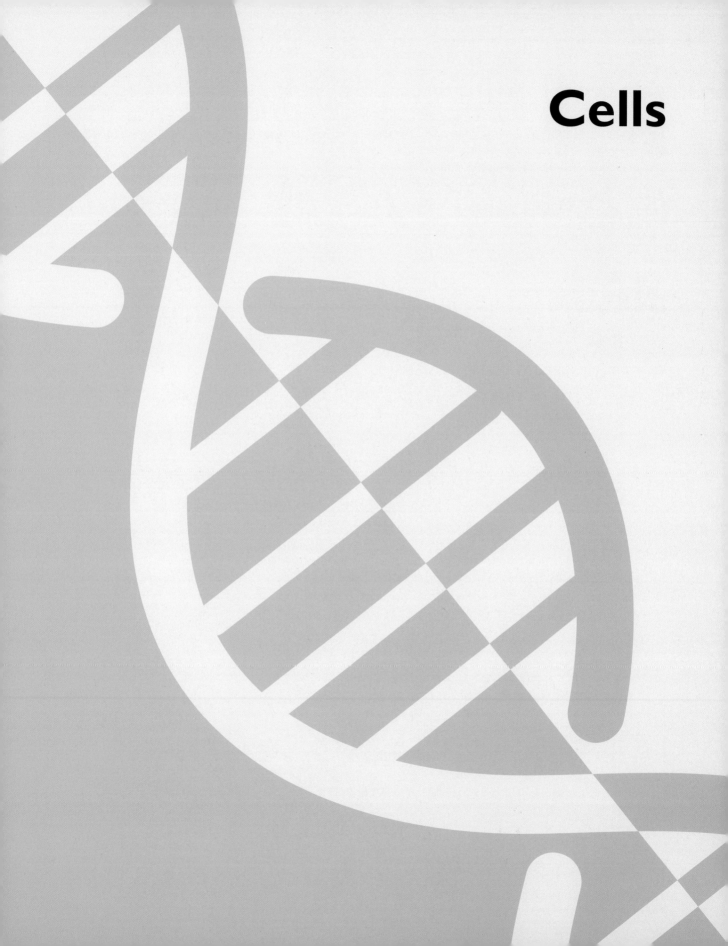

Cells

Animal cells

All living things are made of microscopic building blocks called cells. An organism as complex as a human, for example, is made of trillions of cells working together. Each cell contains smaller structures called organelles, each of which has a specific function.

Key facts

✓ All living things are made of tiny units called cells.

✓ Cells contain smaller structures called organelles.

✓ Most cells in animals are specialized to carry out a particular task.

Human body cell
Many types of cells make up the human body. Like other animal cells, they have an outer covering, or cell membrane, and an internal control center called a nucleus.

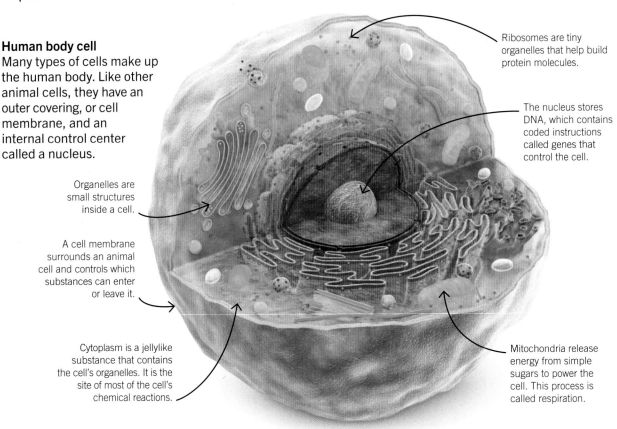

Ribosomes are tiny organelles that help build protein molecules.

The nucleus stores DNA, which contains coded instructions called genes that control the cell.

Organelles are small structures inside a cell.

A cell membrane surrounds an animal cell and controls which substances can enter or leave it.

Cytoplasm is a jellylike substance that contains the cell's organelles. It is the site of most of the cell's chemical reactions.

Mitochondria release energy from simple sugars to power the cell. This process is called respiration.

🔍 Specialized animal cells

As an animal develops from an embryo, its cells multiply and change into many different types of cells—each with a different structure suited to do a specific job.

Long tail for swimming

Sperm cells are produced by male animals. They use their long tail to swim through body fluids to reach female sex cells (eggs).

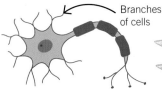

Branches of cells

Nerve cells are specialized to conduct electrical signals. They have tiny branches to connect with other nerve cells.

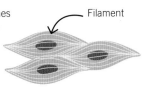

Filament

Muscle cells have filaments that interweave, allowing the cells to contract rapidly and so produce muscle movement.

Plant cells

Like animals, plants are made up of trillions of small units called cells. Plant cells are similar to animal cells, but they have a different structure and contain some organelles not found in animal cells.

Leaf cell
Like most plant cells, leaf cells have a rigid cell wall that surrounds the cell and maintains its shape. Inside the cell is a large fluid-filled structure called a vacuole.

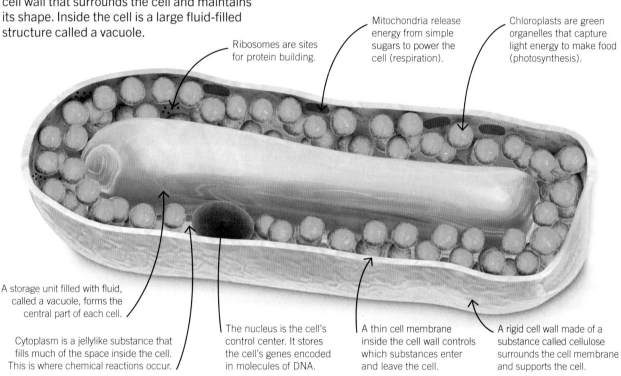

Ribosomes are sites for protein building.

Mitochondria release energy from simple sugars to power the cell (respiration).

Chloroplasts are green organelles that capture light energy to make food (photosynthesis).

A storage unit filled with fluid, called a vacuole, forms the central part of each cell.

Cytoplasm is a jellylike substance that fills much of the space inside the cell. This is where chemical reactions occur.

The nucleus is the cell's control center. It stores the cell's genes encoded in molecules of DNA.

A thin cell membrane inside the cell wall controls which substances enter and leave the cell.

A rigid cell wall made of a substance called cellulose surrounds the cell membrane and supports the cell.

🔍 Specialized plant cells

As a plant grows from a seed, its cells multiply and become specialized for a range of different functions. The plant cells shown here are specialized to transport vital substances, such as water and sugar, around the plant.

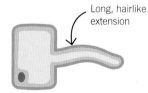

Long, hairlike extension

Root hair cells have long, hairlike extensions that absorb water and minerals from the soil.

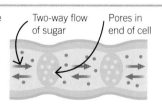

Two-way flow of sugar

Pores in end of cell

Phloem cells transport sugar around the plant. These tubelike cells have porous walls that are joined end-to-end.

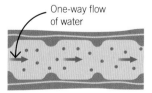

One-way flow of water

Xylem cells carry water up from a plant's roots to its leaves. The cells have open ends that join together to form a tube.

Single-celled organisms

The bodies of plants and animals are made up of billions of cells, but some organisms consist of just one cell. We call these microscopic life forms unicellular (single-celled) organisms. Some kinds of single-celled organisms cause disease in humans.

Key facts

✓ Single-celled organisms consist of one cell.

✓ Some types of single-celled organisms prey on other microscopic life forms.

✓ Some kinds of single-celled organisms can cause disease in humans.

Amoeba
An amoeba is a single-celled organism that lives in water and damp places. It moves by making its cell cytoplasm flow into extensions called pseudopods, causing the cell to change shape.

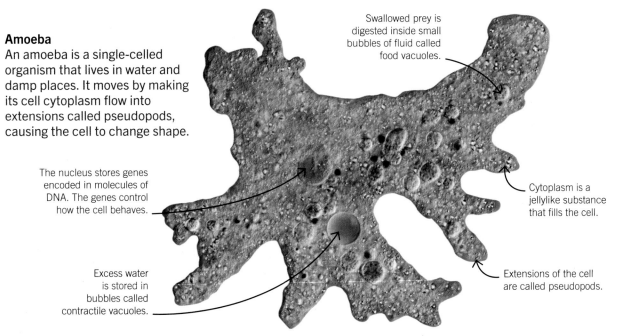

Swallowed prey is digested inside small bubbles of fluid called food vacuoles.

The nucleus stores genes encoded in molecules of DNA. The genes control how the cell behaves.

Cytoplasm is a jellylike substance that fills the cell.

Excess water is stored in bubbles called contractile vacuoles.

Extensions of the cell are called pseudopods.

🔍 Types of single-celled organisms

There are many different types of single-celled organisms. Each type has adaptations to suit its particular way of life.

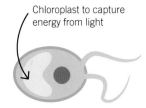

Chloroplast to capture energy from light

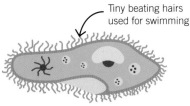

Tiny beating hairs used for swimming

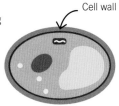

Cell wall

Algae
These are plantlike organisms that can be single-celled or multicellular. *Chlamydomonas* is a single-celled alga. It contains chloroplasts, which are small green organelles that capture energy from sunlight to make food.

Protoctists
Protoctists are a diverse group of organisms that mostly feed by hunting other single-celled organisms. *Paramecium* is a protoctist that lives in water and swims by beating hundreds of tiny hairs on its surface.

Fungi
Yeasts are single-celled fungi. They have a cell wall like plant cells but no chloroplasts. Yeast makes bread rise by making bubbles of carbon dioxide during respiration as it feeds on sugar.

Bacteria

Bacteria are tiny, single-celled life forms that belong to a category of organisms known as prokaryotes. They are very common and live in every kind of habitat, including inside and on the human body.

A protective outer coat called a capsule surrounds a cell wall.

Some bacteria have a long, whiplike extension called a flagellum, which rotates to make them move.

Genes are carried by a closed loop of DNA floating in the cytoplasm.

Some prokaryotic cells also contain small loops of DNA called plasmids.

A cell wall and cell membrane within it surround the cytoplasm.

Inside a bacterium
A typical rod-shaped bacterium has a protective outer capsule, a cell wall, and a thin cell membrane surrounding the cytoplasm.

Prokaryotes and eukaryotes

All organisms are either prokaryotes or eukaryotes. Eukaryotes include organisms such as animals, plants, fungi, and many single-celled organisms. Prokaryotes are tiny, single-celled organisms such as bacteria. While eukaryotic cells have nuclei and membrane-bound organelles, prokaryotic cells are smaller and have no nuclei or membrane-bound organelles. Instead of a nucleus, a prokaryotic cell has a closed loop of DNA that floats in the cytoplasm.

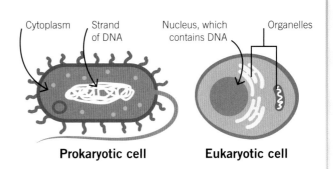

Cytoplasm   Strand of DNA   Nucleus, which contains DNA   Organelles

Prokaryotic cell   **Eukaryotic cell**

Microscopes

Some things are too small to see with the naked eye. Microscopes are instruments that produce magnified images, allowing us to see things as tiny as single cells.

Light microscope
A light microscope uses a series of lenses to magnify a specimen tens or hundreds of times. Light shines through the specimen, so it must be thin and transparent.

Key facts

✓ Microscopes are instruments that produce magnified images.

✓ They are used to study microscopic organisms and living cells.

✓ To produce an image, a light microscope uses light, but an electron microscope uses electron beams.

🔍 Electron microscope

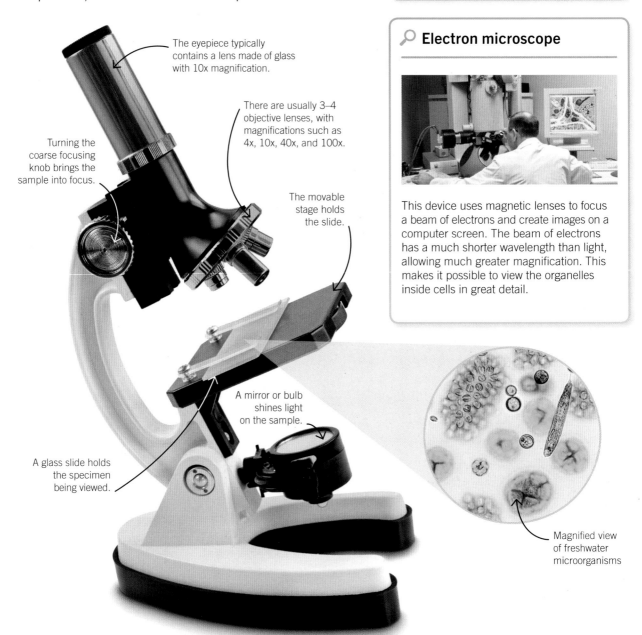

This device uses magnetic lenses to focus a beam of electrons and create images on a computer screen. The beam of electrons has a much shorter wavelength than light, allowing much greater magnification. This makes it possible to view the organelles inside cells in great detail.

The eyepiece typically contains a lens made of glass with 10x magnification.

There are usually 3–4 objective lenses, with magnifications such as 4x, 10x, 40x, and 100x.

Turning the coarse focusing knob brings the sample into focus.

The movable stage holds the slide.

A mirror or bulb shines light on the sample.

A glass slide holds the specimen being viewed.

Magnified view of freshwater microorganisms

Using a microscope

Before using a microscope, you need to prepare your specimen by placing it on a slide. You can then use the microscope's controls to change the magnification and focus the image.

⚙ How to prepare and view a slide

Onion cells make ideal specimens for microscopes because they grow in very thin films that let light shine through them.

1. Dice an onion and use tweezers to peel off a thin film of tissue from the bottom of one piece. Place this tissue on a microscope slide.

2. Using a pipette, add a drop of water to the tissue. Then add a drop of iodine solution, which will darken the cells and make them easier to see.

3. Slowly place a cover slip over the specimen without trapping any air bubbles. Lower the microscope's stage and clip the slide onto it.

4. Select the objective lens with the lowest magnification. Use the coarse adjustment knob to raise the stage to just below the lens.

5. Switch on the light and look through the eyepiece. Now use the coarse adjustment knob to focus the image. Another knob, called the fine adjustment knob, is sometimes used to make small adjustments.

Elodea plant

▤ Calculating magnification

You can calculate the magnification of an image by using the formula below. For example, if a cell is 40 mm wide in a magnified image but the true cell is actually 0.1 mm wide, then:

$$\text{magnification} = \frac{\text{image size}}{\text{true size}} = \frac{40 \text{ mm}}{0.1 \text{ mm}} = 400$$

By rearranging the formula above, you can calculate the true size of the object. For instance, if the magnified image of a plant cell is 20 mm long and the magnification is 100x, then:

$$\text{true size} = \frac{\text{image size}}{\text{magnification}}$$

$$\text{true size} = \frac{20 \text{ mm}}{100} = 0.2 \text{ mm (200 micrometres)}$$

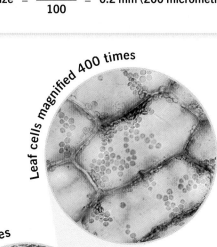

Leaf cells magnified 400 times

Leaf tip magnified 40 times

The cells in a leaf, which are packed together to form tissues, become visible under this magnification.

Magnifying images

You can change how powerfully a microscope magnifies by switching between its different objective lenses. To figure out the total magnification, multiply the power of the eyepiece by the power of the chosen objective lens. For example, if the eyepiece is 10x and the objective lens is 40x, the total magnification is 400x.

Stem cells

Stem cells are cells with the potential to turn into many other kinds of specialized cells in an organism's body. Scientists hope that studying stem cells will lead to new cures for many diseases.

Key facts

- ✓ A stem cell is an unspecialized cell. It has the potential to divide and become one of many other types of cells.
- ✓ Embryonic stem cells can form any type of cell, but adult stem cells have more limited potential.
- ✓ Stem cell research could lead to new treatments for disease, but using embryonic stem cells is controversial.

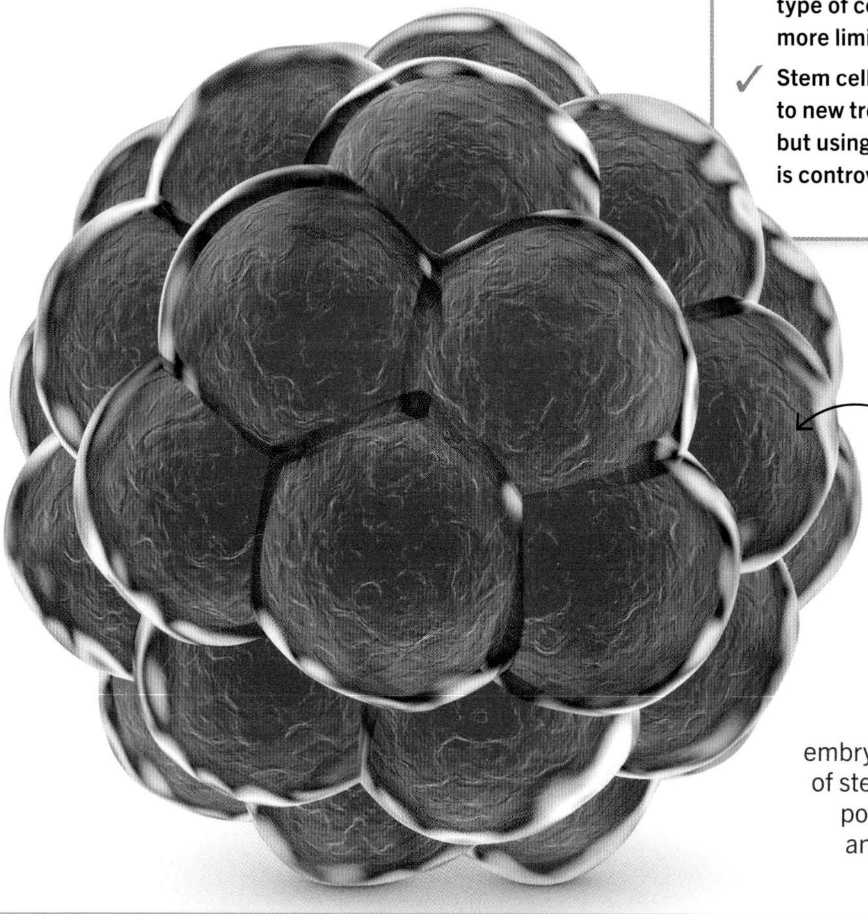

The cells in an embryo are undifferentiated, which means they have not yet formed specialized body cells.

Embryonic stem cells
At a few days old, an animal embryo is nothing more than a ball of stem cells. These cells have the potential to divide and turn into any of the many different kinds of cells in an animal's body.

Stem cell research: pros and cons

Pros

- Stem cells have great potential in medical science. Adult stem cells are already used in bone marrow transplants, which help treat cancers of the blood (leukemia).
- Embryonic stem cells might one day be used to replace faulty cells, such as damaged nerve cells in the spinal cord, to cure conditions such as paralysis.
- Tissue grown from a patient's stem cells is not rejected by the immune system, unlike transplants from a donor.

Cons

- Some people think it is wrong to use human embryos for research or medicine.
- In some countries, embryonic stem cell research is banned.
- Stem cells grown in a laboratory can become infected by viruses, causing disease if they are transplanted into a patient.

Stem cells in animals

A stem cell is a cell that has not yet become specialized. It has the potential to multiply to make more stem cells. These new cells can then differentiate, or become specialized, to serve a particular function, such as carrying oxygen around the body or fighting disease-causing bacteria.

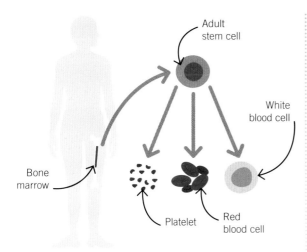

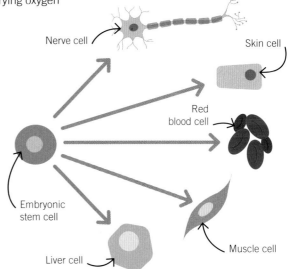

Adult stem cells are found in various parts of the adult human body, such as the bone marrow and intestinal lining. They can divide an unlimited number of times but give rise to only a limited range of cell types, such as blood cells.

Embryonic stem cells are found in embryos in the first few days of development. These cells can develop into all the different specialized cell types that make up the human body.

Stem cells in plants

Plants have clusters of stem cells in parts called meristems. These allow plants to continue growing and changing shape throughout life, unlike animals. Meristems are found in shoot tips, buds, root tips, and around the stem. Plant cuttings that contain meristem tissue can grow into completely new plants.

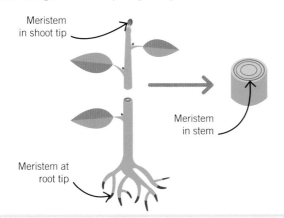

Cuttings grow new roots from meristem tissue in the stem.

Mitosis

The cells in animals and plants divide to produce new cells for growth or to replace cells that are damaged or worn out. This process of dividing to produce genetically identical cells is called mitosis.

Splitting into two

During the last stage of mitosis, the cytoplasm narrows between the two newly formed nuclei and the cell then splits to form two daughter cells. Mitosis produces millions of new cells in the human body every second. Rapidly dividing cells are found in your skin, the roots of your hairs, and in the bone marrow, where new blood cells are made.

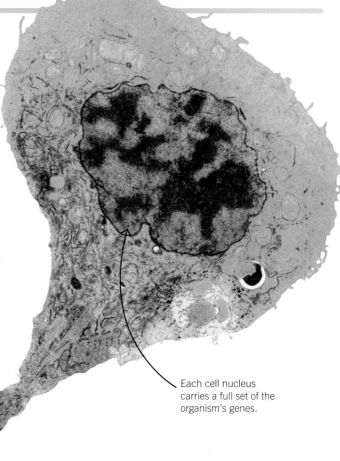

Each cell nucleus carries a full set of the organism's genes.

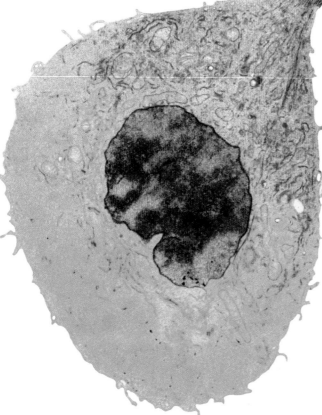

The cytoplasm narrows between the two newly formed nuclei.

How the cell cycle works

Mitosis is the final stage of the cell cycle—the process of cell growth and division. Before mitosis begins, the cell makes a duplicate of all the DNA stored in chromosomes in the nucleus. During mitosis, the duplicate chromosomes are pulled apart. After mitosis, each daughter cell grows and the cell cycle is repeated.

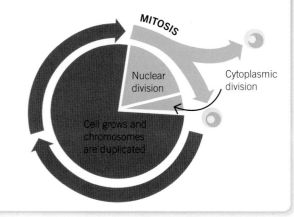

MITOSIS

Nuclear division

Cytoplasmic division

Cell grows and chromosomes are duplicated

Key facts

✓ The process of cell growth and division is called the cell cycle.

✓ Mitosis is the final stage of the cell cycle.

✓ Mitosis produces two genetically identical cells and leaves the number of chromosomes unchanged.

How cells divide

During mitosis, the nucleus of a cell divides to form two new nuclei, with two identical sets of chromosomes. Mitosis has four stages: prophase, metaphase, anaphase, and telophase.

1. Before mitosis

The DNA in a cell is stored in structures called chromosomes in the nucleus. Before mitosis, these look like long, tangled threads.

2. Prophase

The membrane enclosing the nucleus breaks up, and the DNA molecules wind up tightly, making the chromosomes condense (shorten and thicken). The chromosomes look X-shaped because each one is attached to an identical copy. Each side of the X is called a chromatid.

Chromosome

Chromatid

Chromatid

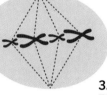

3. Metaphase

The chromosomes are moved to the center of the cell by microscopic fibers (spindle fibers).

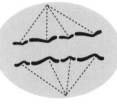

4. Anaphase

The spindle fibers separate each chromosome into chromatids and pull a set of chromatids to each end of the cell.

5. Telophase

Nuclear membranes form around each set of chromatids. The cytoplasm begins to divide (cytokinesis) to form two separate cells.

6. New cells

Two identical daughter cells form and begin to grow. Before the cells are ready to divide again, the chromosomes will be copied to make duplicates of all the cell's genes.

Meiosis

Sexual reproduction involves a special kind of cell division called meiosis, which takes place only in sex organs. It produces sex cells, which have half the usual number of chromosomes but a unique combination of genes.

Key facts

✓ Unlike mitosis, meiosis is a special kind of cell division that produces gametes (sex cells).

✓ After meiosis, cells have half of the usual number of chromosomes.

✓ Meiosis gives each gamete a unique mix of genes, making each offspring different.

Crossing over

In a normal human cell, half of the chromosomes come from the person's mother and half from their father. During meiosis, these maternal and paternal chromosomes pair up and swap random segments of DNA during a process called crossing over.

Segments of DNA are swapped between chromosome pairs.

How meiosis works

Meiosis has two rounds of cell division. First, crossing over takes place and the number of chromosomes is halved. Second, each chromosome is pulled apart into two chromatids, as in mitosis.

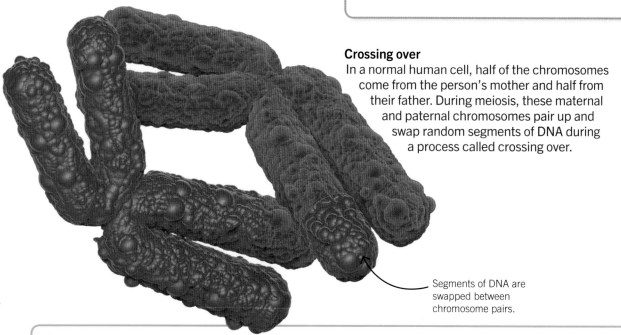

1. Before meiosis begins, the arms of each chromosome duplicate, making the chromosomes X-shaped. Each chromosome now consists of two identical copies, called chromatids.

2. Now X-shaped, maternal and paternal chromosomes pair up. The arms of the paired chromosomes cross over and swap segments of DNA.

3. The cell divides, and one chromosome from each pair goes into each daughter cell. Each chromosome now carries a mixture of genes from the two original parents.

4. A second cell division occurs, separating each chromosome into chromatids.

5. The cells develop into sex cells—sperm and egg cells. Each has half of the usual number of chromosomes. When a sperm joins an egg cell, the usual number will be restored.

Binary fission

Prokaryotic cells such as bacteria divide by a process called binary fission, which means splitting into two. Binary fission is the main way that bacteria reproduce, and it allows them to multiply quickly.

Dividing bacteria
This electron microscope image shows an *E. coli* bacterium dividing. Bacteria have no cell nuclei and usually have just one or two chromosomes. Each chromosome is a closed loop of DNA.

A new cell wall forms between the two cells.

Each daughter cell receives a copy of the original cell's DNA.

⚙ How binary fission works

1. The circular strand of DNA carrying the bacterium's genes is duplicated.

2. The cytoplasm begins to divide and a new cell wall forms in the middle.

3. The two daughter cells separate.

🗐 Calculating number of cells

In ideal growing conditions, bacteria may divide as often as once every 20 minutes, allowing them to multiply in number quickly. If you know how long it takes for a new bacterium to grow and divide (the division time), you can use the formula below to calculate how many bacteria a single cell can produce.

number of cells = 2^n (n = the number of generations)

For example, how many bacteria could a single bacterium produce after 3 hours if the division time is 30 minutes?

1. First calculate how many divisions can fit into 3 hours:

$$n = \frac{180 \text{ minutes}}{30 \text{ minutes}} = 6$$

2. Then work out the number of cells produced:

number of cells = 2^6
= 2 x 2 x 2 x 2 x 2 x 2
= **64**

Culturing bacteria

Bacteria and other microorganisms can be grown and studied in a lab. To prevent contamination of the sample by unwanted microorganisms, it is important to carefully follow a set of procedures known as aseptic techniques.

Agar plates

Bacteria are grown in a nutrient medium—a solution containing all the nutrients they need. This solution is often mixed with hot agar jelly, which is then poured into plates called Petri dishes and allowed to cool and set. The bacteria sample is transferred to the surface of the jelly with an inoculating loop—a loop of wire that is streaked across the surface of the agar. The Petri dish is then kept in a warm place for several days. The individual bacteria from the sample multiply to form visible spots called colonies, each of which contains millions of cells.

Key facts

✓ Bacteria are grown in a culture medium, such as agar jelly.

✓ Bacteria should not be grown at temperatures higher than 25°C.

✓ Aseptic techniques help prevent samples from being contaminated by unwanted microorganisms.

⚙ Aseptic techniques

Aseptic techniques help prevent a culture of microorganisms from being contaminated by unwanted microorganisms from the air, dirt, or your body.

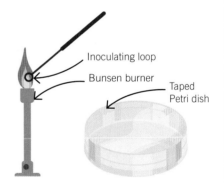

Inoculating loop

Bunsen burner

Taped Petri dish

- Reusable equipment, such as inoculating loops, are sterilized with heat and allowed to cool before use.

- Sterile Petri dishes are opened (as little as possible) near a Bunsen burner flame. The heat of the flame draws air upward, preventing dust from settling on the plate.

- Petri dishes are taped shut to stop microorganisms from getting in.

- After bacteria are transferred to Petri dishes, the dishes are kept upside down to keep condensation from dripping onto the agar.

- Samples of bacteria are cultured at 25°C, a temperature too low for most disease-causing microorganisms to grow.

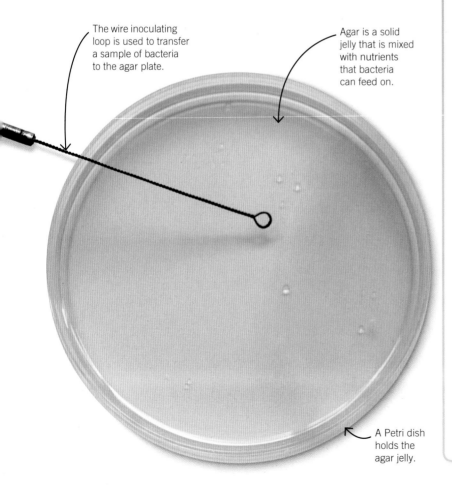

The wire inoculating loop is used to transfer a sample of bacteria to the agar plate.

Agar is a solid jelly that is mixed with nutrients that bacteria can feed on.

A Petri dish holds the agar jelly.

Effect of antibiotics and antiseptics

Antibiotics and antiseptics are chemicals that are harmful to bacteria. This experiment tests the strength of antibiotics by using them to inhibit (slow down) the growth of bacteria on agar plates.

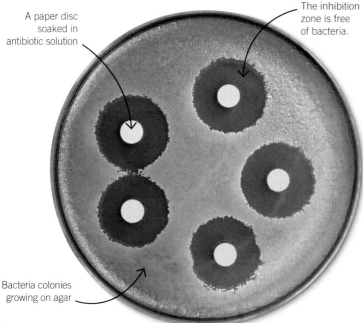

A paper disc soaked in antibiotic solution

The inhibition zone is free of bacteria.

Bacteria colonies growing on agar

Result

The antibiotic on the small discs of paper has seeped into the agar jelly, inhibiting the growth of bacteria and so causing clear circles called inhibition zones. The stronger the antibiotic, the larger the inhibition zone.

Calculating the area of inhibition

The inhibition zones on the agar plate are circular, so you can use the formula for the area of a circle to calculate their size:

$$\textbf{area} = \pi r^2 \quad \text{(where } r \text{ is the radius)}$$

Without opening the dish, use a ruler to measure the diameter of several inhibition zones, and then figure out the average diameter. Halve your result to find the average radius. Put the figure for the average radius into the formula to figure out the answer.

Method

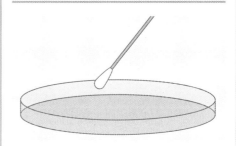

1. Prepared agar plates are covered evenly with bacteria using either a dropping pipette and spreader or a cotton swab.

2. Paper discs that have been soaked in an antibiotic solution are placed on the agar plate.

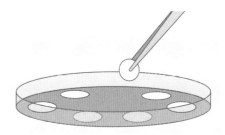

3. Add paper discs soaked in distilled water rather than an antibiotic solution to a second plate. This plate is the control. Any difference between the two plates will be due to the antibiotic, and not the paper.

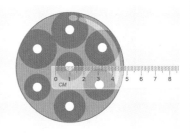

4. Incubate the plates at 25°C for 48 hours, then measure the inhibition zone around each colony.

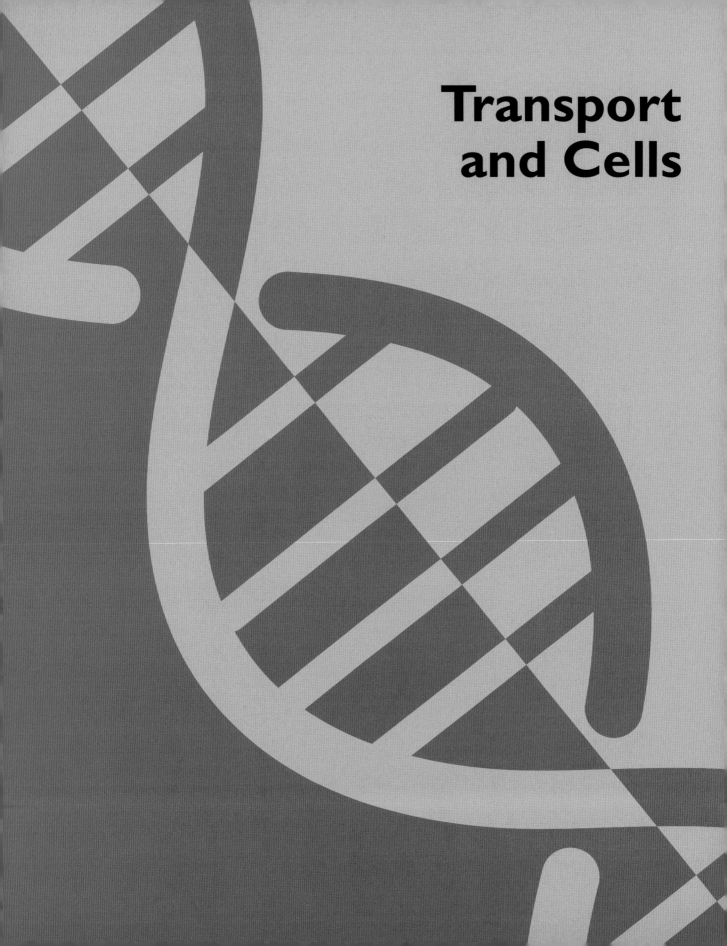

Transport
and Cells

Diffusion

The particles in liquids and gases are continually moving and mingling. As a result, they gradually spread from areas of high concentration to areas of low concentration. This movement is called diffusion. It is the main way that cells exchange substances with their surroundings.

Key facts

✓ Diffusion is the movement of particles from an area of high concentration to an area of low concentration.

✓ Diffusion is the main way cells absorb vital substances and get rid of waste.

✓ Diffusion is a passive process, so it does not require energy.

How diffusion works

Diffusion occurs when there is a difference in concentration of particles between two areas the particles can freely move between. Although the particles move about randomly, over time they become evenly mixed, causing a net (overall) movement from the area of high concentration to the area of low concentration.

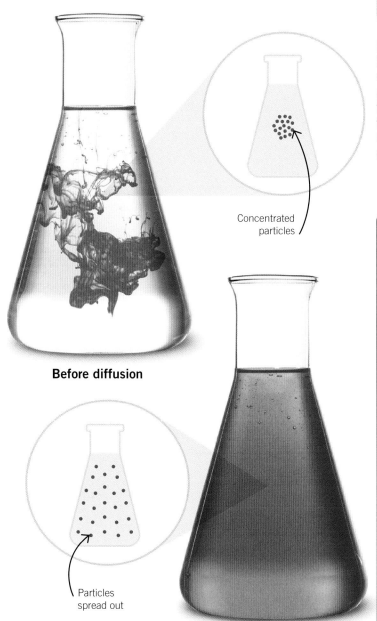

Concentrated particles

Before diffusion

Particles spread out

Fully diffused

🔍 Factors that affect diffusion

Diffusion is the main way that cells absorb substances such as oxygen and get rid of waste such as carbon dioxide. Several factors can speed up or slow down the rate of diffusion.

- **Temperature**
  Particles move faster when they are warmer, so the rate of diffusion speeds up at higher temperatures and slows down at lower temperatures.

- **Concentration gradient**
  The greater the difference in concentration between two places, the faster a substance diffuses between them.

- **Surface area**
  The larger the surface area of a cell or an organ, the faster substances can diffuse into or out of it.

- **Distance**
  The shorter the distance particles have to diffuse, the faster the rate of diffusion. Cell membranes are very thin to allow a high rate of diffusion.

Osmosis

Osmosis is the movement of water across a partially permeable membrane. The water moves from an area with a high water concentration (low solute concentration) to an area with a lower water concentration (high solute concentration), such as a sugar solution.

Partially permeable membrane

A cell's membrane has tiny gaps that allow small molecules such as water to pass freely across, while blocking larger molecules such as sugar. If the liquid inside a cell has a lower concentration of water than the liquid outside it, due to the presence of solutes such as sugar, water molecules will move across the membrane and into the cell. This flow of water is called osmosis.

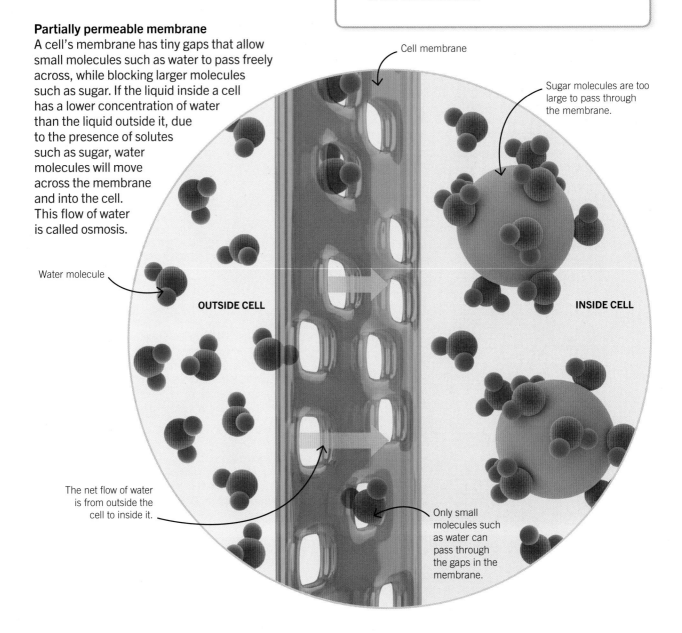

Cell membrane

Sugar molecules are too large to pass through the membrane.

Water molecule

OUTSIDE CELL

INSIDE CELL

The net flow of water is from outside the cell to inside it.

Only small molecules such as water can pass through the gaps in the membrane.

🔍 Osmosis in plants

Plants rely on osmosis to keep their soft tissues rigid so the whole plant stays upright. The fluid in plant cell vacuoles contains dissolved sugars and other solutes, causing the cells to absorb water by osmosis. This keeps cells turgid (plump and firm).

Healthy plant

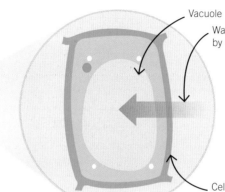

Vacuole

Water drawn in by osmosis

A turgid cell has a large vacuole with lots of water. The vacuole presses outward, putting pressure on the cell wall and making the cell plump.

Cell wall

Wilting plant

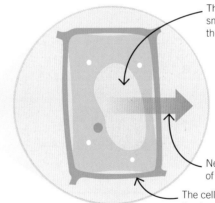

The vacuole is smaller, making the cell less firm.

A flaccid cell has a small vacuole with little water. This makes the cell soft, and the whole plant may soften and wilt.

Net movement of water

The cell loses its plump shape.

Severely wilted plant

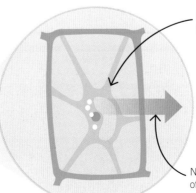

Cytoplasm pulls away from the cell wall.

A plasmolyzed cell has lost so much water by osmosis that its cytoplasm separates from the cell wall. If the plant is not watered, the cell will die.

Net movement of water

Investigating osmosis

You can study the effect of osmosis on plant cells by placing pieces of potato in beakers of sugar solution of varying strength.

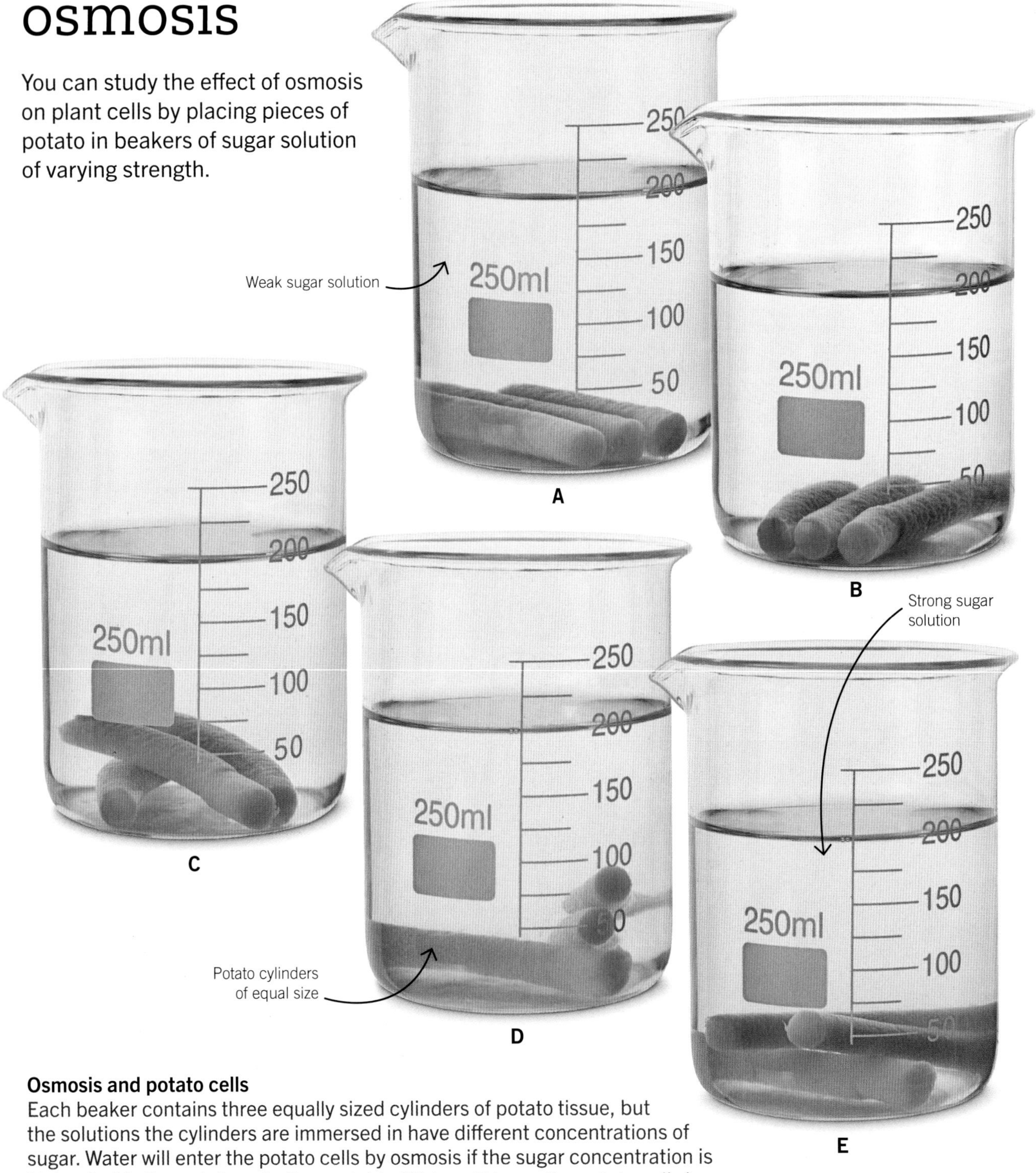

Weak sugar solution

250ml

A

250ml

B

Strong sugar solution

250ml

C

250ml

D

Potato cylinders of equal size

250ml

E

Osmosis and potato cells

Each beaker contains three equally sized cylinders of potato tissue, but the solutions the cylinders are immersed in have different concentrations of sugar. Water will enter the potato cells by osmosis if the sugar concentration is higher inside the potato cells than outside. Water will leave the potato cells by osmosis if the sugar concentration is lower inside the cells than outside.

⚙ Method

1. Label five beakers A to E and put 200 ml of water in each one.

200 ml of water in every beaker

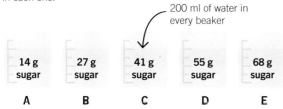

14 g sugar	27 g sugar	41 g sugar	55 g sugar	68 g sugar
A	B	C	D	E

2. Dissolve table sugar (sucrose) in each beaker, following the quantities shown above.

3. Use a cork borer to cut 15 equally long cylinders of potato tissue and arrange these into five groups of three, labeled A to E.

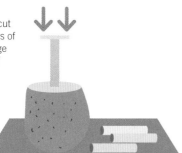

4. Weigh each group and write down the mass.

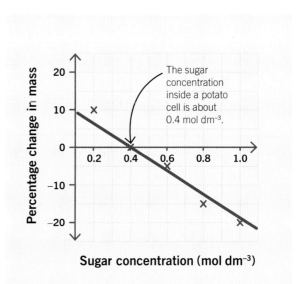

5. Place each group of three cylinders in its beaker and leave for an hour.

6. Remove the potato cylinders, pat dry with tissue paper, and weigh each group again. Write down the results.

7. For each group, figure out the percentage change in mass:

$$\text{percentage (\%) change in mass} = \frac{\text{final mass - original mass}}{\text{original mass}} \times 100$$

🗐 Results

Record your results in a table. The experiment allows you to estimate the concentration of sugar in potato cells by drawing a graph. Make the y-axis the percentage change in mass and the x-axis sugar concentration in moles per liter ($mol\ dm^{-3}$). Mark a cross on the graph for each group of potatoes. Then draw a line of best fit through the points. The point where the line crosses the x axis tells you the sugar concentration that causes no net movement of water into or out of the potato cells. This is equal to the sugar concentration inside the cells.

Table of results	A	B	C	D	E
Sugar concentration ($mol\ dm^{-3}$)	0.2	0.4	0.6	0.8	1.0
Percentage change in mass	10	0	−5	−15	−20

The sugar concentration inside a potato cell is about 0.4 $mol\ dm^{-3}$.

Sugar concentration ($mol\ dm^{-3}$)

Active transport

Living cells can't use diffusion to obtain substances that are more concentrated inside the cell than outside. To absorb such substances, cells use a system called active transport, which uses energy released by cellular respiration.

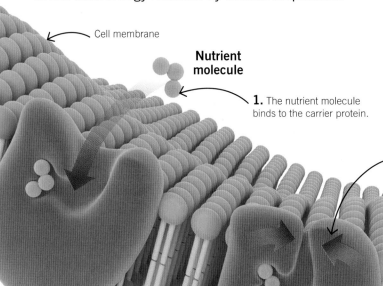

Cell membrane

Nutrient molecule

1. The nutrient molecule binds to the carrier protein.

2. The carrier protein receives energy and begins to change its shape.

Carrier protein

3. The molecule is released inside the cell.

Carrier proteins
Active transport is carried out by protein molecules embedded in the cell's membrane. These "carrier proteins" bind to molecules the cell needs. Energy released by cellular respiration causes the carrier protein to change its shape or rotate, which moves the transported molecule inside the cell.

Root hair cells

Active transport is an important way for animals and plants to obtain nutrients that might be in short supply. Plants obtain minerals from the water in soil, but the concentration of these minerals is often lower in soil moisture than in plant cells. As a result, microscopic hair cells (right) on the roots use active transport to absorb these minerals. The cells lining the human intestine also use active transport to absorb nutrients such as sugars.

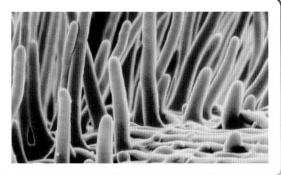

Surface area and volume

The ability of a cell or an organism to exchange vital substances or heat with its surroundings depends on its surface-area-to-volume ratio. Small objects have a larger surface-area-to-volume ratio than large objects.

📌 **Key facts**

✓ Small organisms have a large surface-area-to-volume ratio, so they absorb nutrients quickly by diffusion.

✓ Large organisms have a small surface-area-to-volume ratio, so they need special adaptations to absorb nutrients.

Surface area and temperature

Small animals such as mice have a large surface area relative to their volume, so they lose heat quickly. To make up for this, they eat high-energy food and have dense fur to preserve warmth. Large animals such as elephants, however, have a small surface-area-to-volume ratio. They lose heat slowly, so they don't need fur and can survive on low-energy food.

Large ears increase the surface area of skin and so help elephants cool down in hot weather.

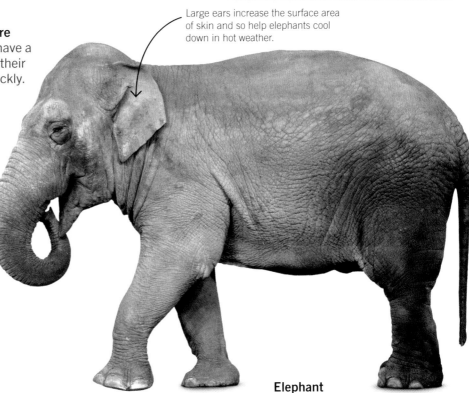

Mouse

Elephant

🔍 **Surface-area-to-volume ratio**

The surface area of an object is the total area of all its outer surfaces. The volume of an object is the amount of space it takes up. The ratio of these two numbers is the surface-area-to-volume ratio.

Small objects have a high surface-area-to-volume ratio.

surface = 3^2 x 6 = 54
volume = 3^3 = 27
surface : volume = 54 : 27
= 2

surface = 2^2 x 6 = 24
volume = 2^3 = 8
surface : volume = 24 : 8
= 3

surface = 1^2 x 6 = 6
volume = 1^3 = 1
surface : volume = 6 : 1
= 6

Exchange and transport

Large multicellular organisms, such as humans, don't have a sufficiently large surface-area-to-volume ratio (see page 57) to absorb vital substances through their body surface by diffusion. Instead, these organisms have special adaptations to increase the surface area of the parts of the body that absorb substances, as well as transport systems to carry substances around the organism.

Key facts

✓ Large organisms need exchange surfaces and transport systems to obtain vital substances such as oxygen and nutrients.

✓ Exchange surfaces have a large surface area to maximize the rate of diffusion.

✓ Transport systems carry vital substances around the bodies of animals and plants.

The small intestine is very long to create a large internal surface area.

Thousands of projections called villi give the intestine a large surface area.

Small intestine
The human small intestine needs a large surface area to absorb nutrients from food efficiently. To maximize its surface area, its inner surface is covered by thousands of fingerlike projections called villi.

🔍 Exchange surfaces and transport systems

Exchange surfaces are parts of organisms that have a high surface area to absorb vital nutrients or get rid of waste. Transport systems are tissues and organs that transport substances around an animal or a plant.

Water flows through a fish's gills.

Gills are organs that aquatic animals use to absorb oxygen from water. They have a folded structure to maximize the surface area in contact with water.

Airways carry oxygen into the lungs.

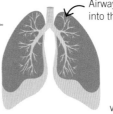

Lungs are organs that air-breathing animals use to obtain oxygen and get rid of carbon dioxide. They have thousands of airways ending in air pockets called alveoli, which create a huge surface area for gas exchange.

Heart

Blood vessels

The blood vessels and heart make up the circulatory system of an animal. Blood flows through this system of tubes, delivering oxygen and nutrients to cells, which absorb these substances by diffusion.

Respiration

Respiration

Every organism needs energy, and this comes from respiration—a chemical reaction that happens all the time inside the cells of all organisms. Respiration is an exothermic reaction, which means it releases stored chemical energy. The energy is used to fuel all sorts of living processes.

Key facts

✓ Respiration is a chemical reaction in cells controlled by enzymes.

✓ Respiration is an exothermic reaction (energy is transferred to surroundings).

✓ The energy released by respiration is stored in a chemical called ATP (adenosine triphosphate).

Energy from food
During respiration, chemical reactions controlled by enzymes break down the chemical bonds in food molecules such as glucose. This releases the energy, which is transferred to a chemical called ATP (adenosine triphosphate). ATP drives many of the processes inside living cells.

Energy from respiration powers muscle contraction.

Movement
Energy is needed to make muscle cells contract so that animals can walk, run, or leap. Some muscles work all the time, such as those that make your heart beat.

Penguins use a considerable amount of energy to maintain a high body temperature.

Keeping warm
Mammals and birds use energy to keep their body temperature constant. When they respire, heat is released and transported around the body through the blood. The rate of respiration increases in colder environments to help maintain body temperature.

Growth
Energy is needed for growth and repair of organisms. Caterpillars grow very quickly. They rely on energy from respiration to create new cells for this growth throughout their life cycle.

Root hairs

Transport of substances
In plants, minerals such as nitrates from the soil are transferred to the root hair cells by active transport—a process that requires energy (see page 56).

Eagles have excellent vision—they can spot prey up to five times further than we can.

Building large molecules
All cells need to make large molecules by joining smaller units together. Trees make large proteins by using small amino acids. Building these large molecules requires energy from respiration.

Relaying information
Nerve signals (impulses) relay information to the brain, allowing animals to respond instantly to changes in the environment—from spotting prey to being alert to danger. Respiration provides the energy needed to send these nerve signals from one part of the body to another within a few milliseconds.

🔍 ATP molecule

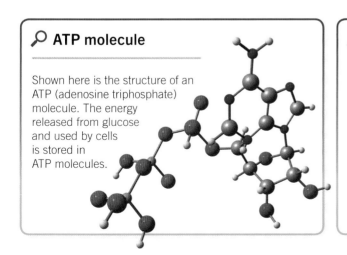

Shown here is the structure of an ATP (adenosine triphosphate) molecule. The energy released from glucose and used by cells is stored in ATP molecules.

🔍 Respiration in plants

During daylight hours, plants make their own food (glucose and starch) through the process of photosynthesis, which needs light energy from the sun, carbon dioxide, and water (see page 76). At night, photosynthesis stops, so the plant breaks down food by respiration—a process that happens both day and night.

Investigating the rate of respiration

An organism respires at different rates depending on certain factors, such as temperature. You can investigate the rate of respiration by measuring how much oxygen an organism takes in from the air.

Effect of temperature on respiration

Germinating seeds respire to provide energy for growth. An apparatus called a respirometer is used to measure how quickly seeds respire at different temperatures.

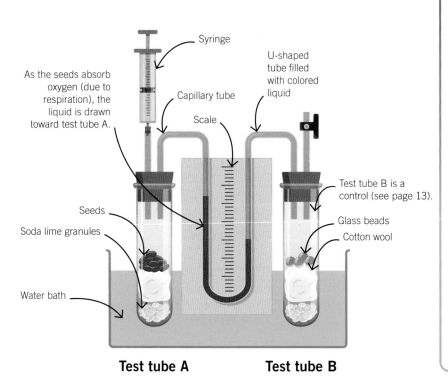

As the seeds absorb oxygen (due to respiration), the liquid is drawn toward test tube A.

Syringe

Capillary tube

Scale

U-shaped tube filled with colored liquid

Test tube B is a control (see page 13).

Glass beads

Cotton wool

Seeds

Soda lime granules

Water bath

Test tube A   **Test tube B**

(see page 13).

📑 Method

1. Place the apparatus in a water bath at 10°C.

2. Add soda lime granules to both the test tubes and cover the granules with cotton wool to protect the seeds from the corrosive soda lime. Soda lime is used because it absorbs carbon dioxide released by the respiring organism, so the organism's oxygen intake (consumption) can be measured.

3. Place some seeds on top of the cotton wool in test tube A and some glass beads of the same mass in test tube B—this is to check that the movement of the fluid in the respirometer is caused by the organism and not by other factors.

4. Using a syringe, fill the U-shaped tube to a chosen level with a colored liquid. Mark the position of the liquid and leave the apparatus for 5 minutes. Then use the scale to measure the distance the liquid has traveled.

5. Repeat the experiment at different temperatures (15°C, 20°C, and 25°C) to compare the rate of respiration. The faster the rate of respiration, the greater the distance the colored liquid moves in a fixed period of time.

📑 Calculating the rate of respiration

The distance traveled by the liquid in the tube represents the volume of oxygen taken in by the organism. This can then be used in the formula below to calculate the rate at which the organism is respiring.

$$\text{rate of respiration} = \frac{\text{volume of oxygen intake (cm}^3)}{\text{time (min)}}$$

Example: A marine biologist measured the rate of respiration of an iguana at different temperatures. She found that the iguana took in 420 cm³ of oxygen in 60 minutes, so the rate of respiration is:

$$\text{rate of respiration} = \frac{420 \text{ cm}^3}{60 \text{ min}} = 7 \text{ cm}^3/\text{min}$$

Aerobic respiration

Aerobic respiration involves a series of enzyme-controlled reactions that take place constantly in every plant cell and animal cell. Aerobic respiration breaks down glucose to release a continuous supply of energy. It is more efficient at transferring energy than anaerobic respiration (see pages 64–65).

Key facts

✓ Aerobic respiration is respiration using oxygen. It is an exothermic reaction (releases energy into the environment).

✓ Glucose and oxygen react inside the mitochondria to produce carbon dioxide, water, and energy.

✓ Aerobic respiration is more efficient at transferring energy than anaerobic respiration.

Mitochondria
Most of the chemical reactions in aerobic respiration take place inside tiny cell structures called mitochondria (singular mitochondrion). A cell that uses a lot of energy, such as a muscle cell, contains a large number of mitochondria.

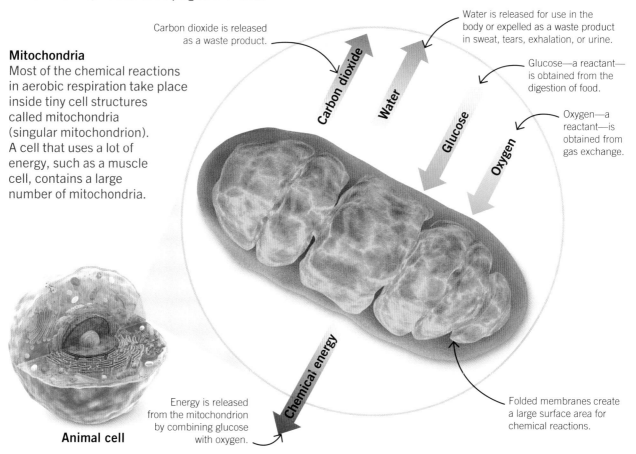

Carbon dioxide is released as a waste product.

Water is released for use in the body or expelled as a waste product in sweat, tears, exhalation, or urine.

Glucose—a reactant—is obtained from the digestion of food.

Oxygen—a reactant—is obtained from gas exchange.

Folded membranes create a large surface area for chemical reactions.

Energy is released from the mitochondrion by combining glucose with oxygen.

Animal cell

Equation for aerobic respiration

Shown here in symbols and words is the equation for aerobic respiration. The equation represents the chemical reaction that releases energy from the glucose.

$$C_6H_{12}O_6 + 6O_2 \longrightarrow 6CO_2 + 6H_2O \; (+ \text{energy})$$

$$\text{glucose} + \text{oxygen} \longrightarrow \text{carbon dioxide} + \text{water} \; (+ \text{energy})$$

Anaerobic respiration

Anaerobic respiration occurs when glucose is partly broken down to release energy without using oxygen. Although it releases far less energy than aerobic respiration (see page 63), it can be used in special circumstances—such as to get a bigger burst of energy during strenuous exercise or when oxygen levels are low.

Key facts

✓ Anaerobic respiration is respiration without oxygen.

✓ Glucose does not completely break down and produces lactic acid in animal cells or carbon dioxide and ethanol in plant and yeast cells.

✓ Less energy is released from each glucose molecule compared to aerobic respiration.

Respiration in working muscles

When muscles work hard, such as during a race, they contract more and so need more energy. This is released from respiration. Much of it comes from aerobic respiration, but some anaerobic respiration also takes place to provide an extra boost of energy.

Getting ready
At the start of the race, the lung and heart supply enough oxygen to the whole body for use in aerobic respiration.

Before activity, muscles are free of lactic acid.

When anaerobic respiration occurs, its waste product— lactic acid—builds up in muscle cells.

Equation for anaerobic respiration

The equation for anaerobic respiration in animals is:

$$C_6H_{12}O_6 \longrightarrow 2C_3H_6O_3$$

glucose $\longrightarrow$ lactic acid (+ energy)

The equation for anaerobic respiration in plants and yeast is:

$$C_6H_{12}O_6 \longrightarrow 2C_2H_5OH + 2CO_2$$

glucose $\longrightarrow$ ethanol + carbon dioxide (+ energy)

Running
During the race, the heart beats faster and breathing speeds up so more oxygen is delivered to muscles for more aerobic respiration. But soon, the heart and lungs are working as fast as they can. Some extra energy then comes from anaerobic respiration, which doesn't need any more oxygen, but produces waste lactic acid.

🔍 Anaerobic respiration in other organisms

Anaerobic respiration happens differently in animal and plant cells. Unlike animals, which produce lactic acid as a waste product during anaerobic respiration, plants and yeast (a type of fungus) produce ethanol and carbon dioxide as wastes when they respire anaerobically.

Carbon dioxide from yeast cells makes the bread rise.

Yeast
In some microorganisms, such as yeast, glucose is broken down into carbon dioxide and ethanol. Anaerobic respiration in yeast is used for making bread and alcoholic drinks—a process called fermentation.

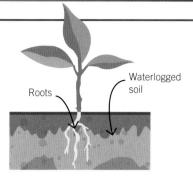

Roots

Waterlogged soil

Plant roots
If soil becomes waterlogged, it reduces the amount of oxygen available for plant root cells. The root cells have to respire anaerobically, producing carbon dioxide and ethanol instead of lactic acid.

Recovery
After the race, the muscles stop working so less energy is needed and anaerobic respiration stops. But the heart and lungs keep working hard for a while—the extra oxygen they deliver now being used to break down the lactic acid.

Oxygen debt
For a short while after the race, the runner continues to take deep breaths until the oxygen debt has been repaid. This is the amount of oxygen needed to break down the lactic acid, producing carbon dioxide and water.

The accumulated lactic acid can sometimes cause cramps, making the muscles painful to move.

The lactic acid level starts to fall.

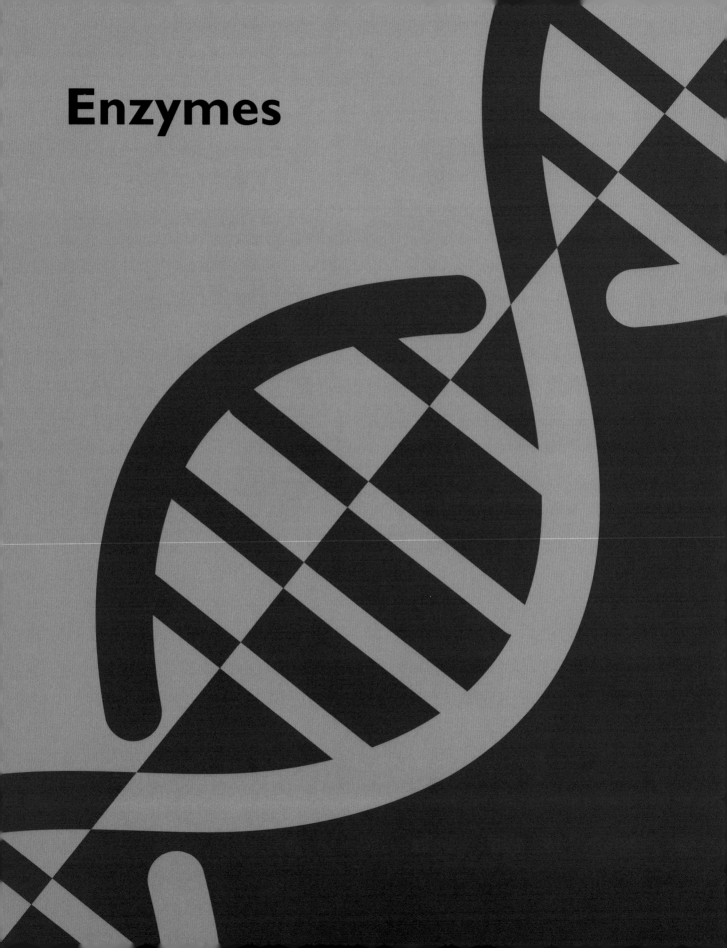

Enzymes

Enzymes

Enzymes are proteins that organisms produce to speed up chemical reactions—from digestion to photosynthesis. Some enzymes break down large substrate molecules into smaller ones, while others join small molecules to form larger ones. Enzymes are catalysts—chemicals that change the rate of a reaction without being changed themselves.

Lock-and-key model

Each enzyme has a unique shape that fits a specific substrate (a chemical changed by the enzyme). This is known as the lock-and-key model. Each type of enzyme can catalyze only one reaction, so the substrate has to fit into the enzyme's active site.

Key facts

✓ Enzymes are large, complex protein molecules.

✓ Enzymes are catalysts— chemicals that change the rate of a chemical reaction without being changed themselves.

✓ The chemicals changed by enzymes are called substrates.

✓ Substrates fit into the active sites of their enzymes because they have complementary shapes.

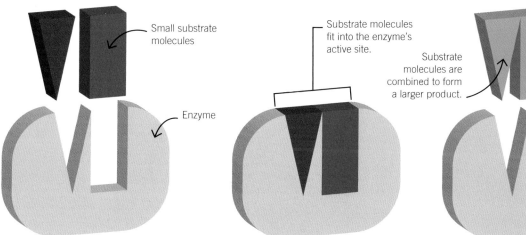

Small substrate molecules

Enzyme

Substrate molecules fit into the enzyme's active site.

Substrate molecules are combined to form a larger product.

Enzyme is unchanged

1. The molecule that an enzyme acts on is called the substrate. Enzyme and substrate molecules have shapes that complement each other.

2. The enzyme's unique shape enables it to form a temporary bond with the substrates. The two substrate molecules then react with each other.

3. The new, larger product separates from the enzyme. The enzyme is unchanged at the end of the reaction and is used over and over again.

🔍 Enzyme structure

Enzymes are made from amino acids that join together to form a long chain. The chain folds into a unique 3-D shape that enables the enzyme to control a specific chemical reaction.

There are about 20 different types of amino acids.

The enzyme's shape determines its function.

Different sequences of amino acids result in different enzymes.

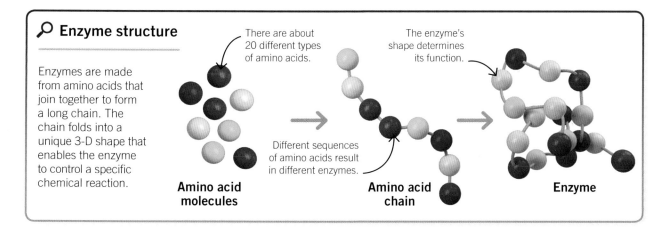

Amino acid molecules

Amino acid chain

Enzyme

Enzymes and temperature

Enzymes need the right conditions to work. Each enzyme needs an optimum temperature to catalyze (speed up) an enzyme-controlled reaction.

Optimum temperature

This graph shows how temperature affects the rate of enzyme activity. If it gets too hot, the enzyme is denatured (its shape changes, preventing it from working), and the reaction rate decreases. If it's too cold, there is not enough energy for reactions to occur fast enough.

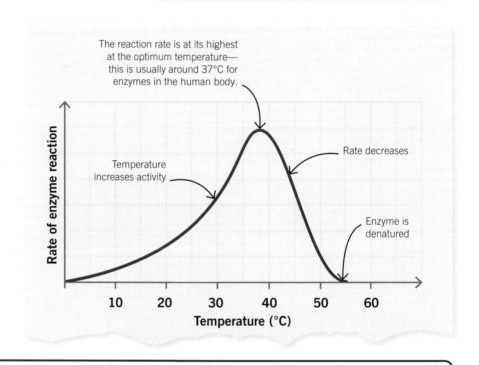

The reaction rate is at its highest at the optimum temperature—this is usually around 37°C for enzymes in the human body.

Temperature increases activity

Rate decreases

Enzyme is denatured

Glow in the dark

Fireflies are winged beetles. They use chemicals within their bodies to create light, which is used to attract breeding partners. The light-emitting reactions are catalyzed by enzymes called luciferases. The optimum temperature for this enzyme is between 22 and 28°C; temperatures above 30°C denature the enzyme.

The tail end of the firefly's body is lined with cells that contain luciferase.

Enzymes and pH

Enzymes are affected by changes in pH (a measure of how acidic or alkaline something is). The pH at which an enzyme is most effective is known as the optimum pH. Extremely low or extremely high pH values affect the rate of reaction by denaturing the enzyme—altering the shape of the active site so that the enzyme can no longer catalyze a reaction.

Key facts

- ✓ Each kind of enzyme has an optimum pH at which it works fastest.
- ✓ The optimum pH for most enzymes that work inside a cell is 7 (neutral).
- ✓ For many digestive enzymes that work outside the cells, the optimum pH is acidic or alkaline.
- ✓ If the pH rises too high or falls too low, an enzyme may be denatured.

Digestive enzymes

The digestive enzyme pepsin works best at a pH of 2 in the acidic conditions of the human stomach. The enzyme trypsin, which helps digest protein, is most effective at a pH of about 8.

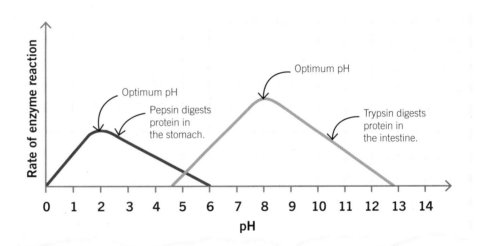

Optimum pH

Pepsin digests protein in the stomach.

Optimum pH

Trypsin digests protein in the intestine.

pH values

The pH scale ranges from pH 0 to pH 14. The pH value indicates whether a substance is an acid or an alkali. Enzymes are affected by how much acid or alkali is present in a substance.

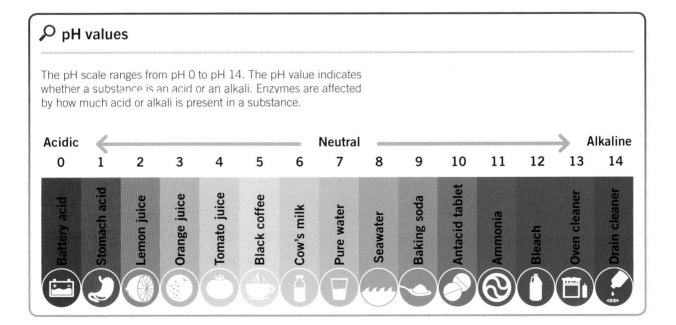

Enzymes and substrates

Concentrations of enzyme and substrate can affect the rate of enzyme-catalyzed reactions. As enzyme or substrate concentration increases, collisions between enzyme and substrate molecules happen more frequently, increasing the rate of reaction up to a maximum point.

Key facts

✓ The rate of enzyme activity increases as substrate concentration increases.

✓ Eventually, no more substrate molecules can fit into the enzyme molecules—the enzyme has become saturated.

✓ As enzyme concentration increases, the rate of reaction increases, but up to a maximum.

Rate of reaction

The higher the substrate concentration, the faster the rate of reaction until there are no more enzyme molecules to which substrates can bind. The same is true for enzyme concentration.

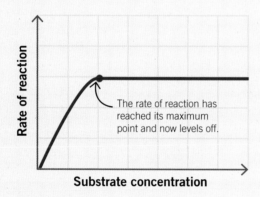

The rate of reaction has reached its maximum point and now levels off.

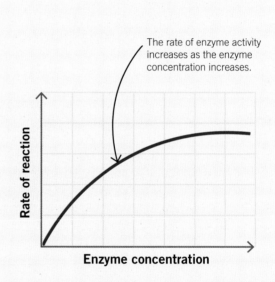

The rate of enzyme activity increases as the enzyme concentration increases.

🔍 Saturation point

When all the enzymes are active, this is called the saturation point—the reaction hasn't stopped; it is just continuing at the same rate. The enzymes are all working but can't go any faster because there are more substrate molecules than open active sites.

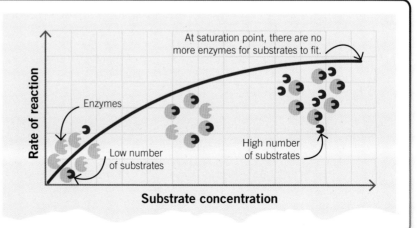

At saturation point, there are no more enzymes for substrates to fit.

Enzymes

Low number of substrates

High number of substrates

Enzymes in industry

Enzymes are widely used in the food industry and in the manufacture of other chemicals. They make the manufacturing process cost-effective because they speed up chemical reactions and can be reused (see page 67)

(see page 67)

Key facts

✓ Enzymes are used in many industries.

✓ Enzymes speed up the rate of chemical reactions.

✓ They can be used over and over again.

Biological washing powder

Enzymes are used in biological washing powder to help break down stains. Stains form from different molecules, so various enzymes are needed to remove them. Enzymes work at low temperatures, reducing the amount of heat needed to wash clothes effectively. They are less harmful to the environment than other stain-removing chemicals because they are biodegradable (break down naturally).

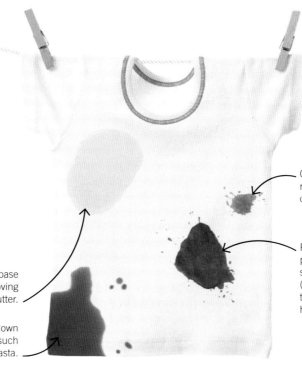

Cellulase helps release dirt from cotton fibers.

Protease removes protein stains such as blood (which contains the protein hemoglobin).

The enzyme lipase is good for removing greasy stains like butter.

Amylase breaks down starch-based foods such as potatoes and pasta.

🔍 Other uses

Breaking down plastic
PETase is an enzyme that digests plastic within a few days. Scientists are trying to make it work even faster.

Fruit juice
Enzymes are used in the production of fruit juice. They help break down cell walls, releasing liquids and sugars. They also break down complex sugars called polysaccharides to make the juice clearer.

Lactose-free milk
People who do not have enough lactase enzyme in their bodies have a problem digesting products that contain lactose (a sugar found in milk). So lactase is used to make lactose-free milk as well as other products that would otherwise contain lactose.

Investigating enzymes

Each enzyme works best at an optimum temperature and pH. In the human body, the optimum temperature is about 37°C. If the temperature is higher or lower than this, the enzyme denatures, and the rate of reaction decreases.

Effect of temperature on enzymes

The effect of temperature on enzyme activity can be tested by measuring the rate of the reaction. This experiment investigates how amylase breaks down starch into glucose under different temperature conditions.

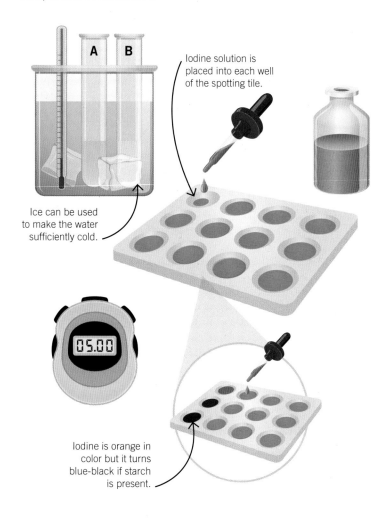

Ice can be used to make the water sufficiently cold.

Iodine solution is placed into each well of the spotting tile.

Iodine is orange in color but it turns blue-black if starch is present.

📌 Key facts

✓ **Each type of enzyme has an optimum temperature and pH at which it works fastest.**

✓ **At a low temperature, the enzyme and substrate molecules move slowly, taking longer to collide and initiate a reaction.**

✓ **As temperature rises, the reaction speeds up—the enzyme and substrate particles collide more often.**

✓ **Above the optimum temperature, the enzyme's active site changes shape—it becomes denatured and the reaction rate decreases.**

📑 Method

1. Prepare a spotting tile by placing a few drops of iodine solution into each well.

2. Place starch solution into test tube A and amylase solution into test tube B.

3. Put both test tubes in a water bath at 4°C until the solutions reach the correct temperature.

4. Mix the solutions in a test tube. Then return the test tube to the water bath and start your timer.

5. After 5 minutes, use a pipette to remove some of the reaction solution and drop it into a well on the spotting tile. Repeat this at 30-second intervals until the iodine no longer turns blue-black.

6. Repeat steps 1–5 using a water bath set at 37°C and 60°C. The sample that takes the shortest length of time to stop testing positive for starch (the iodine color remains orange) indicates the optimum temperature for amylase.

Effect of pH on enzymes

An experiment similar to the one used for temperature can also be used to see how pH affects the rate of enzyme activity. Most enzymes work best in neutral conditions (about pH 7), but the enzyme pepsin, which is found in your stomach, works best in very acidic conditions (about pH 1–2).

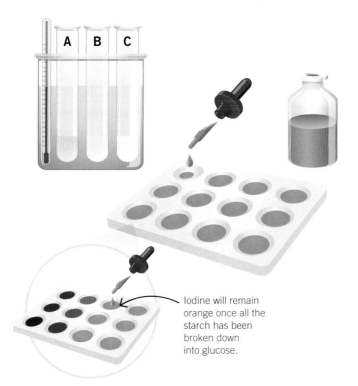

Iodine will remain orange once all the starch has been broken down into glucose.

Method

1. Place some drops of iodine into the wells of a spotting tile.

2. Place starch solution into test tube A, amylase solution into test tube B, and pH 4 buffer solution into test tube C (buffer solution keeps the pH solution stable).

3. Put all three test tubes in a water bath at 37°C (this is the enzyme's optimum temperature) for 10 minutes so that the solutions reach the optimum temperature.

4. Mix all three solutions in a test tube. Return the test tube to the water bath and start your timer.

5. After 5 minutes, use a pipette to remove some of the reaction solution. Add it to the iodine solution in each well of the spotting tile at 30-second intervals until the iodine no longer turns blue-black.

6. Repeat steps 1–5 with buffer solutions of different pH values. The sample that takes the shortest length of time to stop testing positive for starch indicates the optimum pH for amylase.

Calculating the rate of reaction

First equation

The rate of a reaction is a measure of how quickly it happens. One way to calculate reaction rate is to measure how much substrate is used up or how much product is made in a certain time, so:

$$\text{rate of reaction} = \frac{\text{amount of substrate used or product made}}{\text{time}}$$

Example: The enzyme catalase catalyzes the breakdown of hydrogen peroxide into water and oxygen. When investigating the activity of catalase, if 20 cm³ of oxygen was released in 40 seconds, then:

$$\text{rate of reaction} = \frac{20 \text{ cm}^3}{40} = 0.5 \text{ cm}^3/s$$

Second equation

Sometimes we know how long a reaction took but not how the quantities of substrate or product changed. This is the case in the amylase experiment above. To calculate the rate of reaction here, you divide the number 1 by the time taken.

$$\text{rate of reaction} = \frac{1}{\text{time}}$$

Example: If the time taken for amylase to break down the starch in a solution was 10 seconds, then:

The minus 1 sign indicates that we have divided 1 by the seconds.

$$\text{rate of reaction} = \frac{1}{10} = 0.1 \text{ s}^{-1}$$

Metabolism

Metabolism is the sum of all the chemical reactions in a cell or body. Controlled by enzymes (see page 67), metabolism goes on all the time, changing molecules by building them up or breaking them down. Some reactions release energy and others take it in.

Key facts

✓ Metabolism includes all the enzyme-controlled chemical reactions within a cell or body.

✓ Chemical reactions build up or break down molecules.

✓ Enzymes use energy released by respiration to make new molecules in cells.

Breaking down
By breaking chemical bonds in big molecules, some metabolic reactions produce smaller molecules.

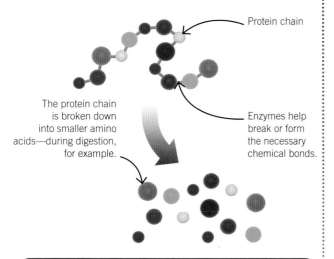

Protein chain

The protein chain is broken down into smaller amino acids—during digestion, for example.

Enzymes help break or form the necessary chemical bonds.

Building up
Some metabolic reactions link smaller molecules with chemical bonds to make bigger molecules.

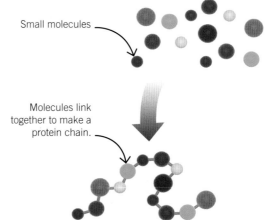

Small molecules

Molecules link together to make a protein chain.

Examples

- All cells break down glucose (a kind of sugar) in respiration to release energy. This energy is used to drive processes that require energy, such as growth and movement.

- Stored carbohydrate (starch in plants, glycogen in animals) gets broken down into glucose whenever glucose is needed by cells.

- Big molecules get broken down into smaller molecules when food is digested—proteins into amino acids, starch into glucose, and lipids into fatty acids and glycerol.

- When animal bodies accumulate too many amino acids, they break the excess down and produce a waste product called urea.

Examples

- Small molecules are joined to make bigger ones to help a body grow—amino acids are joined to make protein molecules, and fatty acids and glycerol are joined to make lipids.

- Glucose molecules are joined to make larger carbohydrates for storage (starch in plants, glycogen in animals).

- Plants also join glucose molecules to make cellulose, which is used to make their cell walls.

- Plants combine carbon dioxide and water molecules to make glucose during photosynthesis. They then build all the other kinds of molecules they need from glucose. For example, they combine glucose with nitrate ions to make amino acids and proteins.

Nutrition
in Plants

Photosynthesis

All organisms need food to survive. Unlike animals, plants don't obtain food by eating—they make their own food chemically, using a process called photosynthesis. This is why green plants are called producers in food chains—they make glucose (a simple sugar) from light energy (sunlight), water, and carbon dioxide.

How photosynthesis works

In photosynthesis, green plants combine carbon dioxide and water to make glucose, which is used as a food source. Oxygen is also produced. Some of it is used by the plant in respiration and the rest is released as a waste product.

Key facts

✓ Plants make their own food by a process called photosynthesis.

✓ Photosynthesis takes place in the green parts of plants.

✓ In photosynthesis, a plant uses light energy to combine carbon dioxide and water to make glucose and oxygen.

✓ Photosynthesis is an endothermic reaction—light energy (from the sun) is taken in during the process.

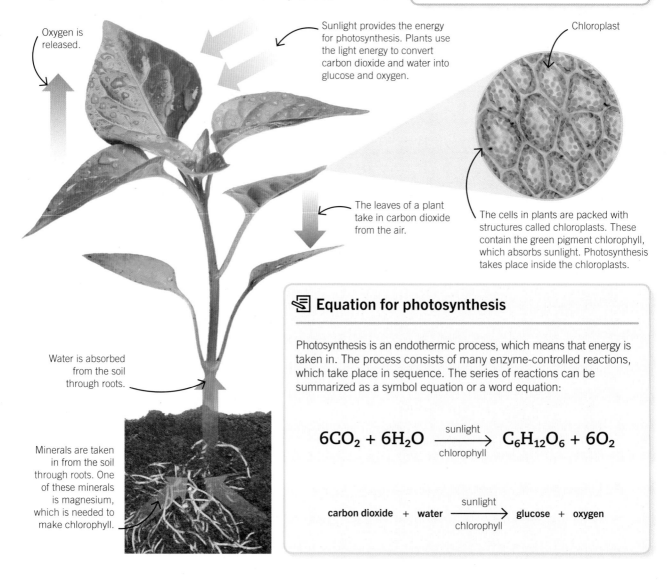

Oxygen is released.

Sunlight provides the energy for photosynthesis. Plants use the light energy to convert carbon dioxide and water into glucose and oxygen.

Chloroplast

The leaves of a plant take in carbon dioxide from the air.

The cells in plants are packed with structures called chloroplasts. These contain the green pigment chlorophyll, which absorbs sunlight. Photosynthesis takes place inside the chloroplasts.

Water is absorbed from the soil through roots.

Minerals are taken in from the soil through roots. One of these minerals is magnesium, which is needed to make chlorophyll.

Equation for photosynthesis

Photosynthesis is an endothermic process, which means that energy is taken in. The process consists of many enzyme-controlled reactions, which take place in sequence. The series of reactions can be summarized as a symbol equation or a word equation:

$$6CO_2 + 6H_2O \xrightarrow[\text{chlorophyll}]{\text{sunlight}} C_6H_{12}O_6 + 6O_2$$

$$\text{carbon dioxide} + \text{water} \xrightarrow[\text{chlorophyll}]{\text{sunlight}} \text{glucose} + \text{oxygen}$$

Leaves

Photosynthesis takes place mainly in a plant's leaves. Leaves have a large surface area so they can make use of as much sunlight as possible. There are more chloroplasts near the top surface of a leaf because this is the part of the leaf that gets the most sunlight.

Leaf structure

A leaf may look incredibly thin, but it is made up of several layers of cells as shown below. The structures within a leaf are adapted to maximize photosynthesis.

Key facts

✓ A leaf is adapted for photosynthesis by having a large surface area and lots of chloroplasts near its upper surface.

✓ Photosynthesis takes place in the palisade layer of the leaf.

✓ Exchange of gases takes place in the spongy mesophyll layer of the leaf.

✓ A stoma (plural stomata) is a hole in the leaf that lets in carbon dioxide and lets out oxygen and water vapor.

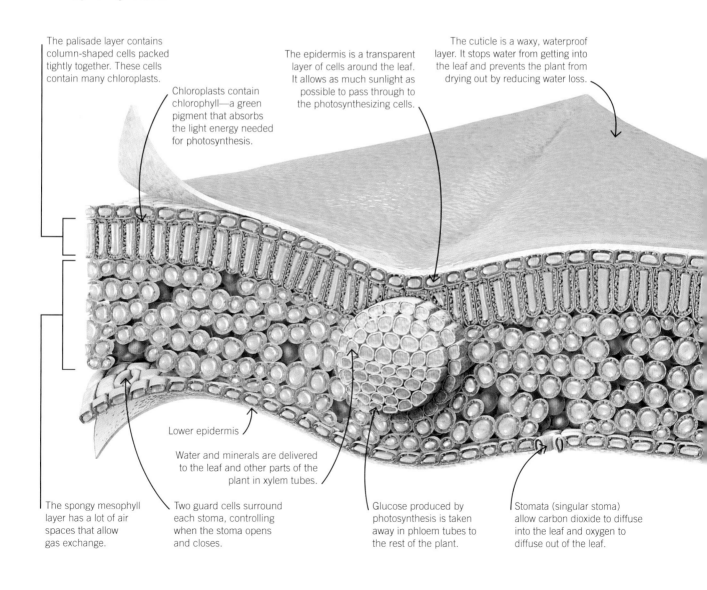

The palisade layer contains column-shaped cells packed tightly together. These cells contain many chloroplasts.

Chloroplasts contain chlorophyll—a green pigment that absorbs the light energy needed for photosynthesis.

The epidermis is a transparent layer of cells around the leaf. It allows as much sunlight as possible to pass through to the photosynthesizing cells.

The cuticle is a waxy, waterproof layer. It stops water from getting into the leaf and prevents the plant from drying out by reducing water loss.

Lower epidermis

Water and minerals are delivered to the leaf and other parts of the plant in xylem tubes.

The spongy mesophyll layer has a lot of air spaces that allow gas exchange.

Two guard cells surround each stoma, controlling when the stoma opens and closes.

Glucose produced by photosynthesis is taken away in phloem tubes to the rest of the plant.

Stomata (singular stoma) allow carbon dioxide to diffuse into the leaf and oxygen to diffuse out of the leaf.

Stomata

The exchange of gases needed for photosynthesis takes place through tiny openings called stomata. These are found mostly on the underside of a leaf and are light-sensitive, closing at night to save water.

Key facts

✓ Oxygen (a waste product of photosynthesis) escapes from the stomata.

✓ Carbon dioxide diffuses into the leaf during photosynthesis.

✓ Water vapor escapes through the stomata during transpiration.

✓ Guard cells control the opening and closing of the stomata.

Opening and closing

Stomata are surrounded by two curved guard cells that change shape to open and close the tiny pore. Shaded from sunlight, the lower surface of a leaf often has a higher number of stomata so that less water is lost through transpiration (see page 106).

Underside of a leaf

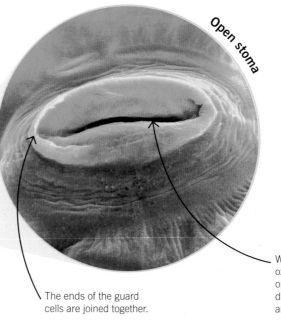

Open stoma

The ends of the guard cells are joined together.

Water vapor and oxygen escape from an open stoma and carbon dioxide enters through an open stoma.

How guard cells work

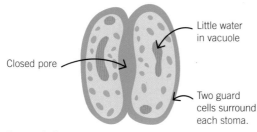

Little water in vacuole

Closed pore

Two guard cells surround each stoma.

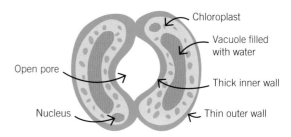

Chloroplast

Vacuole filled with water

Open pore

Thick inner wall

Nucleus

Thin outer wall

Stoma closing
When conditions for photosynthesis are poor, such as when it is dark, water passes out of the guard cells. This makes them flaccid (limp) and causes the stoma to close. This also helps to stop water from escaping when plant water levels are low.

Stoma opening
When plenty of light and water are available, water passes into the guard cells during the day by osmosis (see pages 52–53). This makes the guard cells turgid (swollen). They bend as they swell, causing the stoma to open.

Plants and glucose

Photosynthesis mainly takes place in leaves and produces food in the form of a sugar called glucose, which is used in different ways. Some is used in the cell where it's produced, but much of it ends up in other parts of the plant.

Key facts

✓ All parts of a plant need glucose to grow.

✓ Glucose is stored as starch, used for energy and for making cellulose and proteins, and changed to sucrose.

✓ Respiration is a process that transfers energy from glucose to the cell.

How plants use glucose

Some of the glucose a plant makes is used right away in respiration—to work, cells need energy, which is obtained from respiration. The rest is used in a number of other ways.

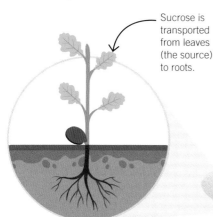

Sucrose is transported from leaves (the source) to roots.

Mitochondrion

Tiny structures within a cell, called mitochondria (singular mitochondrion), transfer the energy stored in glucose to the cell during respiration.

Cell wall

Some of the glucose is used to make a complex sugar called sucrose. This is transported to parts of the plant that need it.

Cellulose, which is made from glucose, is needed to make cell walls. This gives the plant strength and support.

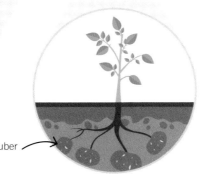

Tuber

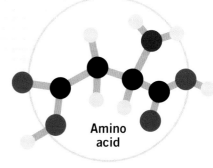

Amino acid

Fats and oils (known as lipids) are made from glucose. They are used as a food store and as a source of food for new seedlings.

The glucose that is not used right away is converted into starch. It is stored in the leaves, roots, and tubers for future use.

Amino acids form when glucose combines with nitrogen, which is absorbed as nitrates from the soil. Proteins are built from these amino acids and used for growth and cell repair.

Plant nutrients

In addition to the glucose made from photosynthesis, plants need minerals for healthy growth. These minerals are dissolved in water in the soil in the form of mineral ions. Plants that do not get enough of these nutrients suffer from deficiency symptoms—they become unhealthy.

Key facts

✓ The three main mineral ions needed for healthy plant growth are nitrates, phosphates, and potassium.

✓ Magnesium (needed in smaller quantities) is very important for photosynthesis.

✓ If a plant doesn't get enough of the right mineral ions, it suffers from deficiency symptoms.

Mineral ion	Role		Healthy plant	Unhealthy plant
Nitrate (contains nitrogen)	Nitrate ions are needed to make amino acids. These in turn are needed to make proteins, which are used for cell growth.	If plants lack nitrates, then plant growth becomes stunted and the leaves turn yellow.		Corn plant
Phosphates (contains phosphorus)	Plants need phosphates for respiration and for making DNA and cell membranes.	A lack of phosphates results in leaves turning purple and poor root growth.		Tomato plant
Potassium	Potassium is needed by the enzymes involved in photosynthesis and respiration.	Potassium-deficient plants have yellow leaves (a condition known as chlorosis) and poor growth of roots, flowers, and fruit.		Grape plant
Magnesium	Magnesium ions are used for making chlorophyll, which is needed for photosynthesis.	Plants that lack chlorophyll have leaves that turn yellow (chlorosis).		Potato plant

Adapting to extreme environments

Most plant species cannot survive in very hot, dry conditions, such as in the desert. Those that do survive here have special adaptations that enable them to carry out photosynthesis and gas exchange.

Desert plants
Cacti have a number of adaptations to enable them to survive in the desert. Plants that are adapted to grow in very arid (dry) environments are known as xerophytes.

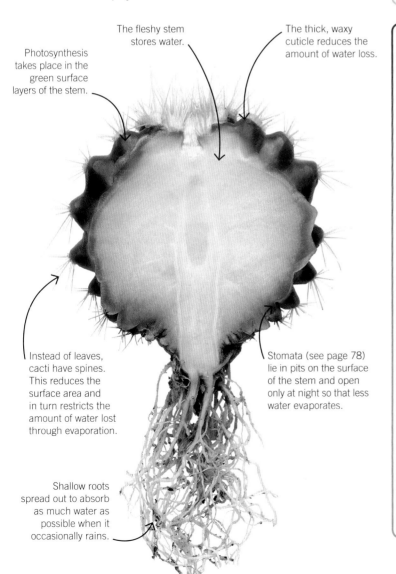

The fleshy stem stores water.

The thick, waxy cuticle reduces the amount of water loss.

Photosynthesis takes place in the green surface layers of the stem.

Instead of leaves, cacti have spines. This reduces the surface area and in turn restricts the amount of water lost through evaporation.

Stomata (see page 78) lie in pits on the surface of the stem and open only at night so that less water evaporates.

Shallow roots spread out to absorb as much water as possible when it occasionally rains.

Key facts

✓ Features of an organism that help it to survive in a particular environment are called adaptations.

✓ Adaptations in plants affect the root system, the shape and size of the leaves, as well as how many stomata a plant has and when they open.

✓ Xerophytes are plants that have adapted to grow in arid environments.

✓ Hydrophytes are plants that have adapted to grow in water.

🔍 How water and Arctic plants survive

Plants that live in water are called hydrophytes. Most have no stomata because dissolved gases can pass directly between the water and the plant's tissue. Water lilies, however, have floating leaves and so have stomata on the upper surface of their leaves.

In the Arctic, plants are small and tend to grow close together to protect them from wind damage. They also have small leaves to reduce water loss and can carry out photosynthesis in extremely cold temperatures.

Investigating photosynthesis

As well as water, green plants need light, chlorophyll, and carbon dioxide for photosynthesis. A starch test can prove that without one of these requirements photosynthesis cannot occur.

Testing leaves for starch

Photosynthesis produces glucose, which plants convert to starch for storage. You can test leaves for the presence of starch by using iodine solution—a leaf that has undergone photosynthesis will test positive for starch.

Iodine solution

Test tube with ethanol

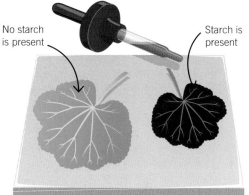

No starch is present

Starch is present

1. Place a leaf in a beaker of boiling water for 1 minute. This softens the cell walls, which helps the iodine penetrate the cells.

2. Put the leaf into a boiling tube half full of ethanol for 5 minutes and place it back into the beaker of water. Ethanol removes the chlorophyll (green pigment), making it easier to see the result of the iodine test.

3. Rinse the leaf in cold water to remove the ethanol and place it on a white tile. Add a few drops of iodine solution—iodine is orange in color and if it changes to blue-black, this shows that starch is present.

🔍 Starch in plants

Any glucose that is not immediately used by a plant is converted to starch. The starch in the leaves is then used at night when the plant cannot photosynthesize. Some plants, such as potatoes, store starch in tubers, which we then use as a source of starch in our food.

Potato plant

Tubers are underground modified plant stems.

New shoots grow

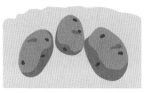

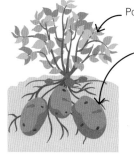

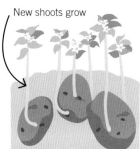

1. In the growing season, sucrose is converted into starch and stored in the tubers.

2. In winter, the leaves die, but the tubers swell because of the stored starch.

3. In spring, the starch that has been stored in the roots is used to produce new shoots and flowers.

Testing for chlorophyll

A variegated leaf can be used to show that chlorophyll is necessary for photosynthesis.

Method

1. You need to destarch a variegated plant by placing it in a dark cupboard for at least 24 hours so that it uses up the stored starch. Then place it in sunlight for about 6 hours.

2. Test the leaf for the presence of starch by using the starch test. When iodine is added, only the green areas of the plant will turn blue-black—the green areas have chlorophyll, which is needed for photosynthesis to occur and make glucose, which is stored as starch.

Variegated leaves are only partly green—these are the areas that have the chlorophyll needed for photosynthesis.

The blue-black area has starch, so photosynthesis has taken place.

Variegated leaf before the test

Variegated leaf after the test

Testing for carbon dioxide

You can show that carbon dioxide is necessary for photosynthesis by removing it from the plant's environment.

Method

1. Enclose a destarched plant in a plastic bag with soda lime—a chemical that absorbs carbon dioxide—and leave the plant in light for several hours. Test a leaf for starch.

2. The leaf should not change color because in the absence of carbon dioxide, the leaf cannot photosynthesize, and therefore no starch is present.

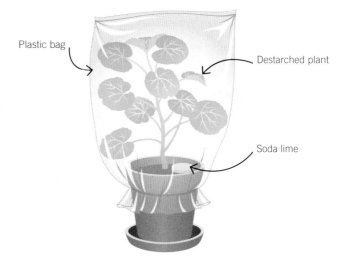

Plastic bag

Destarched plant

Soda lime

Testing for light

By preventing light from reaching a part of a leaf, you can show that light is necessary for photosynthesis.

Method

1. Cover a part of a destarched leaf on a plant with a strip of aluminum foil or black paper, and leave it in light for several hours.

2. Then test the leaf for starch. The part of the leaf that did not receive light should not change color, showing that photosynthesis did not happen.

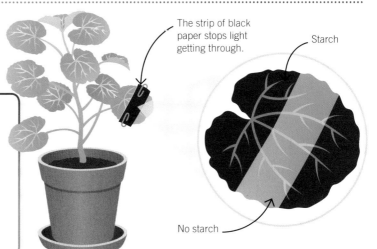

The strip of black paper stops light getting through.

Starch

No starch

Rate of photosynthesis

A plant needs light, carbon dioxide, and warmth for photosynthesis to work. When any of these factors increase, they can make photosynthesis happen faster but only up to a limit when photosynthesis works as fast as it can. Any factor that limits the rate of a process, such as photosynthesis, is called a limiting factor. Faster photosynthesis means a plant makes food more efficiently.

Key facts

✓ The three limiting factors for photosynthesis are light intensity, carbon dioxide, and temperature.

✓ Temperature has an optimal value—photosynthesis stops if it is too hot or too cold.

✓ A combination of limiting factors can affect the rate of photosynthesis.

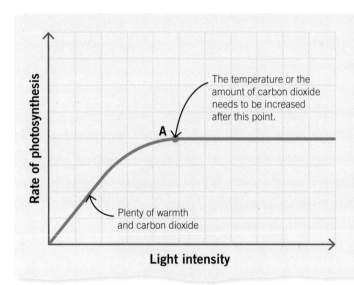

The temperature or the amount of carbon dioxide needs to be increased after this point.

A

Plenty of warmth and carbon dioxide

Light intensity
As light intensity increases, the rate of photosynthesis increases to a maximum and then levels off. The greater intensity provides more energy for faster photosynthesis until it can go no faster and another factor (temperature or carbon dioxide concentration) stops it from going any higher.

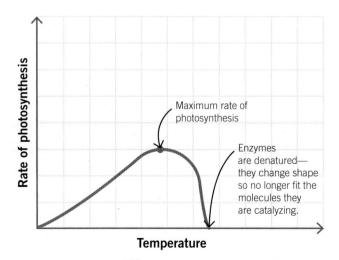

Maximum rate of photosynthesis

Enzymes are denatured— they change shape so no longer fit the molecules they are catalyzing.

Temperature
As temperature increases, the rate of photosynthesis increases to a maximum and then falls. At higher temperatures, the molecules collide faster. This increases the rate of the chemical reactions of photosynthesis. But above the maximum rate, the enzymes used in photosynthesis denature (they change shape), so they can no longer catalyze reactions, and the rate of photosynthesis falls.

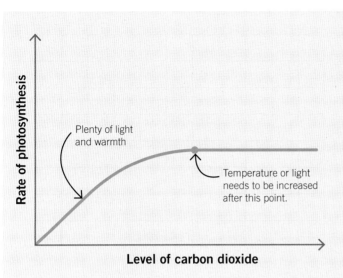

Carbon dioxide

As carbon dioxide concentration increases, the rate of photosynthesis increases to a maximum and then levels off. More carbon dioxide molecules collide with enzymes. This increases the rate of photosynthesis until the enzymes can go no faster and another factor (temperature or light intensity) stops the rate of photosynthesis from going any higher—at the highest rate, the enzymes are filled with carbon dioxide molecules.

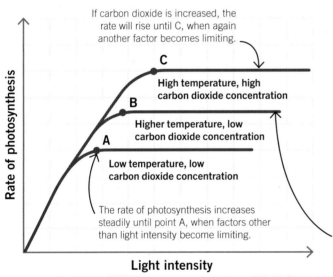

More than one limiting factor

As light intensity increases, it makes the rate of photosynthesis increase up to A. Before point A, light intensity is the limiting factor. The rate then levels off, so other factors (temperature and carbon dioxide concentration) become limiting instead. The higher temperature alone makes it level off a bit higher at point B— but a high temperature combined with a high carbon dioxide concentration can make it level off even higher at point C.

🔎 Features of a plant that affect the rate of photosynthesis

Different features of a plant affect how well it can photosynthesize. For instance, leaves that are bigger or contain more chlorophyll (the green pigment inside chloroplasts) trap more light energy, increasing the amount of glucose a plant can make in a given amount of time. Plants with variegated leaves, for instance, have patches where green chlorophyll is absent, so their overall rate of photosynthesis is likely to be lower than in a plant with all-green leaves, making them less efficient at making food.

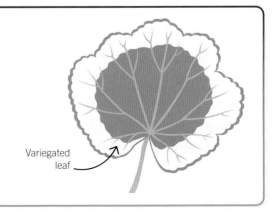

Variegated leaf

Measuring the rate of photosynthesis

You can measure the rate of photosynthesis by finding out how much oxygen is produced in a set amount of time. The more oxygen produced, the faster the rate of photosynthesis.

How light affects the rate of photosynthesis
This experiment allows you to measure the rate of photosynthesis by counting bubbles of oxygen produced by an aquatic plant. Light intensity is varied by changing how close the plant is to a light source.

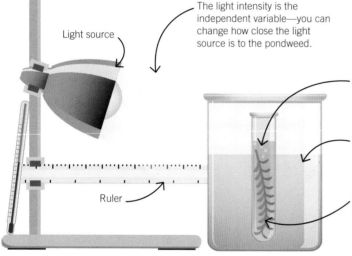

Light source

The light intensity is the independent variable—you can change how close the light source is to the pondweed.

The number of oxygen bubbles produced is the dependent variable.

Water in the beaker insulates the plant in the tube, helping stop the lamp from warming it up.

Ruler

The type of pondweed, temperature, and amount of sodium hydrogen carbonate are all controlled variables. They are kept the same so only the distance from the light source will affect the results.

Method

1. Add sodium hydrogen carbonate solution to a boiling tube—sodium hydrogen carbonate releases carbon dioxide, which the plant needs to photosynthesize.

2. Place the tube in the water beaker and note the temperature in the beaker—this needs to be constant throughout the investigation. Submerge the pondweed in the tube with the cut end at the top. Leave the pondweed for 5 minutes.

3. As the pondweed photosynthesizes, oxygen bubbles are released from the cut end. Using a stopwatch, count how many bubbles are produced in 1 minute when the pondweed is 10 cm from the light. Repeat the count two more times to calculate an average.

4. Repeat the test with the pondweed at 20 cm and 30 cm from the light source. Keep the variables constant (see page 13). When you have finished the test, you will see that the number of bubbles decreases as the distance between the light source and pondweed increases.

Measuring the volume of oxygen

In the first experiment, the bubbles can appear too quickly to count accurately. Bubbles may also be different sizes, and this can affect the amount of oxygen given off. These problems can be solved by collecting all the gas in the tube and measuring the total length of the bubble produced. This will give you a more accurate result for the rate of photosynthesis.

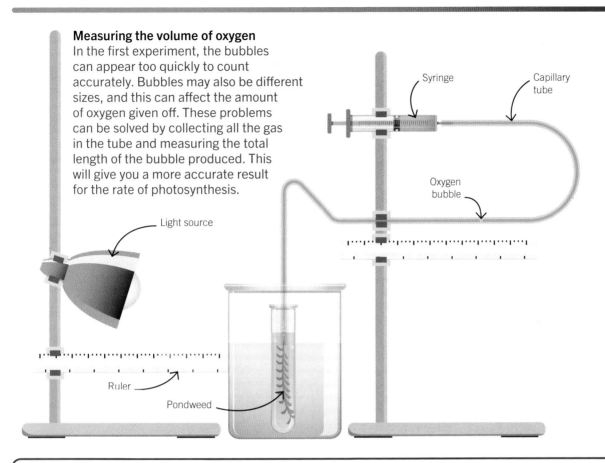

Syringe

Capillary tube

Oxygen bubble

Light source

Ruler

Pondweed

🗐 Method

1. Place the pondweed with the cut end at the top in a tube of sodium hydrogen carbonate solution. Then place the tube in a beaker of water, noting the temperature.

2. Insert the cut end of the pondweed into the end of the capillary tube, and leave it for 5 minutes in front of the light source. When the oxygen is given off, use a syringe to draw the gas bubble into the capillary tube.

3. Measure the length of the oxygen bubble. To reduce errors, repeat the test with the pondweed at the same distance and note the results.

4. Repeat the test with the pondweed at different distances from the light source and record the length of the bubble each time.

🔍 Results

A graph showing number of oxygen bubbles and distance from the light reveals that the rate of photosynthesis falls steeply as the light gets farther away.

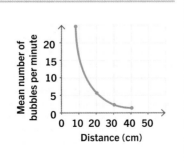

🗐 Calculating the rate of photosynthesis

To calculate the rate of photosynthesis, we need to divide the amount of oxygen produced by the time taken. Example: In an experiment, after 20 minutes, the pondweed produced 4 cm of oxygen gas. Divide the length of the bubble by the time and give your answer in cm/min.

$$\text{rate} = \frac{\text{length of bubble}}{\text{elapsed time}} = \frac{4\ \text{cm}}{20\ \text{mins}} = 0.2\ \text{cm/min}$$

Inverse square law

If you move a plant farther away from a light source, the rate of photosynthesis falls steeply. This is because the rate of photosynthesis is proportional to light intensity, but light intensity falls dramatically with increasing distance. The change in light intensity with distance follows a pattern known as the inverse square law.

Key facts

✓ Light intensity is inversely proportional to the square of the distance.

✓ The inverse square law equation is:

$$\text{light intensity} \propto \frac{1}{\text{distance}^2}$$

✓ The rate of photosynthesis is proportional to light intensity.

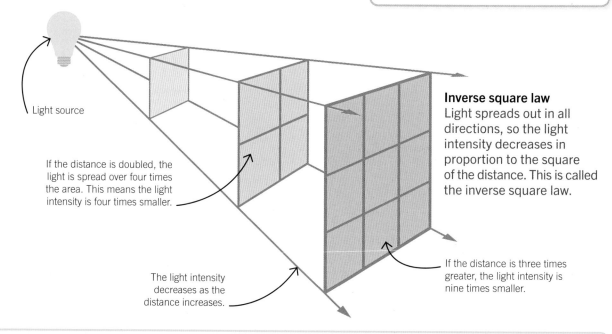

Light source

If the distance is doubled, the light is spread over four times the area. This means the light intensity is four times smaller.

The light intensity decreases as the distance increases.

Inverse square law
Light spreads out in all directions, so the light intensity decreases in proportion to the square of the distance. This is called the inverse square law.

If the distance is three times greater, the light intensity is nine times smaller.

Using the inverse square law

This is how the inverse square law is written:

Proportional symbol

1 over the distance² shows the inverse

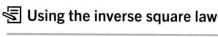

$$\text{light intensity} \propto \frac{1}{\text{distance}^2}$$

Square the value for distance

Example: If a lamp is positioned 20 cm from a plant, calculate the light intensity using the inverse square law.

1. Use the formula: $\text{light intensity} \propto \dfrac{1}{\text{distance}^2}$

2. Substitute in the numbers. $\text{relative light intensity} = \dfrac{1}{20^2}$

3. Square the 20 before finding the inverse. $\text{relative light intensity} = \dfrac{1}{400}$

4. Use a calculator to find the answer. $\text{relative light intensity} = 0.0025$

Greenhouse farming

Greenhouses are used by farmers to create the perfect growing conditions for plants to photosynthesize at the fastest rate possible. This increases the crop yield (how much is produced), but it also increases costs, and this has to be balanced against the income produced by the extra crop.

Key facts

✓ Greenhouses can be used to increase the rate of photosynthesis.

✓ Maximizing the rate of photosynthesis increases the rate of plant growth. This in turn increases the crop yield.

✓ In a greenhouse, the amount of water, light, carbon dioxide, and temperature can be controlled.

Controlled conditions
In sheltered greenhouses, farmers can control pests and the conditions needed for photosynthesis— carbon dioxide, light intensity, and temperature as well as water. Crops can also be grown at any time of the year and in any part of the world.

Carbon dioxide concentrations in the air can be artificially increased. Since carbon dioxide is needed for photosynthesis, the rate of photosynthesis increases when carbon dioxide levels are higher.

Temperatures in a greenhouse are higher due to the insulating effects of the glass. In winter, heaters can be used, and damage caused by frost can be prevented.

Artificial light can be used so that plants photosynthesize for longer than they would in an open field. The intensity of the light can also be increased so that the rate of photosynthesis speeds up.

Watering can be controlled so that plants have the exact amount of water needed for growth. Some farmers also use a system called hydroponics, where plants are grown in nutrient-rich water instead of soil.

Growing plants in a greenhouse allows the farmer to keep out pests such as aphids. This ensures that the plants are kept healthy and maintains a high crop yield.

Nutrition in Humans

Nutrients

Nutrients are the essential substances that an organism needs to survive. These are absorbed by the body when an animal eats or drinks. Some nutrients are used for energy; others are used to build new cells.

Key facts

✓ Nutrients are essential for an organism to survive.

✓ Nutrients include carbohydrates, lipids, proteins, vitamins, minerals, water, and fiber.

✓ Carbohydrates provide energy.

✓ Lipids provide energy and warmth and protect vital organs.

✓ Proteins are used for growth and repair.

Carbohydrates, lipids, and proteins

Besides water, cells are mainly composed of carbohydrates, lipids (solid fats and liquid oils), and proteins. It is therefore essential that these compounds form part of the diet of all consumer organisms. These compounds are also known as macromolecules because their molecules are made of lots of smaller units joined together.

Proteins are used to make new cells for growth. They are also used to repair body tissues. Muscles and body organs are mainly composed of proteins.

Dairy products such as milk are rich in proteins.

Avocados are rich in lipids.

Pasta is a good source of slow-release energy.

Carbohydrates are an organism's main source of energy. Carbohydrates exist in two forms in food—simple sugars and complex carbohydrates such as starch. Sugars provide a quick source of energy. Starches have to be broken down by the body, so they release energy more slowly.

Lipids act as a store of energy and keep an organism warm by providing a layer of insulation under the skin. This layer of fat is also used to protect organs such as the kidneys from damage. Cheese and butter are high in fats while some foods, such as eggs, are sources of both fats and protein.

Other essential dietary nutrients

To function properly, an organism also needs a supply of vitamins and minerals (see page 92), water, and fiber.

Fiber
A type of carbohydrate, fiber provides bulk to keep foods moving through the digestive system. This means waste is pushed out of the body, preventing constipation. Cereals are a good source of fiber.

Water
Your body needs a regular supply of water. It is essential for maintaining cell structure (body cells are composed of approximately 70 percent water) and for body fluids such as blood. Water also helps transport nutrients and remove waste products.

Vitamins and minerals

Vitamins and minerals are essential for good health. They are needed only in small amounts and are usually found in fruits and vegetables. Some vitamins and minerals can be stored in the body, while others have to be eaten.

Key facts

✓ Vitamins and minerals are needed in small amounts to stay healthy.

✓ Fruits and vegetables are rich in vitamins and minerals.

✓ There are 13 essential vitamins.

✓ Calcium and iron are examples of minerals.

Sources of vitamins and minerals

A lack of a particular vitamin or mineral in the diet can lead to deficiency symptoms and can damage a person's health.

🔍 **Vitamin and mineral supplements**

Most people get all the vitamins and minerals they need from their food. However, pregnant women and people with certain medical conditions may need to take supplements. Taking unnecessary supplements for a long period can be harmful to a person's health.

The body converts beta-carotene in carrots into vitamin A. Vitamin A is needed for good eyesight and healthy skin.

Citrus fruits are a good source of vitamin C (ascorbic acid), which is needed to heal wounds and build a strong immune system.

Nuts are rich in iron. Iron is used to make hemoglobin in red blood cells, which is needed to transport oxygen around your body. A lack of iron results in tiredness (anemia).

Dairy products are a good source of calcium. Calcium is needed for healthy bones and teeth.

Differences between vitamins and minerals		
	Vitamin	**Mineral**
Original source	Living organisms: plants and animals	Nonliving material: soil, rocks, and water
Chemical composition	Organic compound	Inorganic compound
Stability/ vulnerability	Broken down by heat (for example when cooking), air, or acid	Not easily destroyed by heat, light, or chemical reactions
Nutritional requirement	All are required to remain healthy	Only some are required to remain healthy

Measuring energy in food

Foods contain a store of chemical energy. The quantity of energy contained in the food can be estimated by burning the food under a test tube of water. The increase in the temperature of the water can then be used to estimate the energy contained in the food.

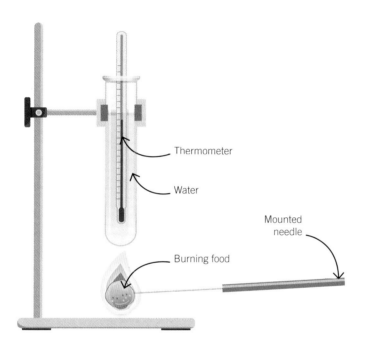

Thermometer

Water

Mounted needle

Burning food

Method

1. Add 20 cm³ of water to a boiling tube clamped to a stand, and calculate the mass of water—1 cm³ of water has a mass of 1 g. Then record the starting temperature of the water.

2. Weigh the food sample and make a note of the mass. Then place it on a mounted needle and ignite the food sample using a Bunsen burner.

3. Hold the burning food sample under the boiling tube of water until it is completely burned. Then record the final temperature of the water.

4. Calculate the change in temperature caused by the burning food sample. A large increase in temperature shows that the food contains a lot of energy.

5. Calculate the energy released by the food (how to do this is shown below). The energy released shows how much energy the food contains.

Burning food practical
The method given here can be used to estimate the energy content of different foods. This method works well for dried foods such as nuts, chips, and bread.

Calculating energy released from food

To calculate the energy released from food, the following formula is used:

$$\text{energy contained in food (J)} = \text{mass of water (g)} \times \text{temperature rise (°C)} \times 4.2$$

To compare different food products, the energy contained per gram is used:

$$\text{energy per gram (J/g)} = \frac{\text{energy contained in food (J)}}{\text{mass of food product (g)}}$$

Example: 15 g of chips are burned underneath a test tube containing 10 g of water. The water temperature changes from 20 °C to 27 °C. Estimate the energy per gram contained within the food.

$$\text{energy contained in food} = \text{mass of water} \times \text{temperature rise} \times 4.2$$

$$\text{energy contained in food} = 10 \times 7 \times 4.2 = 294 \text{ J}$$

$$\text{energy per gram} = \frac{\text{energy contained in food}}{\text{mass of food product}}$$

$$\text{energy per gram} = \frac{294}{15} = 19.6 \text{ J/g}$$

Balanced eating

To remain healthy, a person must eat a balanced diet. This means eating food that contains the nutrients required in the correct amounts. Food provides you with energy for activities such as walking or running and for essential chemical reactions needed to keep your body working properly. The amount of food a person requires depends on their age, sex, and level of physical activity, or if they're pregnant.

Key facts

✓ A balanced diet contains foods that have the required nutrients in the right amounts.

✓ Eating too little food causes a person to become underweight.

✓ Eating too much food can cause a person to become obese.

✓ The amount of food needed by any person is affected by age, sex, pregnancy, and level of physical activity.

Eating a balanced diet

The plate below represents the proportion of your diet that should be made up of each group of foods.

Vegetables are a good source of fiber. They help your digestive system stay healthy and protect you from certain diseases, including heart disease and diabetes.

About a quarter of your food intake per meal should be made of carbohydrate-rich foods. These foods provide you with energy.

Bread, cereal, rice, and pasta

Vegetables

Meat, fish, eggs, dairy products, and nuts

Fruit are a good source of vitamins, minerals, and fiber.

Fruit

Foods rich in protein include meat, fish, nuts, and beans. Your body needs protein to build and repair tissues.

⌨ Body mass

Too little food
Some people do not eat enough food. If a person's energy intake is less than their requirement, they will lose body mass and become underweight. Underweight people often find it harder to fight off disease because they have a poor immune system, lack energy and feel tired, and may suffer from vitamin and mineral deficiencies. A diet that provides less energy than a person needs can lead to starvation, and eventually death.

Too much food
Some people eat too much food, or too many fatty or sugary foods. If a person's intake of energy is greater than the required daily amount, they will gain body mass by storing a layer of fat under the skin and around body organs. If a person becomes very overweight, they are said to be obese. Overweight people have an increased risk of heart disease, stroke, type 2 diabetes, and some types of cancers.

A person's body mass index (BMI) is an indication of whether their body mass is at a healthy level in proportion to their height. If it is too high or too low, it can have health implications. The table to the right shows what a BMI value means. A person's BMI is calculated using the following formula:

$$BMI = \frac{body\ mass\ in\ kg}{(height\ in\ m)^2}$$

Weight categories	BMI (kg/m²)
Underweight	< 18.5
Healthy weight	18.5–24.9
Overweight	25–29.9
Obese	30–34.9

Example: If a 16-year-old boy has a body mass of 65 kg and is 1.8 m tall, his BMI is:

$$BMI = \frac{body\ mass\ in\ kg}{(height\ in\ m)^2} = \frac{65}{1.8^2} = 20.1$$

This BMI indicates that he has a healthy weight.

🔍 Energy content in food

Food labels inform consumers about a food's energy content—kilojoules (kJ) and kilocalories (kcal) tell you how much energy is in the product. The red, amber, and green labels show whether the food is high, medium, or low in fats, saturates, sugars, and salt. This color coding system is used by many countries, and helps people make healthy food choices.

Energy	Fat	Saturated fat	Sugar	Salt
924 kJ 220 kcal	13 g	5.9 g	0.8 g	0.7 g
15%	19%	30%	<1%	12%

This tells you what percent of an adult's recommended daily intake the food contains.

Red labelled foods should only be eaten occasionally.

Green labelled foods are healthier choices.

Food tests

Chemical reagents help scientists detect the presence of carbohydrates, proteins, and lipids in food. The reagent changes color depending on the biological molecules present. Before testing a food product, it may be necessary to crush it using a pestle and mortar. It is then dissolved in distilled water to create a solution.

Key facts

✓ If a food contains starch, it will turn blue-black when iodine is added.

✓ If a food contains sugar (glucose), it will turn brick red when Benedict's solution is added.

✓ If a food contains protein, it will turn purple when Biuret's solution is added.

✓ If a food contains lipids, a white emulsion will form when ethanol is added.

Testing foods for starch

Iodine turns blue-black in the presence of starch (a complex carbohydrate).

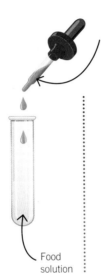

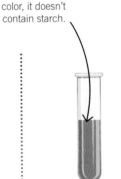

Iodine solution

If the solution doesn't change color, it doesn't contain starch.

If the solution turns blue-black, starch is present.

Food solution

Stir the mixture.

📑 Method

1. Add a few drops of iodine to the food solution. Iodine is an orange solution.

2. Stir the mixture.

3. If the solution turns blue-black, it contains starch.

Testing foods for simple sugars

Benedict's solution turns red in the presence of simple sugars, such as glucose.

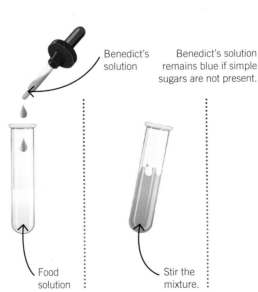

Benedict's solution

Benedict's solution remains blue if simple sugars are not present.

If the solution contains simple sugars, it will change to a red color.

Food solution

Stir the mixture.

📑 Method

1. Add a few drops of Benedict's solution to the food solution. Benedict's solution is bright blue in color.

2. Stir the mixture and heat it in a water bath set at 50°C.

3. If the solution turns red, it contains sugar.

Testing foods for proteins

Biuret's solution turns purple in the presence of protein.

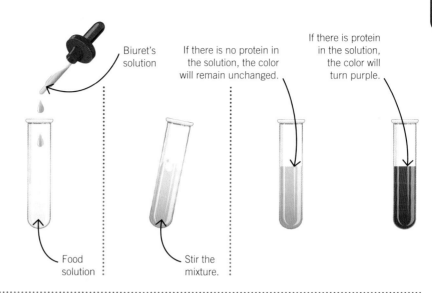

Biuret's solution

If there is no protein in the solution, the color will remain unchanged.

If there is protein in the solution, the color will turn purple.

 Method

1. Add a few drops of Biuret's solution (a mixture of sodium hydroxide and copper sulfate) to the food solution. Biuret's solution is blue.

2. Stir the mixture.

3. If the solution turns purple, it contains protein.

Food solution

Stir the mixture.

Testing foods for lipids

Ethanol causes a white emulsion to appear if lipids are present in the solution.

Ethanol solution

The mixture is added to a test tube of distilled water and mixed again.

A cloudy white emulsion shows a positive test for fats.

 Method

1. Add a few drops of ethanol to the food solution. Ethanol is a clear solution.

2. Stir the mixture.

3. Pour some of the liquid into a test tube of distilled water.

4. If a white emulsion appears, the solution contains lipids.

Food solution

Mix to dissolve some of the food.

Qualitative and quantitative food tests

The more drops of the solution needed, the lower the vitamin C content in the food.

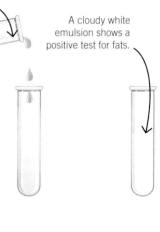

All the tests described here are qualitative food tests. They tell a scientist which nutrients are present in a food but don't convey the quantity of the nutrients. Quantitative food tests measure the amount of a particular nutrient in a food sample.

1. Vitamin C is found in citrus fruits such as oranges. You can use a solution of vitamin C either from the fruit or from vitamin C tablets for this quantitative food test.

2. The concentration of vitamin C in a food can then be determined by measuring how many drops of the solution are required to turn the reagent DCPIP from blue to colorless.

Digestive system

Food is mainly made up of large, insoluble molecules, such as lipids and proteins. These need to be digested: broken down into small, soluble molecules that can be absorbed into the bloodstream and then used by the body. This process takes place in the digestive system.

Organs in the digestive system
The digestive system consists mainly of a long, muscular tube that squeezes food through the body. It begins at the mouth and ends at the anus.

1. Food is broken down in the mouth by chewing. The teeth cut and crush the food into smaller pieces.

2. The food is mixed with saliva produced in the salivary glands. Saliva is a digestive juice—a fluid containing digestive enzymes such as amylase.

3. When you swallow, the esophagus (a muscular tube) moves food to the stomach.

4. Muscles in the stomach wall contract to churn the food. This mixes the food with more digestive juices and acid, breaking down the food further. The acid kills many harmful microorganisms that may have been swallowed with the food, and provides the optimum pH for stomach enzymes to work.

5. In the small intestine, digestive juices from the liver and pancreas are added and digestion is completed. The small, soluble nutrient molecules that have been produced pass through the intestinal wall into the bloodstream. This process is called absorption (see page 102).

6. Only food that cannot be digested reaches the large intestine. Here, water is absorbed into the bloodstream, leaving a mass of undigested food called feces.

7. Feces are stored in the rectum until they leave the body.

The liver is also involved in digestion. It produces bile, which it releases into the small intestine to emulsify lipids. This makes it easier for the enzymes to digest them.

8. The anus is a muscular ring through which feces pass out of the body. This removal of undigested waste is known as egestion.

Peristalsis

Food is moved through the digestive system by a process called peristalsis. Muscles in the wall of the esophagus and intestine contract to make them squeeze. Waves of contraction sweep through the digestive system to push the balls of semidigested food along.

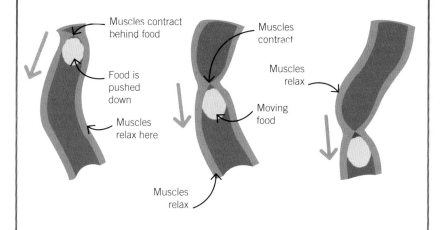

Muscles contract behind food

Food is pushed down

Muscles relax here

Muscles relax

Muscles contract

Muscles relax

Moving food

Key facts

✓ During digestion, large, insoluble molecules are broken down into smaller, soluble molecules.

✓ Food molecules are broken down in the mouth, stomach, and the small intestine.

✓ Soluble food molecules are absorbed into the blood in the small intestine.

✓ Water is absorbed into the bloodstream in the large intestine.

✓ Undigested food leaves the body through the anus.

Physical digestion

There are two types of digestion—physical (also known as mechanical) digestion and chemical digestion (see pages 100–101). Physical digestion involves physically breaking down food into smaller parts through processes such as chewing and crushing. This mainly takes place in the mouth. However, this also includes the churning of food in the stomach and the use of bile (see page 101), a liquid that breaks down large droplets of fat.

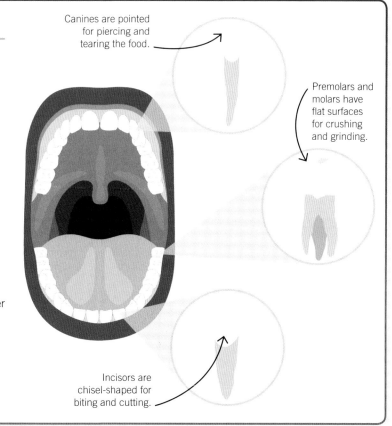

Canines are pointed for piercing and tearing the food.

Premolars and molars have flat surfaces for crushing and grinding.

Incisors are chisel-shaped for biting and cutting.

Teeth

In the mouth, food is broken down into smaller pieces by chewing. It is mixed with saliva before being swallowed and pushed down the esophagus. There are four main types of teeth—the shape of each tooth enables it to perform a different function.

Digestive enzymes

Chemical digestion involves enzymes. These are proteins that function as biological catalysts (see page 67). Digestive enzymes break down large nutrients into small, soluble food molecules that can be absorbed by the body.

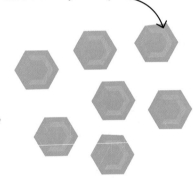

📌 Key facts

✓ Chemical digestion involves enzymes.

✓ Carbohydrase enzymes break down carbohydrates into sugars.

✓ Protease enzymes break down proteins into amino acids.

✓ Lipase enzymes break down lipids into fatty acids and glycerol.

Enzymes in action

Enzymes are produced by glands such as the salivary glands and from cells in the stomach, pancreas, and small intestine. Different types of enzymes break down different groups of nutrients.

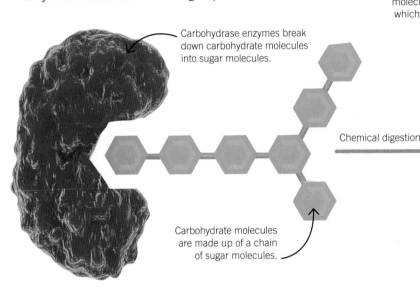

Carbohydrase enzymes break down carbohydrate molecules into sugar molecules.

Enzymes separate the carbohydrate molecules into small sugar molecules, which then pass into the bloodstream and are used by the body.

Chemical digestion

Carbohydrate molecules are made up of a chain of sugar molecules.

Carbohydrase enzymes
Carbohydrate digestion occurs in the mouth and small intestine. Enzymes that break down carbohydrates are called carbohydrases. They break down carbohydrates into simple sugars, which are used for energy. Amylase is an example of a carbohydrase. It breaks down starch in sugar molecules.

🔍 Maintaining optimum enzyme conditions

Each enzyme works best at a certain pH (see page 69). For example, pepsin, a protease enzyme, has an optimum pH of around 2 (acidic). The hydrochloric acid present in the stomach ensures that pepsin can catalyze reactions at its maximum rate.

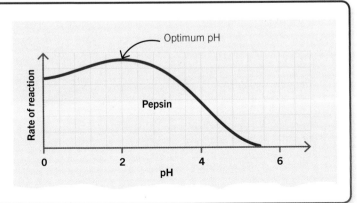

Protease enzymes

Protein digestion occurs in the stomach and small intestine. Enzymes that break down proteins are called proteases. Proteases break down proteins into amino acids, which are used for growth and repair. About 20 different amino acids are used in the human body.

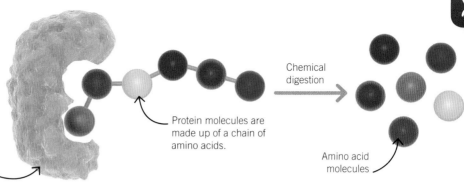

Protease enzymes break down protein molecules into amino acids.

Protein molecules are made up of a chain of amino acids.

Chemical digestion

Amino acid molecules

Lipase enzymes

Lipid digestion occurs in the small intestine. Lipids are used as a store of energy and for insulation. Enzymes that break down lipids are called lipases. They break down lipids into fatty acid and glycerol molecules.

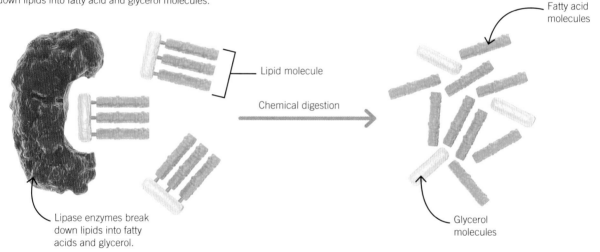

Lipid molecule

Chemical digestion

Fatty acid molecules

Lipase enzymes break down lipids into fatty acids and glycerol.

Glycerol molecules

🔍 Breaking down fats

The enzymes in the small intestine work best in alkaline conditions. However, when the food arrives it is too acidic after being in the stomach. Bile is secreted into the small intestine where it has two effects:

- It neutralizes the acid by providing the alkaline conditions needed.

- It emulsifies fat droplets, which means it breaks them up into hundreds of tiny droplets, providing a larger surface area for the lipase enzymes to work on.

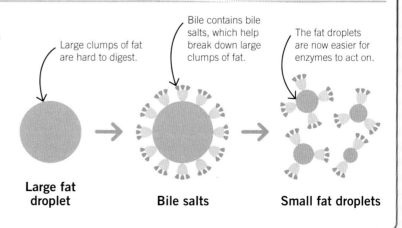

Large clumps of fat are hard to digest.

Bile contains bile salts, which help break down large clumps of fat.

The fat droplets are now easier for enzymes to act on.

Large fat droplet

Bile salts

Small fat droplets

Absorption of food

The small nutrient molecules produced during digestion pass into the bloodstream through the wall of the small intestine. This process is known as absorption. The molecules are then transported to where they are needed in the body. The small intestine has a number of adaptations to ensure that nutrients are absorbed before the undigested food leaves the body.

Key facts

✓ Nutrients are absorbed into the blood in the small intestine by diffusion and active transport.

✓ Villi lining the small intestine create a large surface area for absorption.

✓ Villi have a rich blood supply to maximize diffusion and to transport nutrients away.

Structure of the small intestine

To maximize the rate of absorption, the folded inner lining of the small intestine, which is over 5 m long, is covered in fingerlike projections called villi (singular villus). These increase the surface area of the small intestine, maximizing the rate of nutrient absorption.

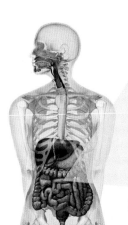

Digestive system in humans

The villus wall is very thin—the short distance allows diffusion to occur easily.

Vessels called lacteals absorb fatty acids and glycerol. These are then transported in lymph fluid before passing into the bloodstream.

Food molecules are absorbed by the villus through diffusion.

Blood capillaries absorb simple sugars, amino acids, and other nutrients, which are carried in the blood to the liver. Nutrients are absorbed into the blood through a combination of diffusion and active transport. By removing these substances quickly, their concentration remains low in the blood. This allows diffusion to occur faster.

🔍 Assimilation of food

The movement of digested food molecules into the cells where they are used is called assimilation. For example, glucose diffuses into body cells where it is used in respiration to release energy.

The liver is an important organ in assimilation:
- It converts excess glucose into glycogen—a complex carbohydrate. Glycogen is stored until additional energy is required, when it is converted back into glucose.
- It converts excess amino acids into carbohydrates and fats, which results in the production of a waste product called urea. This is then removed from the body by the kidneys.

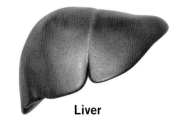
Liver

Transport
in Plants

Transport system

In plants, a series of tiny tubes called xylem tubes carry water and minerals from the roots to the stem and leaves, while phloem tubes carry sugar from leaves to the rest of the plant. Both sets of vessels are made from cells that form a continuous pipe for liquid to flow through.

Key facts

✓ Water and minerals are transported from the roots to the leaves by xylem tubes.

✓ Phloem tubes transport dissolved sugars around the plant.

✓ Xylem and phloem tissue are grouped to form larger structures called vascular bundles.

✓ The upward movement of water to all parts of the plant is called the transpiration stream.

✓ The movement of sugars around the plant is called translocation.

Xylem
Xylem tubes are made from dead cells that have joined together. There is no cytoplasm in these cells. Xylem transports dissolved substances and the water needed for photosynthesis upward to all parts of the plant. This movement of water is called the transpiration stream.

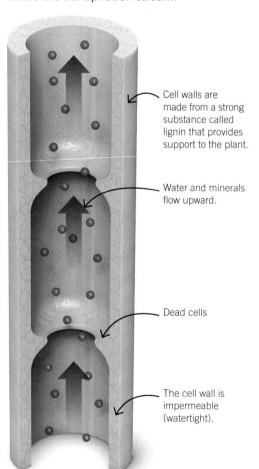

Cell walls are made from a strong substance called lignin that provides support to the plant.

Water and minerals flow upward.

Dead cells

The cell wall is impermeable (watertight).

Phloem
Phloem tubes consist of living cells with small holes in the end walls, forming structures called sieve plates. These allow dissolved sugars produced during photosynthesis to pass through the cell walls. Substances move in both directions. This is called translocation.

Substances flow in both directions.

Sieve plate

Inside a leaf, stem, and root

Xylem and phloem tubes form structures called vascular bundles. The position of vascular bundles varies inside roots, stems, and leaves, as shown in these cross sections.

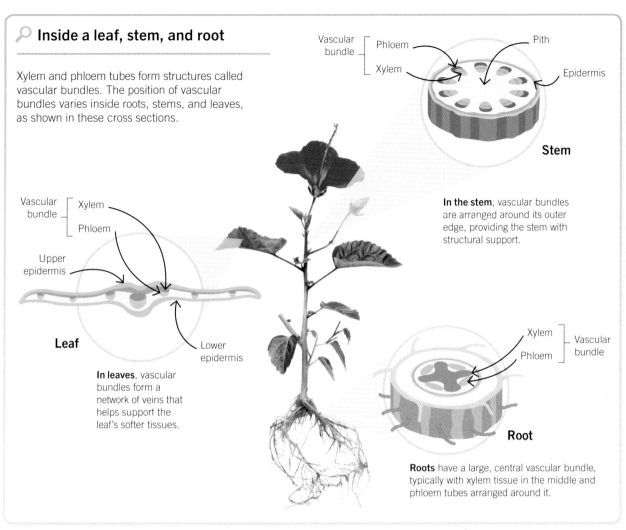

Vascular bundle — Phloem, Xylem

Pith

Epidermis

Stem

In the stem, vascular bundles are arranged around its outer edge, providing the stem with structural support.

Vascular bundle — Xylem, Phloem

Upper epidermis

Leaf

Lower epidermis

In leaves, vascular bundles form a network of veins that helps support the leaf's softer tissues.

Xylem — Vascular bundle
Phloem

Root

Roots have a large, central vascular bundle, typically with xylem tissue in the middle and phloem tubes arranged around it.

Movement of water through a plant

A xylem tube is narrower than a strand of hair. If you place celery in a jar of colored water and let it stand for a day, these microscopic tubes will show the color of the dye.

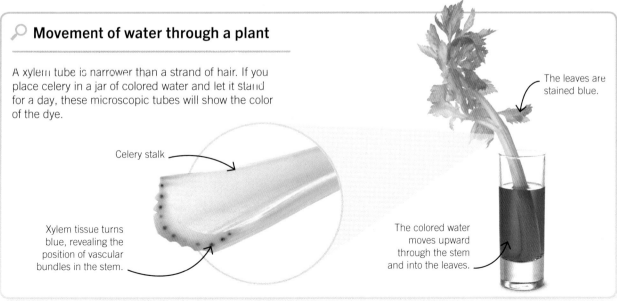

The leaves are stained blue.

Celery stalk

Xylem tissue turns blue, revealing the position of vascular bundles in the stem.

The colored water moves upward through the stem and into the leaves.

Transpiration

Plants absorb water through their roots and lose it from their leaves by evaporation. The loss of water from the leaves draws more water up through the plant. This continual flow of water through a plant, driven by evaporation, is known as transpiration.

Transporting water

When a plant loses water through its leaves, the water is replaced through the roots. The uninterrupted stream of water from the roots to the leaves is called the transpiration stream.

Key facts

✓ Transpiration is the movement of water up through a plant, driven by evaporation from the leaves.

✓ Plants regulate transpiration by opening their stomata (pores in leaves).

✓ Water passes through xylem tubes as it travels through a plant.

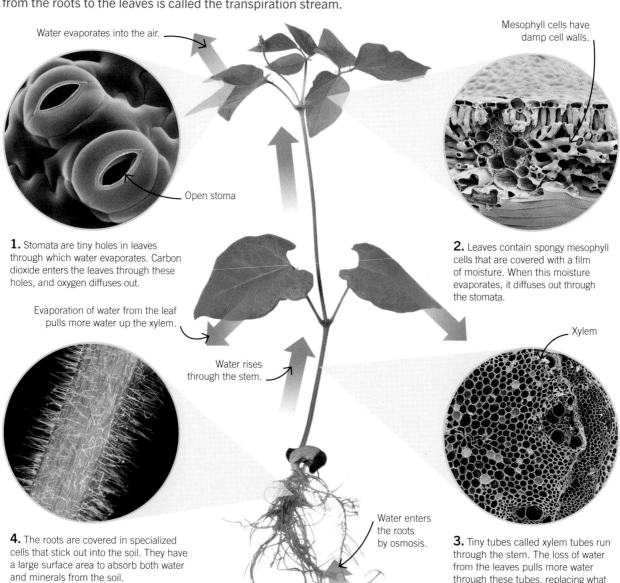

Water evaporates into the air.

Mesophyll cells have damp cell walls.

Open stoma

1. Stomata are tiny holes in leaves through which water evaporates. Carbon dioxide enters the leaves through these holes, and oxygen diffuses out.

2. Leaves contain spongy mesophyll cells that are covered with a film of moisture. When this moisture evaporates, it diffuses out through the stomata.

Evaporation of water from the leaf pulls more water up the xylem.

Xylem

Water rises through the stem.

Water enters the roots by osmosis.

4. The roots are covered in specialized cells that stick out into the soil. They have a large surface area to absorb both water and minerals from the soil.

3. Tiny tubes called xylem tubes run through the stem. The loss of water from the leaves pulls more water through these tubes, replacing what has been lost from the mesophyll cells.

Plant roots

Plant roots are adapted to maximize the absorption of water and minerals from the soil. If a plant loses more water from its leaves than it gains from its roots, the plant starts to wilt (droop) and may eventually die.

Root network

Cells on the surface of roots are covered in millions of fine hairlike extensions that stick out into the soil. These take in water and minerals from the soil. Water is absorbed by osmosis (see pages 52–53) and mineral ions are absorbed by active transport (see page 56).

Wilting

Water is pulled upward from the roots to the stem and leaves. If there isn't enough water, the vacuoles in cells throughout the plant shrink. Pressure is not put on the cell walls to keep the plant upright, so the plant starts to wilt (see page 53).

Root hairs

Roots extend downward into the soil, helping anchor the plant into the ground as well as absorbing water and minerals.

Root hair cell

The root is covered in a layer of cells called the epidermis. Root hairs are long extensions of the epidermal cells. These hairs create a large surface area for absorbing water and minerals from the soil.

⚙ How water and minerals are absorbed

Water and dissolved minerals from the soil are absorbed by root hair cells. These are then passed from cell to cell until they reach the tiny pipelike xylem vessels. From here, water is transported to all parts of the plant.

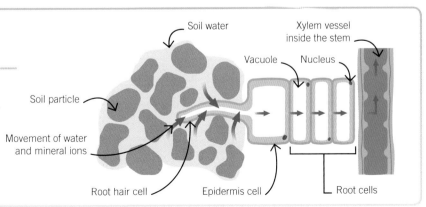

Soil water

Xylem vessel inside the stem

Vacuole   Nucleus

Soil particle

Movement of water and mineral ions

Root hair cell   Epidermis cell   Root cells

Rate of transpiration

The rate of transpiration (how quickly water evaporates from a plant) can be affected by four factors: temperature, humidity, wind speed, and light intensity.

Key facts

✓ Transpiration is the name given to the process of water leaving the plant through the leaves.

✓ More transpiration happens during the day than at night because the stomata are closed in the dark.

✓ Four factors affect the rate of transpiration: temperature, humidity, wind speed, and light intensity.

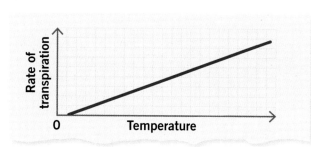

Temperature
An increase in temperature increases the rate of transpiration as it increases the rate at which water evaporates from leaf cells and escapes into the air through stomata (the tiny pores found on the underside of most leaves).

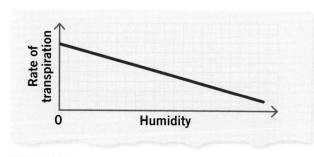

Humidity
Humidity is the amount of water vapor in the air. When humidity is low, the air is dry and water evaporates easily from leaves, resulting in a high rate of transpiration. When humidity is high, water evaporates less easily and transpiration is slower.

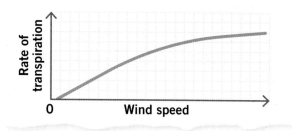

Wind speed
Higher wind speeds cause the rate of transpiration to increase. This is because the water vapor that has diffused out of the leaves is moved away quickly by the wind, preventing humidity from building up around the plant.

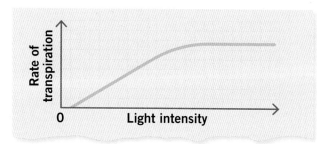

Light intensity
High light intensity increases the rate of photosynthesis, causing stomata to open so that leaf cells can get enough carbon dioxide. When stomata are fully open, water vapor escapes more easily, increasing the rate of transpiration. Bright sunshine also warms leaves, increasing the rate of transpiration by raising the temperature.

Measuring transpiration

You can estimate the rate of transpiration by using an apparatus called a potometer to measure how quickly a plant takes up water. You can change light intensity, temperature, humidity, and wind speed to see how environmental factors affect the rate.

How it works

As water transpires (evaporates) from leaves, it is replaced by water taken up from the tubing. Some water entering the plant is used in photosynthesis, so not all is transpired.

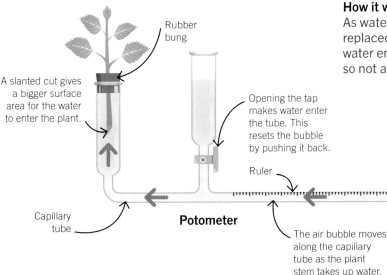

Rubber bung

A slanted cut gives a bigger surface area for the water to enter the plant.

Opening the tap makes water enter the tube. This resets the bubble by pushing it back.

Ruler

Water movement

Capillary tube

Potometer

The air bubble moves along the capillary tube as the plant stem takes up water.

Beaker of water

⚙ Method

1. Put the potometer together underwater to keep air out. Then insert a plant stem into the hole in the bung.

2. To allow an air bubble to form, remove the beaker of water from the capillary tube. Once an air bubble forms, put the water beaker back.

3. Wait until the bubble has reached the start of the ruler and then use a stopwatch to time how long the bubble takes to move a set distance.

4. Repeat the measurement after changing one of the environmental factors that affect transpiration. For example, to increase light intensity, place the potometer by a sunny window.

📑 Calculating the rate of transpiration

If an air bubble moves 30 mm in 60 seconds, the rate of transpiration can be calculated as follows:

$$\text{rate of transpiration} = \frac{\text{distance moved by bubble (mm)}}{\text{time taken (seconds)}}$$

Put the numbers into the equation: $\dfrac{30 \text{ mm}}{60 \text{ s}}$

Calculate the answer using a calculator and include the units:

$$\text{rate of transpiration} = 0.5 \text{ mm/s}$$

Transport
in Animals

The circulatory system

Most animals have a transport system that delivers nutrients and oxygen to every part of the body. It also carries waste products such as carbon dioxide to organs from where they can be removed from the body.

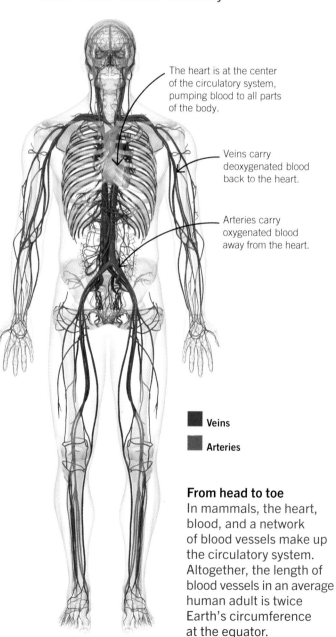

The heart is at the center of the circulatory system, pumping blood to all parts of the body.

Veins carry deoxygenated blood back to the heart.

Arteries carry oxygenated blood away from the heart.

■ Veins

■ Arteries

From head to toe
In mammals, the heart, blood, and a network of blood vessels make up the circulatory system. Altogether, the length of blood vessels in an average human adult is twice Earth's circumference at the equator.

Key facts

✓ Humans have a double circulatory system—blood flows through the heart twice during each circuit of the body.

✓ The circulatory system delivers nutrients and oxygen to every cell in the body. It also transports waste products such as carbon dioxide.

🔍 Types of circulatory systems

Double circulatory system
Humans and other mammals have a double circulatory system. This means that blood passes through the heart twice in one complete circuit.

Lungs

First circuit
The heart pumps deoxygenated blood to the lungs. Here, the blood picks up oxygen before returning to the heart.

Heart

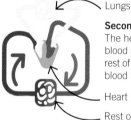

Lungs

Second circuit
The heart pumps oxygenated blood at a higher pressure to the rest of the body, and deoxygenated blood returns to the heart.

Heart

Rest of the body

Single circulatory system
Some animals, such as fish, have a single circulatory system. Deoxygenated blood from the body travels to the heart and then to the gills to become oxygenated, before returning to the body.

Gill capillaries

Heart

Body capillaries

■ Deoxygenated blood

■ Oxygenated blood

Blood vessels

Blood flows through three types of vessels: arteries, veins, and capillaries. These form an extensive network of tubelike structures that transport nutrients and oxygen to every cell in your body.

Transport system

Arteries carry blood away from the heart and veins carry blood back to the heart. Both these vessels are linked by tiny capillaries that go to every part of the body. Capillaries branch out from tiny arteries called arterioles and then merge with venules, which form veins.

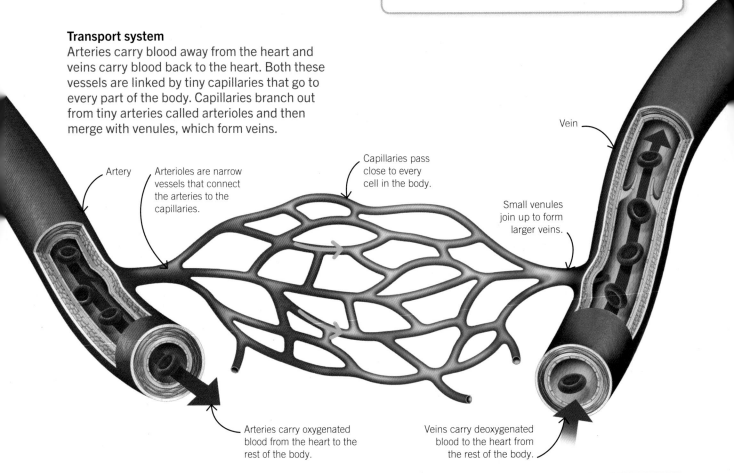

Artery

Arterioles are narrow vessels that connect the arteries to the capillaries.

Capillaries pass close to every cell in the body.

Vein

Small venules join up to form larger veins.

Arteries carry oxygenated blood from the heart to the rest of the body.

Veins carry deoxygenated blood to the heart from the rest of the body.

📑 Calculating the rate of blood flow

Blood flows at different rates depending on the blood vessel it is traveling through. To calculate blood flow, use the following formula:

$$\text{rate of blood flow} = \frac{\text{volume of blood}}{\text{number of minutes}}$$

Example: 1,866 ml of blood passes through an artery in 3 minutes. Calculate the flow of blood.

$$\text{rate of blood flow} = \frac{1{,}866 \text{ ml}}{3 \text{ minutes}}$$

$$= 622 \text{ ml/min}$$

Structure of blood vessels

Blood vessels vary in size and structure depending on their function. Both arteries and veins have walls made up of three main layers, and capillaries have walls with just a single layer of cells.

Key facts

✓ Arteries have thick, muscular, elastic walls to withstand the high blood pressure.

✓ Veins have valves to ensure that blood flows in the right direction.

✓ Capillaries have very thin walls so that substances can pass easily between blood and cells.

Arteries
When the heart contracts, it forces blood through the arteries at very high pressure. Arteries need to be strong to withstand this pressure. They have thick, muscular walls and an elastic (stretchy) layer, enabling them to stretch as the blood surges through the narrow opening (lumen).

Veins
Veins carry blood under low pressure back to the heart, so the walls are not as thick or elastic as those of arteries. To allow blood to flow easily back to the heart, the lumen of a vein is large. Veins also have valves to ensure that blood flows in one direction.

Capillaries
Capillaries are tiny, squeezing through gaps to transport substances to every cell in the body. When blood enters these vessels, it slows down, allowing substances such as nutrients, oxygen, and waste to diffuse through the thin, permeable walls.

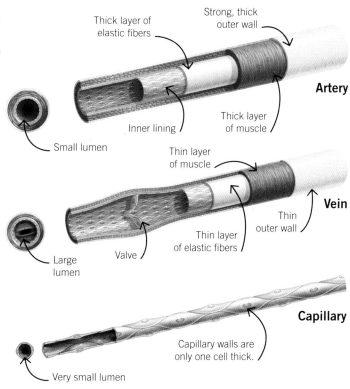

Thick layer of elastic fibers

Strong, thick outer wall

Artery

Inner lining

Thick layer of muscle

Small lumen

Thin layer of muscle

Vein

Thin outer wall

Thin layer of elastic fibers

Valve

Large lumen

Capillary

Capillary walls are only one cell thick.

Very small lumen

⚙ How valves work

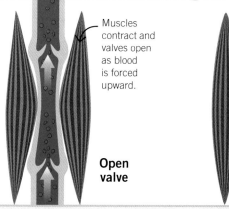

Veins have flaplike structures called valves that open and close so that blood flows in the right direction. Valves open when the blood pushes against them and close when the blood flows back. Pressure from body muscles around the veins also helps keep the blood moving forward. Shown here are valves in the veins of the lower leg.

Muscles contract and valves open as blood is forced upward.

Open valve

Muscles relax and valves close to prevent blood from flowing backward.

Closed valve

Blood

Blood supplies your body with oxygen and the nutrients needed to keep it working. It's made up of trillions of cells and countless substances that float in a straw-colored liquid called plasma.

Composition of blood
Plasma makes up most of your blood, followed by the three types of blood cells: red blood cells, white blood cells, and platelets.

> 📌 **Key facts**
>
> ✓ The four components of blood are red blood cells, white blood cells, platelets, and plasma.
> ✓ Red blood cells contain hemoglobin for transporting oxygen.
> ✓ White blood cells (lymphocytes and phagocytes) defend against pathogens.
> ✓ Platelets help blood clot.
> ✓ Plasma carries dissolved substances.

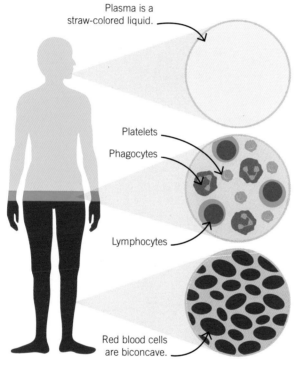

Plasma is a straw-colored liquid.

Platelets

Phagocytes

Lymphocytes

Red blood cells are biconcave.

Plasma
Red and white cells and platelets float in a liquid called plasma, which mainly consists of water. Substances including nutrients, waste (carbon dioxide and urea), hormones, and antibodies are dissolved in this liquid and are transported to all the cells of the body.

White blood cells and platelets
There are two main types of white blood cells—lymphocytes and phagocytes (see pages 264–265). Lymphocytes produce chemicals called antibodies that attack pathogens, while phagocytes engulf and destroy pathogens. White blood cells have a nucleus. Platelets are tiny cell fragments with no nucleus. They clump together to form clots.

Red blood cells
Red blood cells are small, flexible discs that can squeeze through blood vessels. They are described as biconcave because each side of the disc has a concave depression. Red blood cells have no nuclei and are packed with hemoglobin, which carries oxygen.

🔍 Transporting oxygen

Cells need oxygen for respiration—a chemical process that releases energy. Your red blood cells contain hemoglobin molecules that pick up oxygen in the lungs and transport it to all the cells of your body. Iron in hemoglobin helps it carry oxygen.

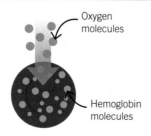

Oxygen molecules

Hemoglobin molecules

1. In the lungs, oxygen diffuses into the blood. It binds with the hemoglobin molecules to form oxyhemoglobin.

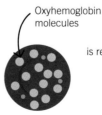

Oxyhemoglobin molecules

2. The oxyhemoglobin molecules are transported to the body's cells.

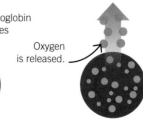

Oxygen is released.

3. In blood capillaries, oxyhemoglobin splits and releases oxygen, which the body's cells absorb.

The heart

The human heart pumps blood around the body. The right side pumps blood to the lungs to collect oxygen, while the left side pumps blood to the rest of the body.

Key facts

✓ The heart has four chambers: the right and left atria, and the right and left ventricles.

✓ The atria receive blood from the lungs and body.

✓ The ventricles pump blood out of the heart.

Structure of the heart

The heart consists of four chambers—two small upper chambers called atria (singular atrium) and two lower chambers called ventricles. The four major blood vessels that carry blood in and out of the heart are vena cava, pulmonary artery, aorta, and pulmonary vein. Valves inside the heart ensure that blood flows in one direction.

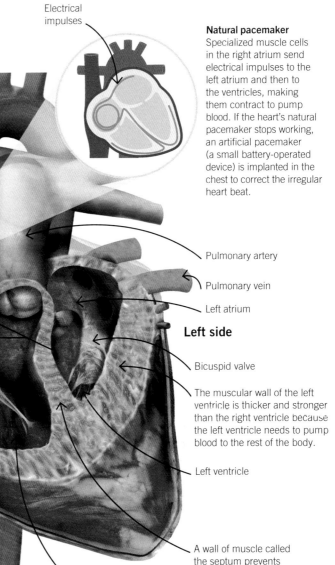

Electrical impulses

Natural pacemaker
Specialized muscle cells in the right atrium send electrical impulses to the left atrium and then to the ventricles, making them contract to pump blood. If the heart's natural pacemaker stops working, an artificial pacemaker (a small battery-operated device) is implanted in the chest to correct the irregular heart beat.

Vena cava

Aorta

Right atrium

Right side

Semilunar valves

Tricuspid valve

Pulmonary artery

Pulmonary vein

Left atrium

Left side

Bicuspid valve

The muscular wall of the left ventricle is thicker and stronger than the right ventricle because the left ventricle needs to pump blood to the rest of the body.

Left ventricle

A wall of muscle called the septum prevents oxygenated blood and deoxygenated blood from mixing.

Right ventricle

Coronary arteries

Coronary arteries
These supply the heart muscle with oxygenated blood and nutrients. If they become blocked, the heart is starved of oxygen, resulting in a heart attack.

How the heart works

Every heartbeat consists of a cycle of carefully controlled steps, which takes less than a second to complete. During each cycle, deoxygenated blood is forced through the right side of the heart to the lungs, while oxygenated blood is forced through the left side of the heart to the rest of the body.

Controlled sequence

Heartbeats are controlled by electrical impulses generated in the heart. Each heartbeat has three phases. When muscles contract, the chambers get smaller, squeezing the blood out. The chambers relax and fill up again with blood.

■ Deoxygenated blood

■ Oxygenated blood

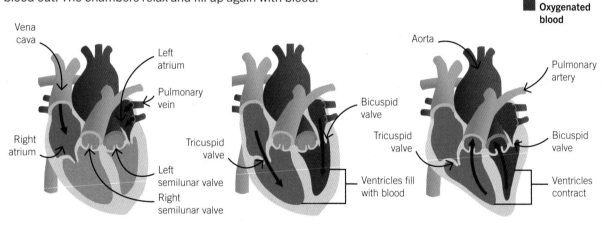

Vena cava · Left atrium · Pulmonary vein · Right atrium · Tricuspid valve · Left semilunar valve · Right semilunar valve · Bicuspid valve · Tricuspid valve · Ventricles fill with blood · Aorta · Pulmonary artery · Bicuspid valve · Ventricles contract

1. When the muscles of the heart relax, the atria (the upper chambers) fill with blood from the vena cava and pulmonary vein. The semilunar valves shut, preventing blood from flowing into the ventricles.

2. When the atria contract, blood is forced through the tricuspid and bicuspid valves into the ventricles (the lower chambers).

3. The ventricles contract and the semilunar valves open as blood surges out of the heart through the pulmonary artery and aorta. At the same time, the bicuspid and tricuspid valves shut.

🖩 Calculating cardiac output

Cardiac output is the total volume of blood that is pumped out every minute by the left ventricle. The heart rate (this is the same as your pulse rate) is the number of times the heart beats per minute (bpm). You can calculate the cardiac output using the following equation:

cardiac output = heart rate x stroke volume

Example: Calculate the cardiac output of a heart that pumps out 60 cm³ of blood with a heart rate of 55 bpm.

cardiac output = heart rate x stroke volume

= 55 x 60

= 3,300 cm³/min

Heart rate

Heart rate is a measure of how many times the heart beats each minute. The typical resting heart rate is between 60 and 100 beats per minute (bpm). This is affected by age, sex, and how fit a person is.

The pulse

Every time the muscle of your heart contracts to pump, a surge of blood moves through the arteries as blood is carried around the body. This can be felt wherever an artery comes close to the skin's surface, such as in the wrists.

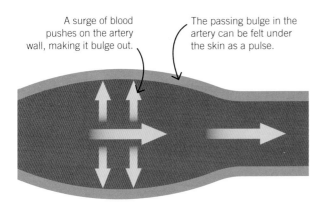

A surge of blood pushes on the artery wall, making it bulge out.

The passing bulge in the artery can be felt under the skin as a pulse.

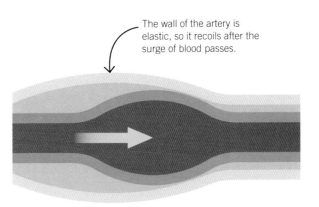

The wall of the artery is elastic, so it recoils after the surge of blood passes.

⚙ Measuring your pulse rate

Because a pulse is felt for each pumping action of the heart, the pulse rate is the same as the heart rate and so is affected by the same things, such as exercise.

1. A pulse can be taken by using two fingers. Put the first and middle fingers gently on the inside of the wrist and press the skin until you feel the pulse.

2. Count the number of beats felt in 30 seconds. Multiply the number by two to calculate the number of times the heart beats per minute. Repeat at least 3 times and calculate an average.

🔍 Heart sounds

A normal heart beat makes a "lub-dub" sound. The noise comes from the heart's valves closing to stop blood flowing backward. "Lub" is caused by the tricuspid and bicuspid valves closing to prevent backflow into the atrium, and "dub" is caused by the semilunar valves closing.

A stethoscope can be used to listen to the heart as it beats.

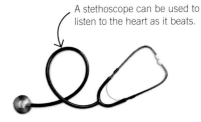

Changing heart rate

Your heart rate speeds up when you exercise and your muscles work harder. It can also rise when the heart is stimulated by a hormone called adrenaline, which is released into the bloodstream when we get excited, angry, or afraid.

Heart rate and exercise

Your heart beats more rapidly during strenuous exercise. This increases the volume of blood pumped around the body and the speed at which it reaches your cells. The graph below shows how a typical person's heart rate changes during a mixture of walking and running.

Key facts

✓ **Heart rate increases with the level of exercise.**

✓ **As the heart beats faster, it pumps more oxygenated blood to working muscles.**

✓ **The hormone adrenaline makes the heart rate go faster when a person is excited, angry, or afraid.**

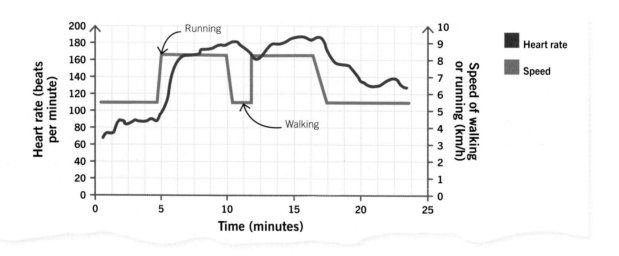

Heart rate

Speed

⚙ Measuring how heart rate changes with exercise

The more intense the exercise, the greater the increase in heart rate. People who exercise regularly are fitter and tend to have a lower resting heart rate. Their heart rate also returns to its resting rate more rapidly after exercise. To see how the heart rate changes with exercise, you can carry out this practical by checking your pulse rate. You can feel your pulse on the inside of your wrist (see page 117).

1. Sit for a period of at least 5 minutes. Then measure your pulse rate by counting the number of beats in 30 seconds.

2. Next, do some light exercise. This can be walking or jumping for 2 minutes. After this period, make a note of your pulse rate.

3. After a rest period, more strenuous exercise can be undertaken for 2 minutes. Then check your pulse rate.

4. Multiply the number of beats by two for beats per minute. Record the results in a table. You will see how your heart rate varies.

Beats per minute	
Sitting	70
Walking	85
Skipping	105

Lymphatic system

The lymphatic system is a network of vessels that carry a fluid called lymph around the body. Scattered throughout the lymphatic system are clumps of tissue called lymph nodes. These contain cells called lymphocytes, which fight pathogens.

Key facts

✓ The fluid carried by the lymphatic system is called lymph.

✓ The lymphatic system returns lymph to the blood.

✓ Lymph contains lymphocytes.

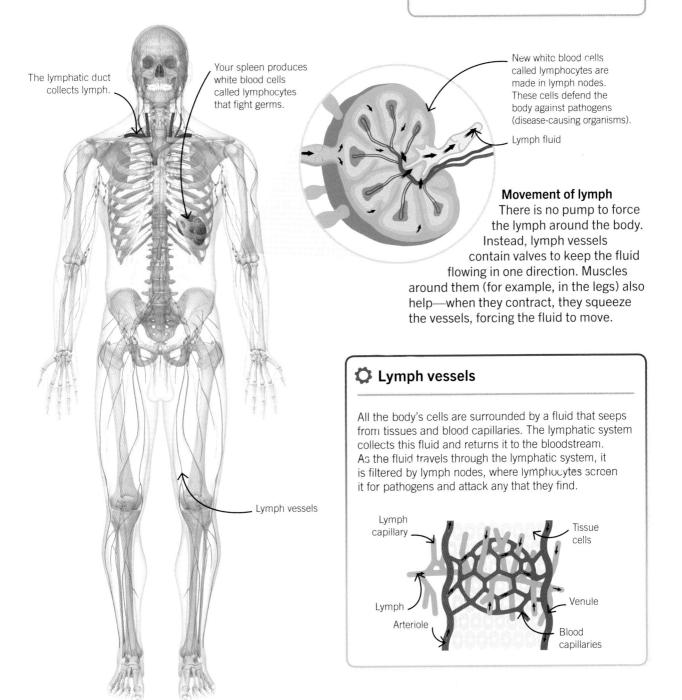

The lymphatic duct collects lymph.

Your spleen produces white blood cells called lymphocytes that fight germs.

New white blood cells called lymphocytes are made in lymph nodes. These cells defend the body against pathogens (disease-causing organisms).

Lymph fluid

Movement of lymph

There is no pump to force the lymph around the body. Instead, lymph vessels contain valves to keep the fluid flowing in one direction. Muscles around them (for example, in the legs) also help—when they contract, they squeeze the vessels, forcing the fluid to move.

Lymph vessels

⚙ Lymph vessels

All the body's cells are surrounded by a fluid that seeps from tissues and blood capillaries. The lymphatic system collects this fluid and returns it to the bloodstream. As the fluid travels through the lymphatic system, it is filtered by lymph nodes, where lymphocytes screen it for pathogens and attack any that they find.

Lymph capillary

Tissue cells

Lymph

Venule

Arteriole

Blood capillaries

The lungs

Your lungs are part of the respiratory system. They play an important role in the exchange of gases—oxygen from the air enters the bloodstream when you breathe in, and waste carbon dioxide leaves the bloodstream when you breathe out.

Key facts

✓ Air mostly enters through the nose and passes through the trachea, bronchi, and bronchioles, before reaching the alveoli.

✓ Gas exchange takes place in the alveoli.

✓ Gas exchange surfaces are areas where oxygen enters the bloodstream and carbon dioxide leaves the bloodstream.

The respiratory system
Inhaled air enters the trachea (windpipe), which is split into two tubes called bronchi (singular bronchus). Inside the two spongelike lungs, these tubes divide into smaller tubes called bronchioles.

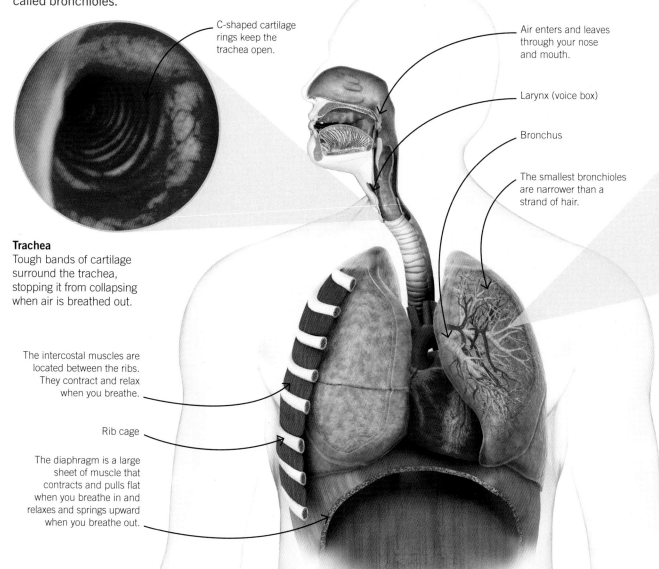

C-shaped cartilage rings keep the trachea open.

Air enters and leaves through your nose and mouth.

Larynx (voice box)

Bronchus

The smallest bronchioles are narrower than a strand of hair.

Trachea
Tough bands of cartilage surround the trachea, stopping it from collapsing when air is breathed out.

The intercostal muscles are located between the ribs. They contract and relax when you breathe.

Rib cage

The diaphragm is a large sheet of muscle that contracts and pulls flat when you breathe in and relaxes and springs upward when you breathe out.

Gas exchange

All living organisms have gas exchange surfaces, such as in the lungs, where gases enter and leave the blood. At the end of each bronchiole are tiny air sacs called alveoli (singular alveolus). This is where gas exchange takes place; oxygen moves from the alveoli into the blood, and carbon dioxide moves from the blood into the alveoli. Both gases move by diffusion (see page 51).

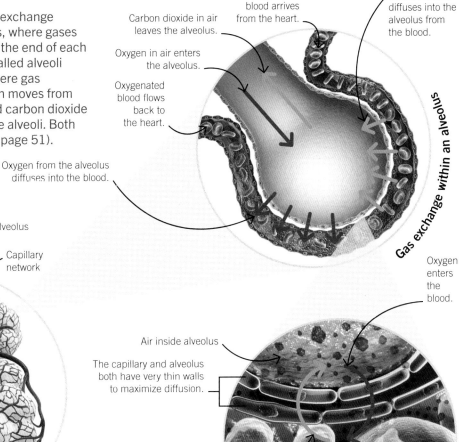

Deoxygenated blood arrives from the heart.

Carbon dioxide in air leaves the alveolus.

Oxygen in air enters the alveolus.

Oxygenated blood flows back to the heart.

Carbon dioxide diffuses into the alveolus from the blood.

Oxygen from the alveolus diffuses into the blood.

Gas exchange within an alveolus

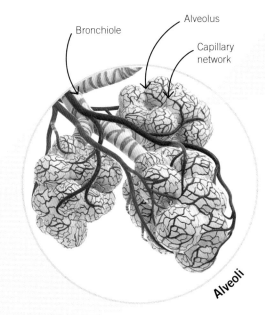

Bronchiole

Alveolus

Capillary network

Alveoli

Oxygen enters the blood.

Air inside alveolus

The capillary and alveolus both have very thin walls to maximize diffusion.

Carbon dioxide enters the alveolus.

Red blood cell

Alveolus and capillary walls

🔍 Gas exchange in fish

In a fish, the gills are the gas exchange surfaces. Gills are made up of lots of gill filaments. This increases the surface area for gas exchange by diffusion— just as the countless alveoli in the lungs increase the gas exchange area for a human.

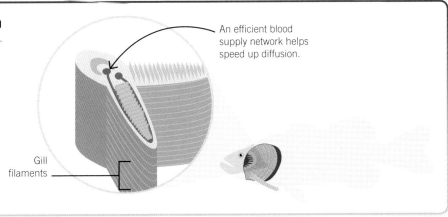

An efficient blood supply network helps speed up diffusion.

Gill filaments

Breathing

When you breathe in, oxygen-rich air enters your lungs so the oxygen can enter your bloodstream. When you breathe out, the air contains less oxygen but more waste carbon dioxide that has entered the air from the bloodstream.

Breathing in and out

Breathing is controlled by a set of muscles that work together to make the volume of the chest (thorax) cavity increase and decrease. This in turn makes air move in and out.

Key facts

✓ Breathing in is called inhalation (or inspiration); breathing out is called exhalation (or expiration).

✓ The ribs, intercostal muscles, and diaphragm control your breathing.

✓ Air enters and leaves the lungs because of changes in pressure and volume.

✓ Sticky mucus traps dust and particles.

✓ Ciliated cells lining the airways sweep away dust and microorganisms trapped in the mucus.

Inhalation (breathing in)

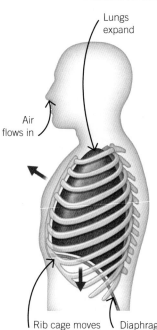

Lungs expand

Air flows in

Rib cage moves outward

Diaphragm is pulled downward

1. The outer set of muscles between the ribs (external intercostal muscles) contract. This makes the ribs move upward and outward.

2. At the same time, the muscles of the diaphragm contract. This flattens and pulls the dome-shaped diaphragm down.

3. The volume of the chest cavity increases. This causes pressure inside the chest cavity to fall below the pressure outside the lungs. As a result, air is drawn into the lungs.

Exhalation (breathing out)

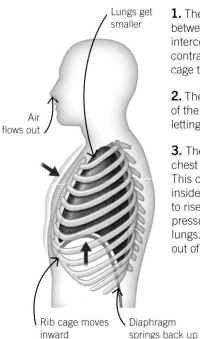

Lungs get smaller

Air flows out

Rib cage moves inward

Diaphragm springs back up

1. The inner set of muscles between the ribs (internal intercostal muscles) contract, causing the rib cage to move downward.

2. The muscles of the diaphragm relax, letting it move back up.

3. The volume of the chest cavity decreases. This causes pressure inside the chest cavity to rise above the pressure outside the lungs. Air is now forced out of the lungs.

🔍 Cilia and mucus

When you breathe in, hairs inside the nose trap dust particles and microorganisms. The trachea and bronchi are also lined with cells that have microscopic hairlike structures called cilia and cells that release mucus. Together, these help prevent dust particles and microorganisms from getting into the lungs.

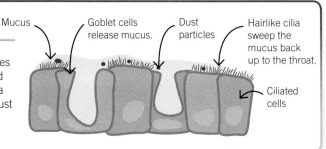

Mucus

Goblet cells release mucus.

Dust particles

Hairlike cilia sweep the mucus back up to the throat.

Ciliated cells

Effects of exercise on breathing

During exercise, a person breathes more rapidly and more deeply. This allows more oxygen to be taken into the body and more carbon dioxide to be removed. The extra oxygen is used to meet the increased respiration demands in the muscle cells.

Changes to depth and rate of breathing
For a person at rest, the volume of air that moves in and out of the lungs is around 500 cm³. The graph below shows how this changes during exercise. Not only does the volume breathed in and out (the depth of breathing) increase, but the rate of breathing increases, too—breathing gets faster as more breaths happen each minute.

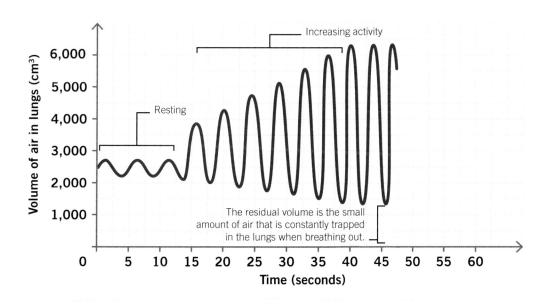

Increasing activity

Resting

The residual volume is the small amount of air that is constantly trapped in the lungs when breathing out.

Measuring breathing rate

A person's breathing rate (also known as the respiratory rate) can be measured by counting the number of breaths taken in one minute. The typical resting respiratory rate for a healthy adult is between 12 and 18 breaths per minute.

1. Count the number of breaths taken when resting for one minute. Repeat three times, and calculate the mean breathing rate.

2. Exercise for one minute and measure the breathing rate again. You will see that the harder you exercise, the faster your breathing rate.

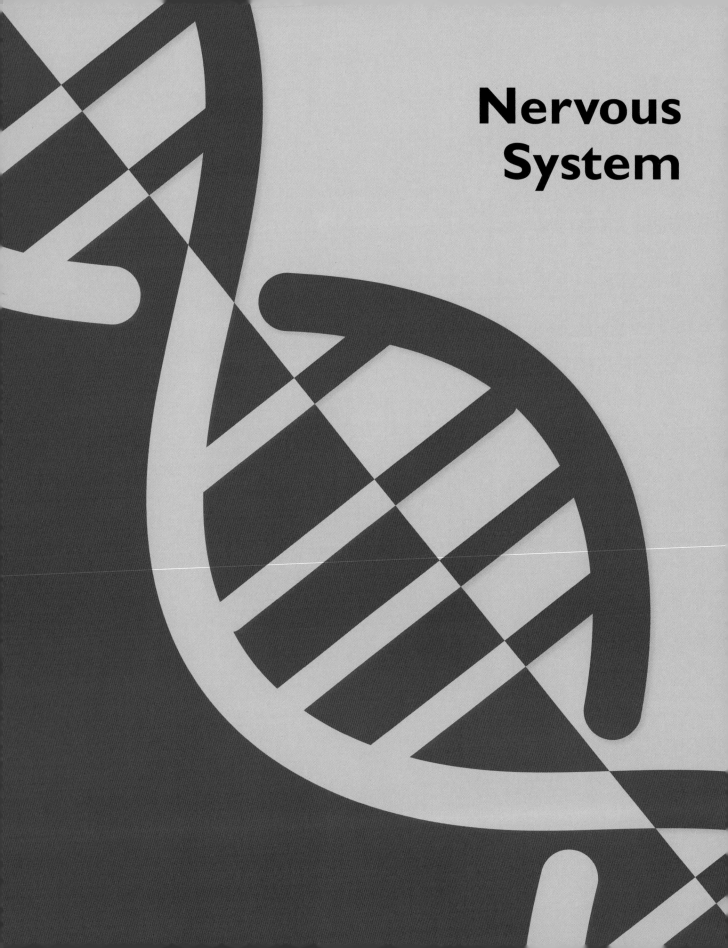

Nervous System

Stimulus and response

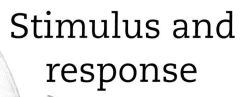

Organisms need to react to changing situations in order to survive. Animals may need to escape from predators or find food, for example. Any change that triggers a response in an organism is called a stimulus.

1. The sight of a predator, such as an owl, is a powerful stimulus for a harvest mouse.

2. The mouse uses receptors, such as the ones in its eyes, to detect stimuli, such as light. The receptors send signals to the brain, which figures out how to respond.

3. The mouse's brain sends signals to effectors—parts of the body, such as leg muscles, that produce a response. The mouse responds by running away and hiding.

🔍 Receptors and effectors

The main receptors that animals use to detect stimuli are their sense organs. For a mouse, these are its eyes, ears, whiskers, nose, and mouth. Effectors include not just the muscles the mouse uses to escape but also glands inside its body. For example, at the sight of a predator, the mouse's adrenal glands produce a hormone called adrenaline, which prepares the mouse's body for sudden action.

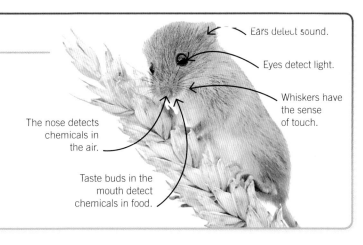

Ears detect sound.

Eyes detect light.

Whiskers have the sense of touch.

The nose detects chemicals in the air.

Taste buds in the mouth detect chemicals in food.

Nervous system

An animal's nervous system allows it to detect changes in its surroundings (stimuli) and respond quickly. It is made up of cells called neurons, which carry electrical impulses around the body at high speed.

Key facts

✓ Sense organs contain neurons called receptors that respond to specific stimuli.

✓ The brain and spinal cord make up the central nervous system (CNS), the nervous system's control center.

✓ Nerves carry electrical impulses between the CNS and the rest of the body.

⚙ How the nervous system works

Sensory neurons, such as light-sensitive cells in the human eye, detect changes in our surroundings. They then send electrical signals to the brain or spinal cord, which together form the central nervous system (CNS)—the nervous system's control center. The CNS processes the information and figures out how to respond. It then sends electrical signals along motor neurons to effectors, such as muscles, which respond.

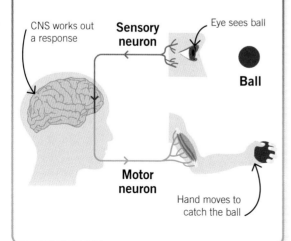

CNS works out a response

Sensory neuron

Eye sees ball

Ball

Motor neuron

Hand moves to catch the ball

The brain is the largest organ in the human nervous system.

Nerves are large bundles of neurons that carry electrical impulses to every part of the body.

The bones of the spine protect the delicate nervous tissue in the spinal cord.

The spinal cord connects the brain to the peripheral nervous system.

■ Central nervous system (CNS)

□ Peripheral nervous system

Human nervous system

The human nervous system has two main parts. The central nervous system (CNS) is made up of the brain and spinal cord. The peripheral nervous system is made up of all the nerves outside the CNS.

Neurons

The cells that make up the nervous system are called neurons or nerve cells. They carry information from the senses to the central nervous system (CNS) and from the CNS to muscles and glands. The information is sent as an electrical signal called a nerve impulse.

Key facts

✓ The electrical messages that neurons carry are called nerve signals or nerve impulses.

✓ The three main types of neurons are sensory neurons, motor neurons, and relay neurons.

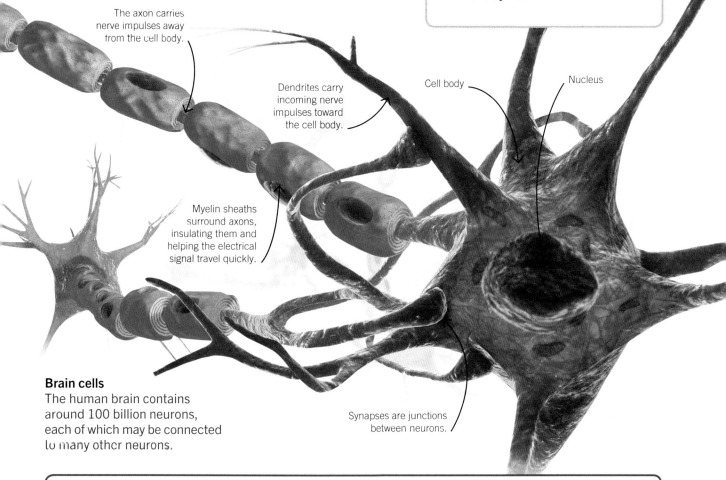

The axon carries nerve impulses away from the cell body.

Dendrites carry incoming nerve impulses toward the cell body.

Cell body

Nucleus

Myelin sheaths surround axons, insulating them and helping the electrical signal travel quickly.

Synapses are junctions between neurons.

Brain cells
The human brain contains around 100 billion neurons, each of which may be connected to many other neurons.

Types of neurons

Neurons can be more than 1 m long. There are three main types of neurons, each found in a different part of the nervous system.

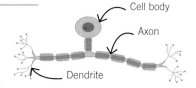

Cell body

Axon

Dendrite

Sensory neurons detect stimuli, such as light, and send electrical impulses to the CNS.

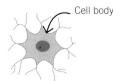

Cell body

Relay neurons pass on signals from sensory neurons to motor neurons.

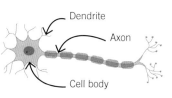

Dendrite

Axon

Cell body

Motor neurons carry signals from the CNS to effector organs.

Synapses

Nerve cells join to each other at junctions called synapses. A nerve impulse cannot cross a synapse directly because there is a tiny gap between the neighboring cells. Instead, the signal is passed across the junction by chemicals called neurotransmitters.

Key facts

✓ Neurons are connected at junctions called synapses.

✓ When an electrical signal arrives at a synapse, it triggers the release of chemicals called neurotransmitters.

✓ Neurotransmitters bind to receptors on the receiving neuron, which may trigger a new nerve impulse.

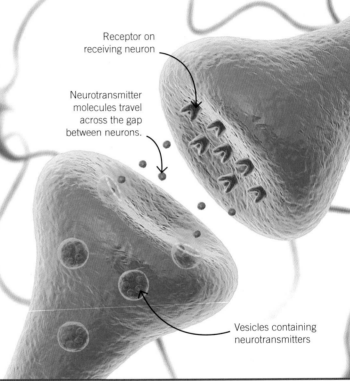

Receptor on receiving neuron

Neurotransmitter molecules travel across the gap between neurons.

Vesicles containing neurotransmitters

Meeting point

A synapse is the junction between two neurons. Nerve impulses trigger the release of chemicals called neurotransmitters, which travel across this gap. This sets off a new electrical impulse in the receiving neuron, so the message continues to travel through the nervous system.

🔍 Neurotransmitters

Neurotransmitters are produced only at the outgoing end of a neuron, so the nerve impulse can pass only in one direction across a synapse. Drugs that affect the nervous system often work by interfering with the neurotransmitters and their receptors.

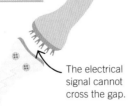

The electrical signal cannot cross the gap.

1. An electrical impulse travels along a neuron until it reaches the end of the cell.

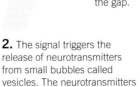

Neurotransmitters diffuse across the gap.

2. The signal triggers the release of neurotransmitters from small bubbles called vesicles. The neurotransmitters diffuse across the tiny gap between neighboring cells.

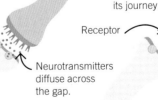

The signal continues its journey.

Receptor

3. The neurotransmitter molecules bind to receptors on the next cell, which may trigger a new electrical signal.

Reflex arc

If you touch something that causes pain, your hand withdraws immediately, without you having to think. This is called a reflex action. To save time, reflex actions are often controlled by nerve signals that take a shortcut through the body, bypassing the brain. This pathway is called a reflex arc.

Key facts

✓ A reflex action does not usually involve the brain.

✓ A reflex arc is the pathway taken by the nerve signal that triggers a reflex action.

✓ Many reflex actions are coordinated by the spinal cord.

Pain reflex

The withdrawal reflex is one of the fastest reflexes. It quickly pulls away (withdraws) the affected body part from a source of pain or from an unusual or unexpected sensation.

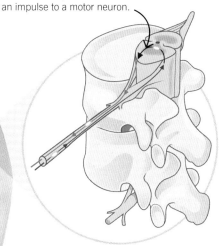

3. Spinal cord
A relay neuron in the spinal cord receives the impulse and sends an impulse to a motor neuron.

2. Receptor
Receptor cells in the skin detect the stimulus. This causes an impulse to travel along the sensory neuron to the spinal cord.

1. Stimulus
A thorn on the cactus pierces the skin. This is the stimulus.

4. Effector
The motor neuron sends a nerve impulse to a muscle in the arm (the effector), which then contracts, pulling the hand away from the source of pain.

🔍 Reflex actions

Reflex actions are faster than normal voluntary responses, as the nerve signal doesn't have to travel to the brain. You may not be consciously aware of the stimulus until after your body has reacted. Many reflexes happen to protect you from harm.

The fight or flight response is a reaction to dangerous stimuli, such as a poisonous snake. It makes your heart rate accelerate and your breathing deepen, enabling you to run away from the danger.

The eye closing reflex closes your eyelids tightly if a rapidly moving object approaches your face. This reflex protects your eyes from injury.

Pupils constrict automatically in bright light and widen again in the dark. This reflex protects the light-sensitive cells inside the eye from damage.

Measuring reaction time

Reaction time is the length of time a person takes to respond to a stimulus. This experiment allows you to measure a person's reaction time using a ruler and some simple math.

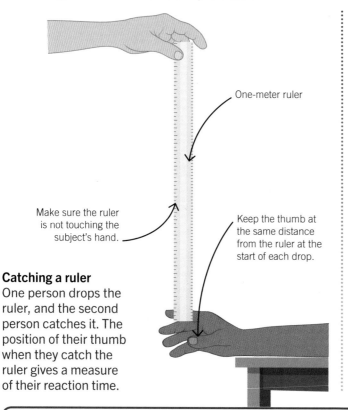

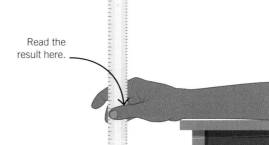

One-meter ruler

Make sure the ruler is not touching the subject's hand.

Keep the thumb at the same distance from the ruler at the start of each drop.

Read the result here.

Catching a ruler
One person drops the ruler, and the second person catches it. The position of their thumb when they catch the ruler gives a measure of their reaction time.

⚙ Method

1. Ask your test subject to sit upright with their arm resting on a flat surface, such as a table, and their hand free.

2. Hold a one-meter ruler so that the zero mark is between the test subject's finger and thumb, without the ruler touching the hand.

3. Tell your subject to prepare to grab the ruler when they see it drop, but don't give them any indication of when it will fall.

4. After a random length of time, release the ruler.

5. Read the number above your subject's thumb and record the result.

6. You can use this test to compare the reaction times of different people or to compare one person's reaction times at different times of day.

🖩 Calculating reaction time

Use the formula below to convert the distance (d) fallen in centimeters into reaction time (t) in seconds.

$$t = \sqrt{\dfrac{d}{500}}$$

To get a more accurate result, repeat the test several times. Figure out the mean (average) distance by adding up the readings from each test and dividing the total by the number of tests.

The brain

The human brain is made up of around 100 billion neurons connected in complex circuits. It controls mental processes, including conscious thought, memory, language, and emotions. It also coordinates body muscle movement and controls unconscious processes, such as breathing.

Parts of the brain

The brain is made up of different regions, each of which is involved in a particular function. Deep folds in its outer surface increase the brain's surface area, creating more room for neurons and so increasing the brain's processing power.

📌 **Key facts**

✓ **The brain, along with the spinal cord, is part of the central nervous system.**

✓ **The brain controls many complex processes, such as language and memory.**

✓ **Different parts of the brain have different functions.**

🔍 A brain of two halves

Seen from the top, the outer part of the brain (the cerebrum) is made of two halves (cerebral hemispheres) that look like mirror images. Some functions are controlled by only one hemisphere. For instance, the right hemisphere controls the muscles on the left side of the body. However, for most functions, the two halves work together. If one side is damaged, the other can often take over the job of the lost tissue.

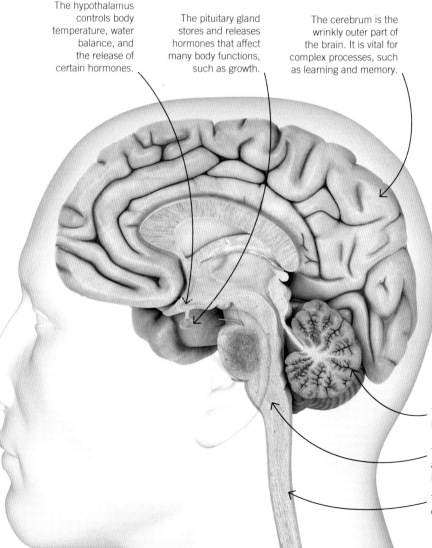

The hypothalamus controls body temperature, water balance, and the release of certain hormones.

The pituitary gland stores and releases hormones that affect many body functions, such as growth.

The cerebrum is the wrinkly outer part of the brain. It is vital for complex processes, such as learning and memory.

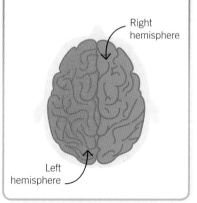

Right hemisphere

Left hemisphere

The cerebellum coordinates muscles and helps control body movement and balance.

The brainstem controls unconscious activities, such as heartbeat and breathing rate.

The spinal cord and brain make up the central nervous system.

Studying the brain

The brain is the most complex organ in the human body. Scientists studying the brain have tried to assign specific functions, such as memory, to different parts of the brain. However, many mental functions involve different areas of the brain working together.

fMRI brain scan

This fMRI (functional magnetic resonance imaging) scan of a person's brain shows small areas lighting up with activity during speech. Brain scanners allow scientists to investigate how different parts of the brain contribute to complex mental functions, such as speech. They can also be used to detect damage caused by a stroke, brain tumor, or other disease.

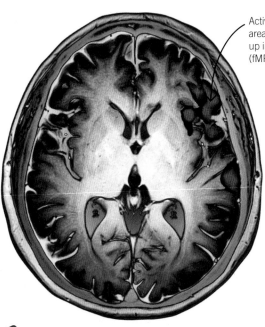

Actively respiring areas of the brain light up in a functional MRI (fMRI) scan.

✎ Key facts

✓ **In the past, scientists investigating the brain relied on studying people with brain injuries.**

✓ **Today, brain scanners can reveal which parts of a healthy brain are active during a mental task.**

✓ **Many mental functions involve multiple areas of the brain working together.**

🔍 Investigating brain function

Scientists use a wide variety of methods to investigate the brain's function. Each method has its own advantages and disadvantages.

Brain injury

In the past, scientists studying the brain relied on finding patients whose brains were damaged by disease or injury to see what effect the damage had on mental functions such as memory.

Brain scan

Scientists and doctors use several different kinds of scanning machines to create images of the brain. The images reveal which brain cells are respiring most actively and therefore working hardest.

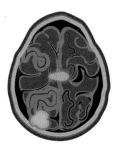

Electrodes

Stimulating the surface of the brain with electrodes has helped scientists figure out which parts of the brain control muscles. However, this technique can be used only during surgery.

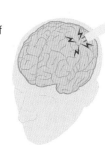

EEG

An electroencephalogram (EEG) machine detects the faint waves of electrical activity that sweep across the whole brain. EEGs have helped scientists study what happens to the brain during sleep and dreaming.

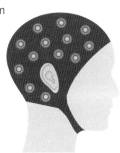

Nervous system damage

Damage to the nervous system can cause many problems, from memory loss to lack of sensation. Some nerves can regrow after damage, but damage to the central nervous system is often permanent.

🔍 Gamma knife

Brain tumors are cancers that grow in the brain. They can be difficult to remove surgically without damaging the surrounding healthy tissue. One technique used to treat brain tumors is called gamma knife. The patient lies in a machine that focuses about 200 beams of gamma radiation from different angles, all coinciding at the tumor. This gives the tumor a lethal dose of radiation but leaves surrounding brain tissue unharmed.

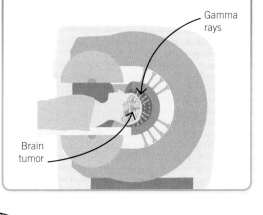

Gamma rays

Brain tumor

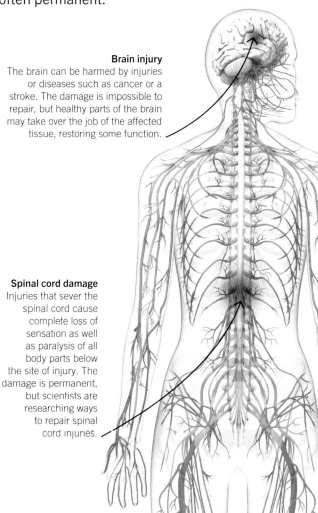

Brain injury
The brain can be harmed by injuries or diseases such as cancer or a stroke. The damage is impossible to repair, but healthy parts of the brain may take over the job of the affected tissue, restoring some function.

Spinal cord damage
Injuries that sever the spinal cord cause complete loss of sensation as well as paralysis of all body parts below the site of injury. The damage is permanent, but scientists are researching ways to repair spinal cord injuries.

Peripheral nerve damage
Damage to motor nerves causes loss of movement in muscles attached to the nerve, while damage to sensory nerves causes loss of sensation.

Nervous system
Any part of the nervous system can be damaged by disease or injury. Damage to the central nervous system causes greater disability than damage to peripheral nerves.

The eye

The human eye works a bit like a camera. It uses a curved, transparent lens to focus captured light onto a light-sensitive film—called the retina—on its back surface, forming an image.

Key facts

✓ **Eyes create images by focusing light rays.**

✓ **Light-sensitive receptor cells in the eye react to light and send nerve impulses to the brain.**

✓ **One set of muscles regulates how much light enters the eye. Another set of muscles controls the lens's focusing power.**

Inside the eye

Most of the structures inside the eye are transparent to let light pass through. When light lands on the retina at the back of the eye, it stimulates light-sensitive receptor cells. They send nerve impulses to the brain, where the image is processed.

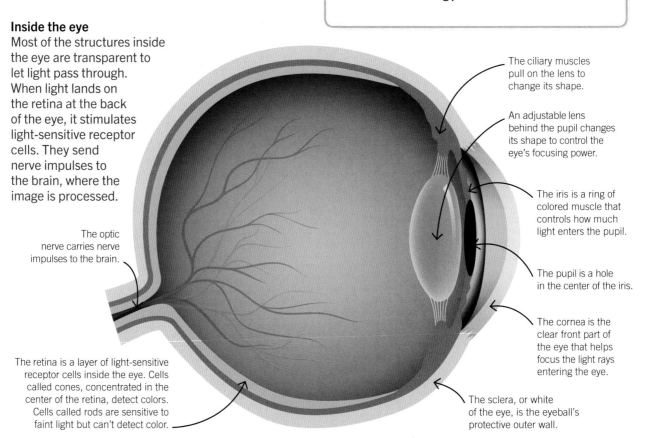

The ciliary muscles pull on the lens to change its shape.

An adjustable lens behind the pupil changes its shape to control the eye's focusing power.

The iris is a ring of colored muscle that controls how much light enters the pupil.

The optic nerve carries nerve impulses to the brain.

The pupil is a hole in the center of the iris.

The cornea is the clear front part of the eye that helps focus the light rays entering the eye.

The retina is a layer of light-sensitive receptor cells inside the eye. Cells called cones, concentrated in the center of the retina, detect colors. Cells called rods are sensitive to faint light but can't detect color.

The sclera, or white of the eye, is the eyeball's protective outer wall.

⚙ Iris reflex

The iris is a ring of muscle fibers that are oriented in two patterns—circular and radial. When the circular muscle fibers contract, the pupil constricts, letting less light into the eye. When the radial fibers contract, the pupil widens, letting in more light. The size of the pupil changes automatically in response to the amount of light entering the eye.

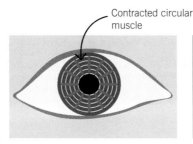

Contracted circular muscle

Constricted pupil

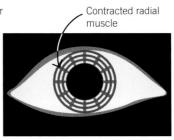

Contracted radial muscle

Dilated pupil

Seeing

To create an image, the eye bends the diverging rays of light from objects so that they converge at a point on the retina. This is called focusing. Most of the focusing is done by the cornea. The eye's adjustable lens makes fine adjustments depending on whether the object being viewed is near or far away.

Key facts

✓ The cornea and lens focus light on the retina.

✓ Ciliary muscles contract and relax to change the shape of the lens and its focusing power.

✓ The lens becomes fatter to focus on nearby objects and thinner to focus on distant objects.

Forming images on the retina

As light rays pass through the cornea and the lens, they are bent (refracted). The rays cross inside the eye and project a clear but inverted view of the object on the retina. The optic nerve carries this information to the brain, which then flips the image the right way up.

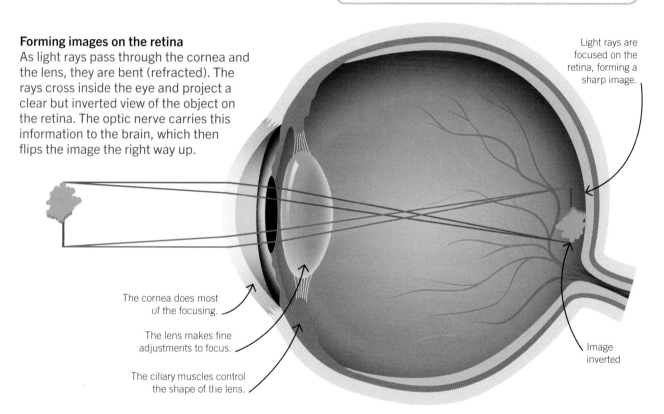

Light rays are focused on the retina, forming a sharp image.

The cornea does most of the focusing.

The lens makes fine adjustments to focus.

The ciliary muscles control the shape of the lens.

Image inverted

Near and far vision

To focus on objects at different distances, the lens in the eye needs to change shape. Its shape is controlled by the ciliary muscles. When these muscles contract, the lens becomes fatter and focuses on nearby objects. When the ciliary muscles relax, the lens becomes thinner and focuses on distant objects.

Near vision

Thick lens

Rays of light brought into focus on retina

Far vision

Thin lens

Rays of light brought into focus on retina

Nearsightedness

Some people have a visual defect called nearsightedness, which makes distant objects look blurred. Nearsightedness can occur if the eyeball is slightly too long or if the lens or cornea are too curved and focus light rays too strongly.

Key facts

✓ **Nearsightedness makes distant objects look blurred.**

✓ **In a nearsighted eye, light rays are brought into focus in front of the retina.**

✓ **A concave (inwardly curving) lens can correct nearsightedness.**

Correcting nearsightedness
In a nearsighted eye, light rays are brought into focus before they reach the retina. A concave lens corrects this by making the light rays diverge before they enter the eye.

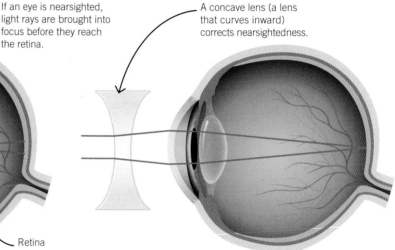

If an eye is nearsighted, light rays are brought into focus before they reach the retina.

A concave lens (a lens that curves inward) corrects nearsightedness.

Retina

Nearsighted eye

Corrected vision

⚙ How laser eye surgery works

Visual defects such as nearsightedness, farsightedness, and astigmatism can be corrected by laser eye surgery. One of the most common techniques to correct nearsightedness involves reshaping the cornea to make it less curved, which reduces its focusing power.

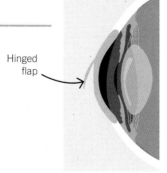

Hinged flap

1. A small flap is cut in the front of the cornea and folded out of the way.

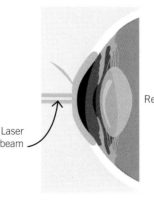

Laser beam

2. A computer-controlled laser beam burns away a patch of corneal tissue, making the cornea less curved.

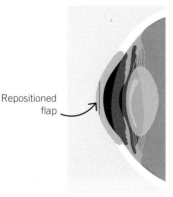

Repositioned flap

3. The flap is then folded back in place and allowed to heal.

Farsightedness

Some people have a visual defect called farsightedness, which makes nearby objects appear blurred. This condition can occur if the eyeball is too short or if the lens or cornea are not sufficiently curved and so don't bend light rays strongly enough. Aging can also cause farsightedness by making the lens stiffer.

Key facts

✓ Farsightedness makes nearby objects look blurred.

✓ In a farsighted eye, light rays are brought into focus behind the retina.

✓ A convex (outwardly curving) lens can correct farsightedness.

Correcting farsightedness

In a farsighted eye, the focal point is behind the retina, making images on the retina blurred. A convex lens corrects vision by causing light rays to converge (bend inward) before they enter the eye.

A convex lens (a lens that curves outward) corrects farsightedness.

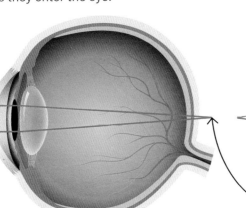

Farsighted eye

If an eye is farsighted, light rays are brought to a focal point behind the retina.

Corrected vision

⚙ Replacement lens surgery

Visual defects such as farsightedness and nearsightedness can be corrected by surgery that replaces the lens in the eye. The eye's natural crystalline lens is removed through an incision, and a synthetic lens is inserted in its place. Another option is to insert a synthetic lens in front of the natural lens, which is left in place.

The synthetic lens is made of transparent plastic.

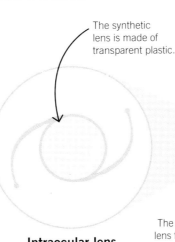

Intraocular lens

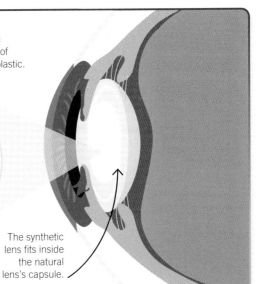

The synthetic lens fits inside the natural lens's capsule.

Astigmatism

Astigmatism is a visual problem caused by uneven curvature of either the cornea or the eye's lens. This causes the eye to focus some rays of light (such as those traveling in the vertical plane) more strongly than others (such as those traveling in the horizontal plane). As a result, images are blurred.

Correcting astigmatism

An astigmatic eye can't focus light properly to form an image on the retina. This causes blurred vision, which is fixed with unevenly curved lenses that bend light in one direction more than in another.

Key facts

✓ In an astigmatic eye, the dome-shaped cornea or the eye's lens is slightly oval rather than evenly rounded.

✓ The eye's focusing power varies depending on the orientation of incoming light rays.

✓ Images are blurred at any distance from the viewer.

The cornea is not evenly rounded.

The image on the retina is unevenly focused.

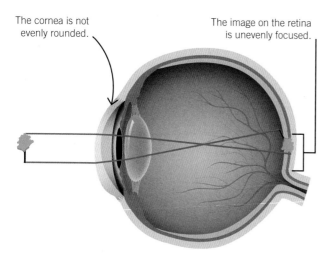

Astigmatic eye

An unevenly curved lens compensates for the cornea's abnormal shape, correcting vision.

The image on the retina is now clear.

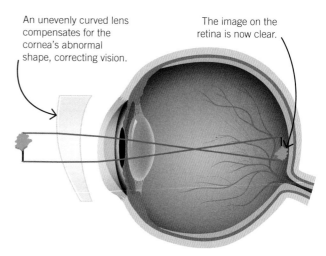

Corrected vision

🔍 Testing for astigmatism

Astigmatism causes light rays in certain orientations to focus incorrectly. One way to figure out which orientation is affected is to look at a sunburst chart, which is made of lines arranged like the spokes on a wheel. To an astigmatic eye, lines in some directions will appear sharp, while others will look blurred.

Lines seen by normal eye

Blurring in the vertical plane

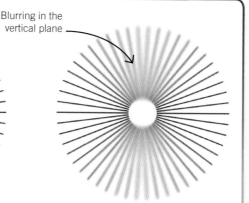

Lines seen by astigmatic eye

The ear

Sound consists of invisible waves that travel through air. The ear collects these waves, magnifies them, and transmits them to the fluid-filled inner ear, where sensory cells respond by sending nerve impulses to the brain.

Key facts

✓ Sound waves are invisible vibrations that travel through the air.

✓ The outer ear collects sound waves and funnels them toward the middle ear and inner ear.

✓ Sensory cells inside the inner ear detect sound and send nerve impulses to the brain.

Inside the ear

The ear has three parts: the visible outer ear, the middle ear, and the inner ear. The delicate structures of the middle and inner ear are located inside hollows in the bone of the skull. Sound travels through the middle ear as vibrations in tiny bones and through the inner ear as vibrations in fluid.

🔍 **Cochlear implants**

A cochlear implant can restore lost hearing. An external microphone picks up sound and converts it into a signal that is transmitted to a receiver surgically implanted under the skin. The receiver then sends electrical impulses along a tiny wire threaded through the cochlea. This stimulates the sensory cells in the cochlea, which send nerve impulses to the brain.

Transmitter

Microphone

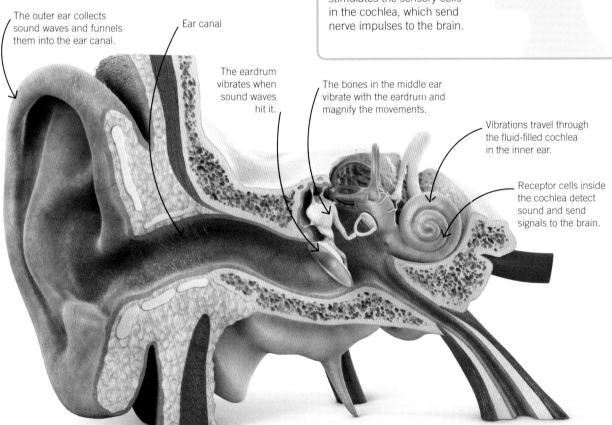

The outer ear collects sound waves and funnels them into the ear canal.

Ear canal

The eardrum vibrates when sound waves hit it.

The bones in the middle ear vibrate with the eardrum and magnify the movements.

Vibrations travel through the fluid-filled cochlea in the inner ear.

Receptor cells inside the cochlea detect sound and send signals to the brain.

Temperature control

The nervous system keeps the inside of the human body at a constant 37°C, as this is the temperature at which enzymes work best. If body temperature rises or falls, the nervous system sends signals to effector organs, which then restore the body's normal temperature.

Key facts

- ✓ The maintenance of a constant environment inside the body is called homeostasis.
- ✓ Body temperature is controlled by a negative feedback system.
- ✓ The part of the brain that controls temperature is called the hypothalamus.

The skin

Skin responds to temperature changes in several ways. It helps release excess heat when body temperature rises, and it retains heat when body temperature falls. In cold weather, the body can also generate heat by shivering—a reflex that causes body muscles to contract quickly.

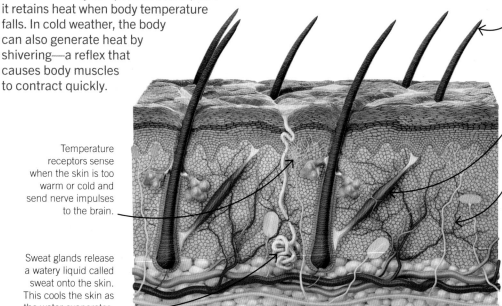

Temperature receptors sense when the skin is too warm or cold and send nerve impulses to the brain.

Sweat glands release a watery liquid called sweat onto the skin. This cools the skin as the water evaporates.

Hairs stand up when body temperature falls, trapping air close to the skin for insulation. This also causes goose bumps.

Hair erector muscles raise and lower hairs.

Blood vessels in the skin dilate when the body is warm. This allows more blood to flow closer to the surface of the skin, allowing heat to escape. In cold weather, the blood vessels constrict, helping the body retain heat.

⚙ The body's thermostat

Body temperature is monitored and controlled by a part of the brain called the hypothalamus. When body temperature is too high, the hypothalamus sends nerve impulses to effectors that lower body temperature. When body temperature is low, it sends nerve impulses to effectors that raise body temperature. Responding to a change by reversing it is called negative feedback.

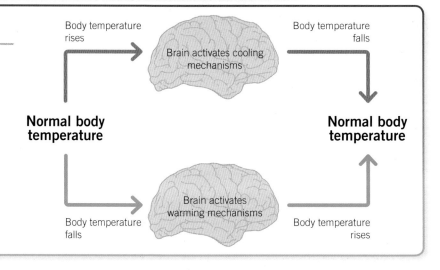

Body temperature rises

Brain activates cooling mechanisms

Body temperature falls

Normal body temperature

Normal body temperature

Body temperature falls

Brain activates warming mechanisms

Body temperature rises

Hormones

The endocrine system

The endocrine system works together with the nervous system to control and coordinate the body. Endocrine glands secrete chemicals called hormones into the bloodstream. Blood then transports the hormones to target organs, where they cause an effect.

Endocrine glands

Hormones are produced by endocrine glands—organs that synthesize hormones and secrete them into blood vessels. Endocrine glands are found in many parts of the body and together make up the endocrine system.

The pituitary gland in the brain is often referred to as a master gland. It secretes several hormones, some of which control other endocrine glands.

The thyroid gland produces thyroxine, which controls the body's metabolic rate.

The adrenal glands produce adrenaline, which prepares the body for rapid action in stressful situations.

The pancreas produces insulin and glucagon, which regulate blood glucose levels.

The ovaries produce estrogen and progesterone in females. These cause the development of female secondary sexual characteristics. They also control the menstrual cycle.

The testes produce testosterone in males, stimulating the development of male secondary sexual characteristics.

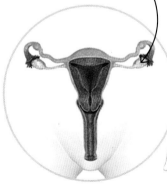

Ovaries in female endocrine system

Homeostasis

Homeostasis is the maintenance of a constant internal environment. This provides the optimum conditions for enzyme actions and all body functions. In humans, this includes the control of blood glucose levels, body temperature, and water levels.

Key facts

✓ Homeostasis is the maintenance of a constant internal environment.

✓ Many homeostasis control systems involve negative feedback.

✓ Negative feedback systems control body temperature, blood glucose levels, and water levels.

Water levels
The level of water in the human body is controlled by a negative feedback system: when the water level is too high, the body reacts to lower it; when the water level is too low, the body reacts to raise it. This cycle operates all the time to maintain optimum water levels.

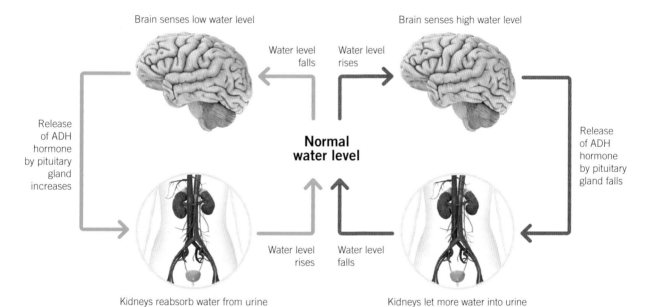

Brain senses low water level

Water level falls

Water level rises

Brain senses high water level

Release of ADH hormone by pituitary gland increases

Normal water level

Release of ADH hormone by pituitary gland falls

Water level rises

Water level falls

Kidneys reabsorb water from urine

Kidneys let more water into urine

🔍 Feedback systems

The human body uses negative feedback to control internal temperature, water levels, and blood glucose levels. In each case, the level of something is continually monitored. If it rises or falls too much, either hormones or nerve signals are used to bring the levels back to normal.

Blood glucose
The hormones insulin and glucagon are used to control glucose levels in the blood. When blood glucose is too high, the hormone insulin is released to lower it. When blood glucose is too low, the hormone glucagon is released to raise it.

Temperature
If body temperature rises above 37°C, the brain reacts by sending nerve signals that trigger the release of sweat and an increase in blood flow to the skin's surface. If body temperature falls, nerve signals trigger shivering, reduced blood flow to the skin, and rising of body hairs to trap warmth.

Insulin and glucagon

The cells in the human body need a constant supply of the sugar glucose for respiration. The concentration of glucose in the blood is monitored and controlled by an organ called the pancreas. Without this mechanism, blood glucose levels would rise dramatically after eating and would fall too low for respiration several hours later.

Key facts

✓ Blood glucose levels are monitored and controlled by the pancreas.

✓ The pancreas releases the hormones insulin and glucagon.

✓ Insulin causes blood glucose levels to fall.

✓ Glucagon causes blood glucose levels to rise.

Negative feedback system

When blood glucose levels rise, such as after eating, the pancreas releases the hormone insulin. This causes body cells to absorb glucose from the blood, and it makes the liver convert glucose to glycogen for storage. Blood glucose levels then fall. When blood glucose is too low, such as after exercise, the pancreas releases glucagon. Glucagon makes the liver convert glycogen back to glucose, raising blood glucose levels.

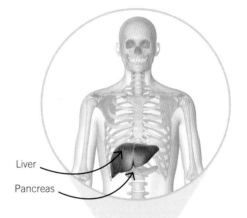

Liver

Pancreas

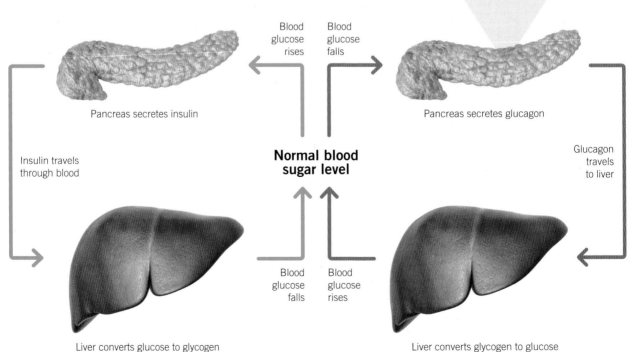

Blood glucose rises

Blood glucose falls

Pancreas secretes insulin

Pancreas secretes glucagon

Insulin travels through blood

Glucagon travels to liver

Normal blood sugar level

Blood glucose falls

Blood glucose rises

Liver converts glucose to glycogen and body cells take up glucose

Liver converts glycogen to glucose

Diabetes

Diabetes is a medical condition in which the body's blood glucose control system stops working properly. The blood glucose level rises too much, and injections of the hormone insulin may be needed to lower it. There are two types of diabetes: type 1 and type 2 diabetes.

Key facts

✓ Diabetes causes abnormally high blood glucose levels.

✓ People with type 1 diabetes do not produce any insulin.

✓ Type 1 diabetes can be treated with regular insulin injections.

✓ The body cells of a person with type 2 diabetes do not respond properly to insulin.

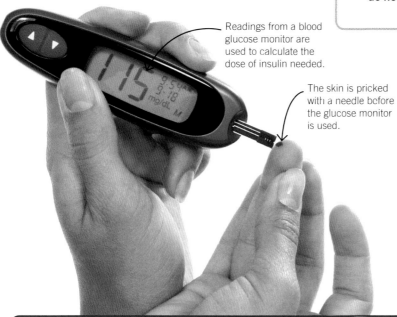

Readings from a blood glucose monitor are used to calculate the dose of insulin needed.

The skin is pricked with a needle before the glucose monitor is used.

Living with diabetes

Many people with diabetes have to regularly monitor their blood glucose level by taking small samples of blood 4–10 times a day. In type 1 diabetes, which usually begins in childhood, the pancreas stops producing insulin. Regular insulin injections are essential to keep blood glucose in a healthy range. In type 2 diabetes, which usually begins in adulthood, the pancreas still makes insulin, but the body's cells become resistant to the hormone. Type 2 diabetes can often be treated by weight loss and a change in diet.

🔍 Blood glucose levels

This graph shows the blood glucose level of a person with diabetes (red) and an unaffected person (green). An unaffected person's blood glucose level varies but remains within a narrow range. In contrast, the glucose level of a person with diabetes rises dramatically. Regular insulin injections are needed to lower it to within normal range. Insulin injections do not completely mimic natural control but allow diabetics to live active lives.

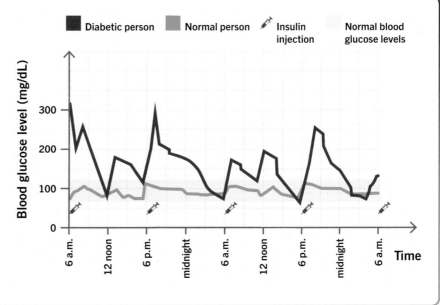

■ Diabetic person   ■ Normal person   ✒ Insulin injection   Normal blood glucose levels

Blood glucose level (mg/dL)

The kidneys

The kidneys play an important role in homeostasis by maintaining the correct water balance in the body. They are also responsible for removing toxic waste from the blood. They do both jobs by producing urine—a solution containing water, urea, and other waste substances, such as excess mineral ions.

Key facts

- ✓ Urea is a toxic substance produced by the breakdown of excess amino acids in the liver.
- ✓ The kidneys filter blood to remove urea and other waste products.
- ✓ The kidneys maintain water balance by controlling the amount of water in urine.
- ✓ Urine is a solution containing urea, water, and other waste substances.

Urine production

About a quarter of the body's blood volume passes through the kidneys each minute. They filter out excess water and waste products such as urea—a chemical produced by the breakdown of amino acids in the liver. The kidneys reabsorb some of the water before urine drains to the bladder. The amount of water they reabsorb varies and is controlled by a hormone called ADH (antidiuretic hormone), which helps the body maintain the right water level (see page 143).

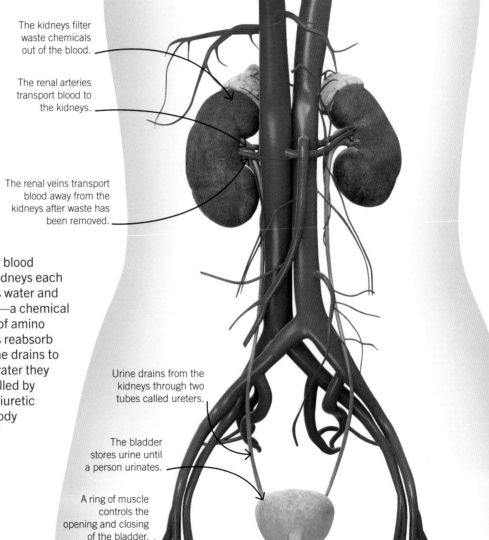

The kidneys filter waste chemicals out of the blood.

The renal arteries transport blood to the kidneys.

The renal veins transport blood away from the kidneys after waste has been removed.

Urine drains from the kidneys through two tubes called ureters.

The bladder stores urine until a person urinates.

A ring of muscle controls the opening and closing of the bladder.

⚙ Filtering the blood

1. Inside the kidney, blood vessels branch into a network of fine vessels called capillaries. The capillaries form thousands of ball-shaped clusters called glomeruli.

2. As blood flows through a glomerulus, small molecules such as water, glucose, salts, and urea pass out into a cup-shaped sac called a Bowman's capsule. Blood cells and large molecules such as proteins remain in the blood as they are too big to escape.

3. Next, selective reabsorption occurs. The liquid in the Bowman's capsule drains though a tubule surrounded by blood vessels that reabsorb all the glucose, some mineral ions, and a variable quantity of water. The hormone ADH makes the tubule walls more permeable when more water needs to be reabsorbed.

4. The remaining waste drains through a collecting duct and eventually reaches the bladder.

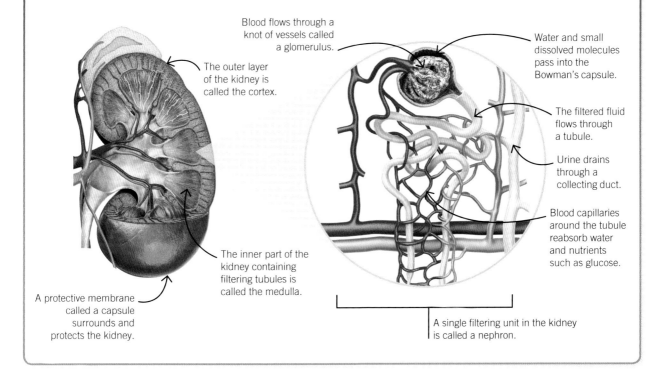

The outer layer of the kidney is called the cortex.

A protective membrane called a capsule surrounds and protects the kidney.

The inner part of the kidney containing filtering tubules is called the medulla.

Blood flows through a knot of vessels called a glomerulus.

Water and small dissolved molecules pass into the Bowman's capsule.

The filtered fluid flows through a tubule.

Urine drains through a collecting duct.

Blood capillaries around the tubule reabsorb water and nutrients such as glucose.

A single filtering unit in the kidney is called a nephron.

🔍 Treating kidney failure

The kidneys can be damaged by disease or injury, sometimes permanently. Kidney failure can be treated by a kidney transplant or by dialysis. A dialysis machine works like a natural kidney. A patient's blood flows into the machine and between partially permeable membranes surrounded by dialysate (dialysis fluid), which contains the same concentration of useful substances as blood. Harmful waste products, such as urea, diffuse out of the blood into the dialysis fluid. Glucose and other useful substances do not diffuse out of the blood as they are at the same concentration in the fluid.

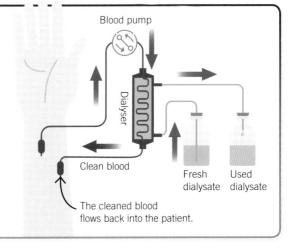

Blood pump

Dialyser

Clean blood

Fresh dialysate

Used dialysate

The cleaned blood flows back into the patient.

Puberty in males

During puberty, sex hormones cause the male body to undergo a number of physical changes. The sex hormone testosterone triggers the development of male secondary sexual characteristics, such as facial hair and a deeper voice. Testosterone is produced by two small organs called testes.

Key facts

✓ Testosterone is produced by the testes.

✓ A rise in the testosterone level triggers the development of male secondary sexual characteristics.

✓ Male secondary sexual characteristics include facial hair, a deeper voice, and a larger penis and testes.

Male secondary sexual characteristics
Puberty in males usually begins between the ages of 9 and 15, which is slightly later than in females. The process is triggered by a rise in testosterone levels.

🔍 How does a voice break?

Several changes cause a male's voice to deepen during puberty. The cavities inside the nose and throat become larger, giving the voice more space in which to resonate. The larynx (voice box) grows larger and thicker, and the vocal cords within it, which create sound when they vibrate, grow longer. This means they vibrate more slowly, producing a lower pitch. The larynx grows so quickly during puberty that it can stretch the vocal cords, resulting in high-pitched squeaks, cracks, and croaks—similar to a guitar string pulled too tight.

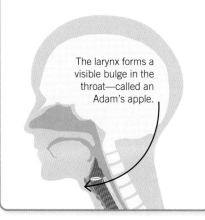

The larynx forms a visible bulge in the throat—called an Adam's apple.

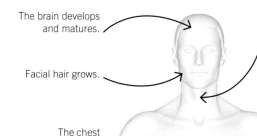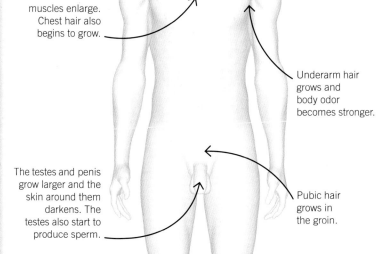

The brain develops and matures.

Facial hair grows.

The larynx (voice box) gets bigger and the voice deepens. This is often referred to as the voice breaking.

The chest broadens and muscles enlarge. Chest hair also begins to grow.

Underarm hair grows and body odor becomes stronger.

The testes and penis grow larger and the skin around them darkens. The testes also start to produce sperm.

Pubic hair grows in the groin.

Puberty in females

During puberty, sex hormones cause the female body to undergo a number of physical changes. The hormone estrogen, produced by the ovaries, triggers the development of female secondary sexual characteristics, such as larger breasts and wider hips. These changes prepare the female body for pregnancy and childbirth.

Key facts

✓ A rise in the estrogen level triggers the development of female secondary sexual characteristics.

✓ Estrogen is produced by the ovaries.

✓ Secondary sexual characteristics in females include breasts, wider hips, and menstruation (periods) starting.

Female secondary sexual characteristics
Puberty in females is triggered by a rise in estrogen levels. It usually begins between the ages of 8 and 14.

What causes acne?

Acne affects both males and females, particularly during puberty. Spots form when the small pits that hairs grow out of become blocked by an oily substance called sebum. Sebum helps lubricate and protect the skin, but too much may be made during puberty. The excess sebum forms a plug that may become infected with bacteria. This results in inflammation (swelling), causing a spot.

1. Sebum from a sebaceous gland blocks the opening around a hair.

Sebaceous gland

2. The sebum accumulates and becomes infected by bacteria.

3. The presence of bacteria causes inflammation, producing a red spot.

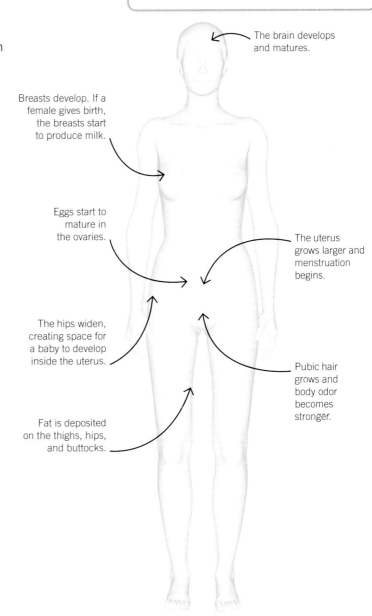

The brain develops and matures.

Breasts develop. If a female gives birth, the breasts start to produce milk.

Eggs start to mature in the ovaries.

The uterus grows larger and menstruation begins.

The hips widen, creating space for a baby to develop inside the uterus.

Pubic hair grows and body odor becomes stronger.

Fat is deposited on the thighs, hips, and buttocks.

The menstrual cycle

During puberty, females start having periods. Around once a month, the lining of the uterus is lost from the body through the vagina. The body then undergoes a number of changes that prepare it for a possible pregnancy. This series of events is known as the menstrual cycle. The stages of the menstrual cycle are controlled by hormones.

Key facts

✓ The menstrual cycle lasts about 28 days.

✓ The menstrual cycle is controlled by the hormones estrogen, progesterone, FSH, and LH.

✓ During a period, the lining of the uterus is shed from the body.

✓ During ovulation (around day 14 of the cycle), an egg is released from an ovary.

Stages of the menstrual cycle

The menstrual cycle lasts for around 28 days, though the length and timing of stages in the cycle can vary from person to person.

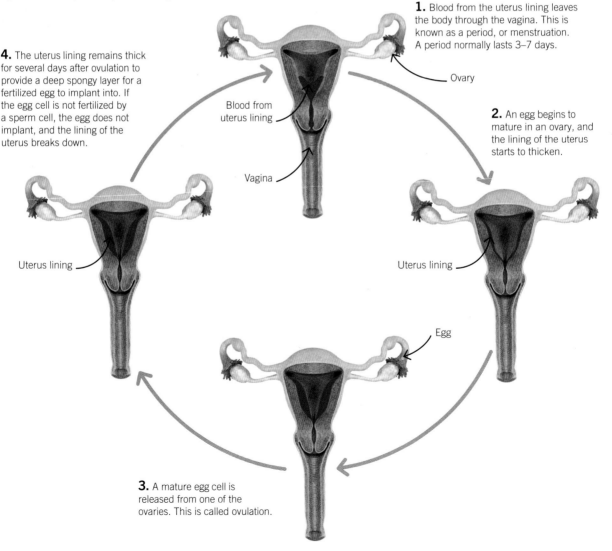

1. Blood from the uterus lining leaves the body through the vagina. This is known as a period, or menstruation. A period normally lasts 3–7 days.

Ovary

Blood from uterus lining

Vagina

2. An egg begins to mature in an ovary, and the lining of the uterus starts to thicken.

Uterus lining

4. The uterus lining remains thick for several days after ovulation to provide a deep spongy layer for a fertilized egg to implant into. If the egg cell is not fertilized by a sperm cell, the egg does not implant, and the lining of the uterus breaks down.

Uterus lining

Egg

3. A mature egg cell is released from one of the ovaries. This is called ovulation.

⚙ Hormones and the menstrual cycle

The menstrual cycle is controlled by the interaction of four hormones: estrogen, progesterone, follicle-stimulating hormone (FSH), and luteinizing hormone (LH). Throughout the cycle, the levels of these hormones rise and fall as they interact with the body and each other. If an egg is not fertilized, the levels of all four hormones drop. This results in the lining of the uterus being shed from the body, and the cycle repeats.

Hormone level during the menstrual cycle

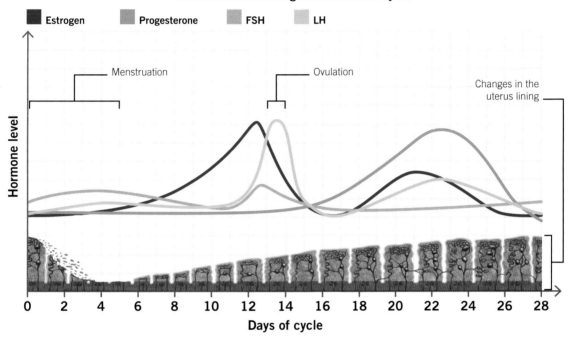

Hormones in the menstrual cycle		
Hormone	**Produced by**	**Effects**
Estrogen	Ovaries	Makes the lining of the uterus thicken. High levels inhibit FSH production (to stop more than one egg from maturing) and stimulate LH release.
Progesterone	Ovaries	Maintains the lining of the uterus and inhibits the release of FSH and LH (so no more eggs develop if a woman is pregnant).
Follicle-stimulating hormone (FSH)	Pituitary gland	Causes an egg to mature in an ovary and stimulates the ovaries to release estrogen.
Luteinizing hormone (LH)	Pituitary gland	Triggers ovulation (release of an egg).

Contraceptives

Any technique used to prevent pregnancy is known as contraception. There are many different forms of contraceptives. Hormonal methods such as the contraceptive pill disrupt the menstrual cycle, whereas barrier methods such as condoms prevent sperm cells from reaching the egg.

Key facts

- ✓ Methods used to prevent pregnancy are called contraception.
- ✓ Hormonal methods disrupt the menstrual cycle. They include the contraceptive pill and some IUDs.
- ✓ Barrier methods prevent the sperm and egg from meeting. They include condoms and diaphragms.
- ✓ Sterilization involves clipping the oviducts in females and cutting the sperm ducts in males.

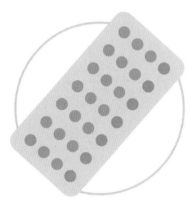

Hormonal pills
These pills contain low doses of estrogen and progesterone. They prevent the release of follicle-stimulating hormone (FSH) by the pituitary gland in the brain, so no eggs mature or are released. The hormones also prevent the lining of the uterus from developing.

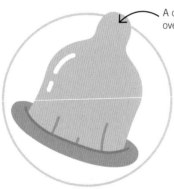

A condom fits over a male's penis.

Condom
A condom is a thin latex sheath placed over a male's penis. It collects semen and prevents sperm from entering the vagina. Condoms also provide protection against sexually transmitted infections.

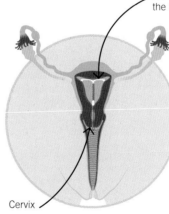

An IUD in the uterus

Cervix

Intrauterine device
Intrauterine devices (IUDs) are small devices that are placed inside the uterus. Some IUDs have a copper coil—copper is toxic to sperm. Others work by releasing the hormone progesterone. This thickens the mucus produced by the cervix and stops sperm from reaching an egg. Progesterone also stops the uterus lining from building up, preventing implantation.

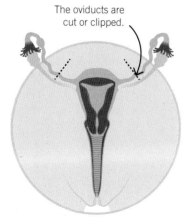

The oviducts are cut or clipped.

Sterilization
This involves an operation to prevent people from having babies. In females, the oviducts are cut or clipped, preventing eggs from reaching the uterus. In males, the sperm ducts are cut, preventing sperm from entering semen.

Diaphragm
A diaphragm is a thin rubber cap placed over a female's cervix before sex. It prevents sperm from entering the uterus. It is often used with a spermicide cream that kills sperm.

Fertility treatment

Some people have difficulty becoming pregnant. There are many causes of infertility, including blocked sperm ducts or low sperm numbers in males and blocked oviducts or eggs that don't mature in females. Doctors can help such people conceive by using a technique called in vitro fertilization (IVF).

IVF

During IVF treatment, eggs are collected from a female's ovaries and fertilized with a male's sperm in a laboratory to produce embryos. If a healthy embryo develops, it is placed in the mother's uterus. In certain cases, a special technique called intracytoplasmic sperm injection is required. This involves injecting a single sperm cell directly into an egg cell rather than letting sperm penetrate the egg naturally.

Key facts

✓ Blocked sperm ducts or low sperm numbers are causes of infertility in males.

✓ Blocked oviducts or lack of egg maturation are causes of infertility in females.

✓ In vitro fertilization (IVF) is used to treat infertility.

✓ During IVF, an egg cell is fertilized with a sperm cell outside the body. The resulting embryo is then placed into the uterus.

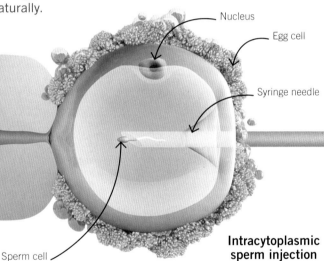

Nucleus

Egg cell

Syringe needle

Sperm cell

Intracytoplasmic sperm injection

🔍 Stages in IVF treatment

1. Fertility drugs are given to the female. These contain hormones that stimulate many eggs to mature in the ovaries.

2. A number of eggs are collected from the female's ovaries, and a sample of semen is collected from the male.

3. The sperm and egg cells are mixed in a Petri dish and left for several hours.

4. The fertilized eggs are monitored as they divide to form embryos.

5. After around five days, the best embryo is placed into the female's uterus. If the embryo implants successfully, it will develop into a baby.

Adrenaline

When a person feels threatened or scared, their adrenal glands release the hormone adrenaline. This triggers the fight or flight response, which prepares the body to confront danger.

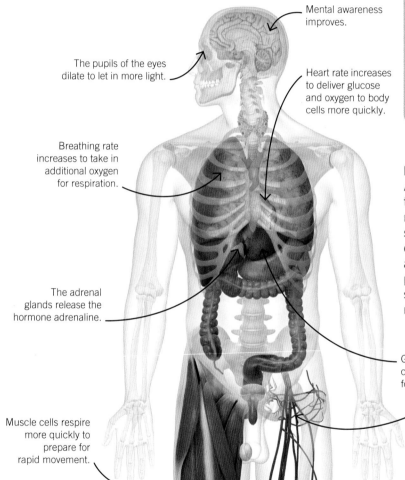

Mental awareness improves.

The pupils of the eyes dilate to let in more light.

Heart rate increases to deliver glucose and oxygen to body cells more quickly.

Breathing rate increases to take in additional oxygen for respiration.

The adrenal glands release the hormone adrenaline.

Muscle cells respire more quickly to prepare for rapid movement.

Glycogen in the liver is converted to glucose for respiration.

Blood is diverted away from the digestive system and toward the large muscles in the limbs.

Effects of adrenaline

Adrenaline affects many parts of the body. It deepens breathing and makes the heart beat faster and stronger, boosting the delivery of oxygen and glucose to the brain and muscles. These changes prepare the body for rapid action in situations where a quick response may be essential for survival.

🔍 Fear reaction

Adrenaline is produced in the bodies of many animals, preparing them for sudden action when they are frightened or angry. The fight or flight response also activates the nervous system, with effects all over the body. In animals with fur, for example, nerve impulses make hairs stand on end to make the animal look larger and more threatening. The same reflex occurs in humans, giving us goose bumps when we are frightened.

A cat's hairs stand on end when it's frightened.

Thyroxine

Thyroxine is a hormone produced by the thyroid gland in the neck. It regulates the body's metabolic rate— the rate at which the body uses energy. Thyroxine affects how quickly cells respire and how quickly molecules are broken down or built up in cells.

Key facts

✓ Thyroxine is a hormone produced by the thyroid gland.

✓ Thyroxine controls the body's metabolic rate.

✓ The hypothalamus stimulates the pituitary gland to release thyroid-stimulating hormone (TSH), which acts on the thyroid gland to release thyroxine.

Thyroxine production

When the body needs more energy, the hypothalamus in the brain causes the pituitary gland to release thyroid-stimulating hormone (TSH). TSH travels in the blood to the thyroid gland, triggering the release of thyroxine. Thyroxine then raises the body's metabolic rate, giving cells more energy.

The hypothalamus monitors energy use and the level of thyroxine in the blood. If the level falls or the body needs more energy, the hypothalamus stimulates the pituitary gland to release TSH.

The pituitary gland releases TSH, which travels in the blood to the thyroid gland.

The thyroid gland produces the hormone thyroxine, which raises the body's metabolic rate.

Negative feedback

A negative feedback system helps keep the body's metabolic rate stable. When cells have enough energy, thyroxine production stops, and the metabolic rate slows down. If it slows too much, this triggers the release of thyroxine, raising the metabolic rate again.

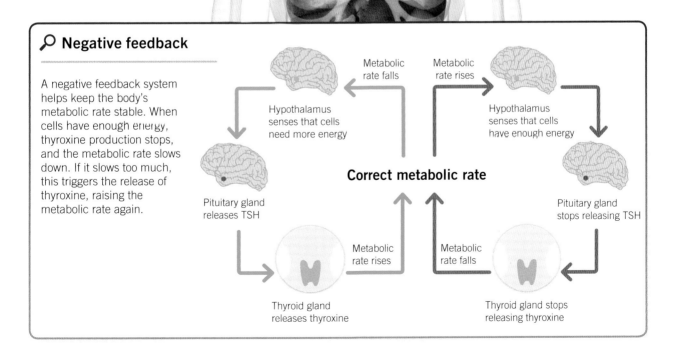

Metabolic rate falls

Metabolic rate rises

Hypothalamus senses that cells need more energy

Hypothalamus senses that cells have enough energy

Correct metabolic rate

Pituitary gland releases TSH

Pituitary gland stops releasing TSH

Metabolic rate rises

Metabolic rate falls

Thyroid gland releases thyroxine

Thyroid gland stops releasing thyroxine

Plant hormones

Plants use hormones to respond to certain stimuli, such as light and gravity. The hormone auxin affects the way plants grow, making shoots grow upward toward the light and roots grow downward away from it.

Tropisms

Plants respond to light and gravity by changing the way they grow. Growing in response to light is called phototropism, and growing in response to gravity is called gravitropism. Shoots grow toward the light (positive phototropism) and away from gravity (negative gravitropism), whereas roots grow away from light (negative phototropism) and toward gravity (positive gravitropism).

The shoot bends upward, growing toward the light and away from gravity.

The root bends downward, growing toward gravity and away from the light.

Key facts

✓ **The plant hormone auxin controls the way plants respond to light and gravity.**

✓ **Phototropism is growth in response to the direction of light.**

✓ **Gravitropism is growth in response to the direction of gravity.**

🔍 Auxin

Tropisms are controlled by the hormone auxin. Made in the tips of growing shoots and roots, it diffuses through the plant. In shoots, auxin stimulates growth by making cells elongate. In roots, it inhibits growth.

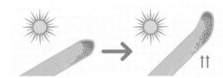

In shoots, auxin moves to the shaded side of the plant. Cells elongate more here, making the shoot grow toward the light.

If a shoot grows sideways, gravity makes auxin concentrate at the bottom. Cells elongate here and the shoot grows upward.

In roots, gravity makes auxin concentrate at the bottom. It inhibits growth here, and the root bends downward.

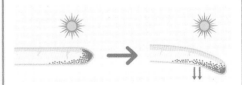

If a root is exposed to light, auxin concentrates at the bottom. It inhibits growth and the root grows downward.

Using plant hormones

Plant hormones can be very useful to farmers or gardeners. They can be used to speed up or slow down the ripening of fruits, make seeds germinate and flower buds open, and kill weeds.

Key facts

✓ Auxins are used to kill weeds, delay fruit ripening, and trigger growth of seedless fruit.

✓ Ethene is a gas used to speed up the ripening of fruit.

✓ Gibberellins are used to end dormancy in seeds and flower buds.

Ripening fruit

Ethene is a gas that plants produce as a hormone to trigger the ripening of fruit. It breaks down cell walls and converts starch to sugar, making fruit sweeter. Ethene produced naturally by bananas speeds up the ripening of other fruit kept in the same bowl. Fruit suppliers harvest bananas when unripe and use ethene to trigger ripening just before they are sold.

Bananas change color from green to yellow and then brown as they ripen.

🔍 Useful hormones

Plant hormones have many different uses. Some of the hormones used in gardening and agriculture are natural compounds, but others are synthetic chemicals that mimic the effect of natural hormones.

Synthetic auxins are often used as weed killers. They make the affected plants grow uncontrollably fast, which kills them. Auxins are also used to slow down fruit ripening and to trigger the growth of seedless fruit from unpollinated flowers.

Gibberellins are hormones that trigger the end of dormancy in seeds and flower buds. They are used to make seeds grow and to make flowers open. Some flowers and fruits, such as seedless grapes, grow larger after being sprayed with gibberellins.

Effect of light on seedlings

Hormones allow plants to respond to their environment as soon as they start growing. This experiment investigates the way seedlings grow after they germinate.

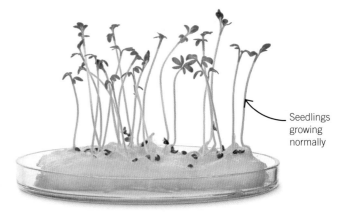

Seedlings growing normally

Full sunlight

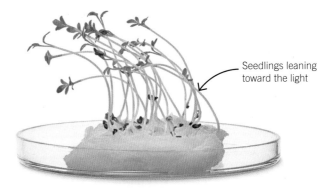

Seedlings leaning toward the light

Partial light

⚙ Method

1. Put cotton wool in three Petri dishes and soak with equal volumes of water.

2. Put the same number of mustard seeds or cress seeds on the cotton wool in each dish and place in a warm place. Water the seeds every day for 2–3 days until they germinate.

3. Once the seeds have germinated, make sure each dish has the same number of seedlings by removing spares from the dishes with too many.

4. Measure the height of each seedling with a ruler and make a record of the measurements.

5. Place one dish in a bright place, such as a windowsill. Place another in a place with partial light, such as the end of a room farthest from a window. Place the third in a dark place.

6. Water the seedlings and measure their heights every day for at least 5 days. Record the results in a table.

7. Calculate the mean seedling height for each dish for each day, and note any differences in the direction of growth.

Seedlings growing tall and yellow

Darkness

Result

The seedlings on the windowsill grow normally, but those grown far from a window lean toward the light. This is called tropism and is caused by the hormone auxin (see page 156). The seedlings kept in the dark have grown unusually tall as they try to reach the light. However, they cannot make the green pigment chlorophyll without light, so their leaves are yellow.

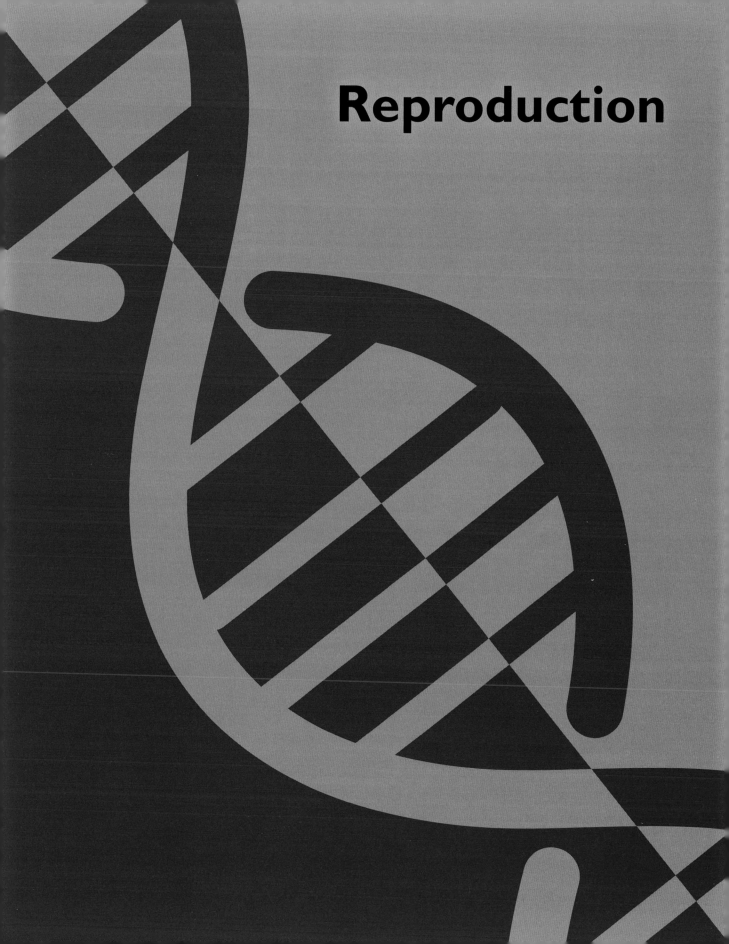

Reproduction

Sexual reproduction

Sexual reproduction is the production of new offspring by two parents. Each parent contributes a unique selection of their genes, making every offspring genetically unique. This variation makes sexually reproducing populations better able to adapt to changes, such as the appearance of new diseases.

Key facts

✓ **Sexual reproduction requires two parents.**

✓ **Male and female gametes (sex cells) fuse to create a zygote. This is called fertilization.**

✓ **The offspring produced by sexual reproduction are all genetically different, creating variation.**

Male sex cells are called sperm.

Female sex cells are called egg cells or ova.

Sperm cells are smaller but much more numerous than egg cells.

Sex cells

Sex cells are produced by a type of cell division called meiosis (see page 46), which gives each sex cell half of the usual number of chromosomes (the haploid number). When a sperm and egg cell fuse to form a zygote, the chromosomes combine in the nucleus, restoring the full number (the diploid number). Each embryo has a unique blend of maternal and paternal genes, which results in genetically varied offspring.

Human sperm
23 chromosomes

Human egg
23 chromosomes

Zygote
46 chromosomes

Embryo
46 chromosomes

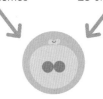

Fertilization

Sexual reproduction involves the production of special cells called sex cells (gametes). In animals, female sex cells are called egg cells, and male sex cells are called sperm. When a male sex cell meets a female sex cell, they fuse with one another—a process known as fertilization. The fertilized egg is called a zygote and may develop into a new organism.

Sperm cell

Animals and some plants produce male sex cells called sperm. A sperm cell has a tail that it beats to swim toward an egg cell.

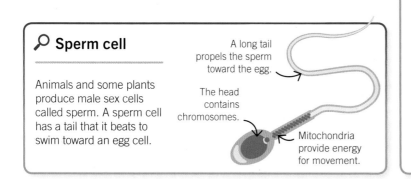

A long tail propels the sperm toward the egg.

The head contains chromosomes.

Mitochondria provide energy for movement.

Asexual reproduction

Asexual reproduction is the production of new offspring by a single parent. This form of reproduction is very common in microorganisms, plants, and many small animals. All the offspring produced by asexual reproduction are genetically identical both to each other and to the parent.

Budding in yeasts
Yeasts are single-celled fungi that can multiply in number very quickly thanks to a form of asexual reproduction known as budding. A new yeast cell develops as a small outgrowth, or bud, of the parent cell. Corals, sponges, and small freshwater animals called hydras also reproduce by budding.

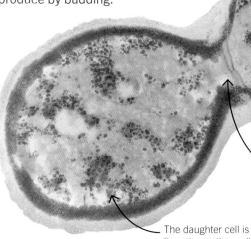

A wall forms between the two cells before the daughter cell separates.

The daughter cell is smaller than the mother cell.

🔍 Advantages of asexual reproduction

Asexual reproduction has many advantages over sexual reproduction. Only one parent is needed, so there is no need to find a mate. It is faster than sexual reproduction, allowing organisms to multiply quickly under favorable conditions. However, unlike sexual reproduction, which produces varied offspring, asexual reproduction produces genetically identical clones. This makes all members of the population equally vulnerable to the same disease or to a change in the environment.

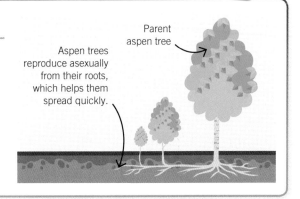

Parent aspen tree

Aspen trees reproduce asexually from their roots, which helps them spread quickly.

Flowers

Flowers are the reproductive organs of flowering plants. Many flowers are brightly colored to attract small animals called pollinators. These animals carry sex cells from the male parts of a flower to the female parts of another flower.

Pollination

The male parts of a flower are called stamens. The top of a stamen makes a powdery substance called pollen, which contains male sex cells. Pollinating animals accidentally pick up this powder and carry it to other flowers, where it rubs off on the stigma—the top of the female part of the flower.

Key facts

✓ Flowers are the reproductive organs of flowering plants and make male and female sex cells.

✓ Pollination is the transfer of pollen grains from the male parts of flowers to the female parts of flowers.

✓ A flower must be pollinated in order to make seeds.

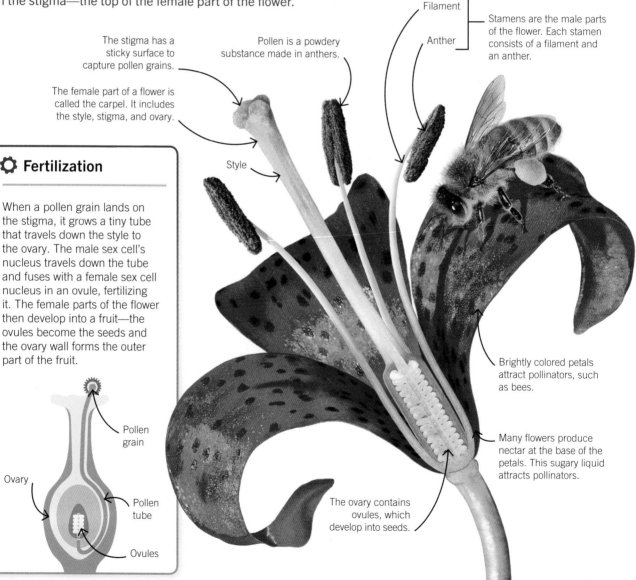

Filament

Anther

Stamens are the male parts of the flower. Each stamen consists of a filament and an anther.

The stigma has a sticky surface to capture pollen grains.

Pollen is a powdery substance made in anthers.

The female part of a flower is called the carpel. It includes the style, stigma, and ovary.

Style

⚙ Fertilization

When a pollen grain lands on the stigma, it grows a tiny tube that travels down the style to the ovary. The male sex cell's nucleus travels down the tube and fuses with a female sex cell nucleus in an ovule, fertilizing it. The female parts of the flower then develop into a fruit—the ovules become the seeds and the ovary wall forms the outer part of the fruit.

Pollen grain

Ovary

Pollen tube

Ovules

Brightly colored petals attract pollinators, such as bees.

Many flowers produce nectar at the base of the petals. This sugary liquid attracts pollinators.

The ovary contains ovules, which develop into seeds.

Wind pollination

The flowers of many plants, such as grasses, are pollinated not by animals but by wind. Wind-pollinated flowers don't need to attract pollinators and so don't have scents, bright colors, or nectar. They produce masses of tiny pollen grains that float in the air.

Key facts

✓ Some flowers are pollinated by wind rather than by animals.

✓ Wind-pollinated flowers are small and drab.

✓ Wind-pollinated flowers produce millions of tiny pollen grains.

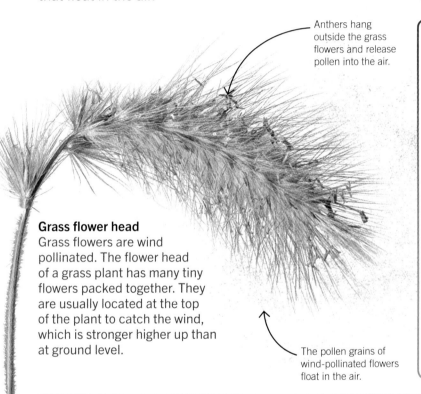

Anthers hang outside the grass flowers and release pollen into the air.

Grass flower head
Grass flowers are wind pollinated. The flower head of a grass plant has many tiny flowers packed together. They are usually located at the top of the plant to catch the wind, which is stronger higher up than at ground level.

The pollen grains of wind-pollinated flowers float in the air.

Grass floret

The flower head of a grass plant is made of many tiny flowers called florets. These have large anthers that hang outside the flower to scatter pollen into the air. Feathery stigmas also hang outside the flower to catch wind-blown pollen.

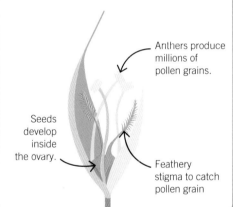

Anthers produce millions of pollen grains.

Seeds develop inside the ovary.

Feathery stigma to catch pollen grain

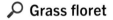

Comparing animal- and wind-pollinated flowers		
	Animal pollinated	**Wind pollinated**
Petals	Large and colorful	Tiny and dull
Anthers	Inside the flower	Hang outside the flower
Stigma	Inside the flower, sticky	Outside the flower, feathery
Pollen	Thousands of sticky or spiky pollen grains that stick to animals	Millions of tiny, smooth pollen grains that are carried by the wind
Scent and nectar	Has scent and nectar	No scent or nectar

Fruit

After a flower has been pollinated, the petals fall off and the ovary grows to form a fruit, with seeds developing inside it. Some fruits have bright colors and sweet, edible flesh to attract animals, which help disperse the seeds. However, fruits can also develop into nuts, pods, wings, or other structures.

Key facts

✓ **A fruit is a seed-bearing structure formed from the ovary of a flower.**

✓ **Some fruits have sweet, edible flesh to attract animal dispersers.**

Inside a tomato

A tomato is a simple fruit formed from a single ovary that contains many seeds. The seeds are trapped in a slippery, jellylike flesh that makes them hard to remove, so animals swallow the seeds with the flesh. The seeds later pass out of the animal's body in its droppings, usually far away from the parent plant.

A fruit is attached to the parent plant by a pedicel (stalk).

The ovary wall becomes fleshy.

Bright colors and sweet flesh attract animals, which disperse the seeds.

Seeds develop inside the ovary.

⚙ How a fruit develops

As a fruit begins to form, it stores nutrients such as starch in its ovary wall, which at first is very hard. As the fruit ripens, the starch turns into sugar, the ovary wall softens, and the skin changes color. All these changes make the fruit more attractive to animals.

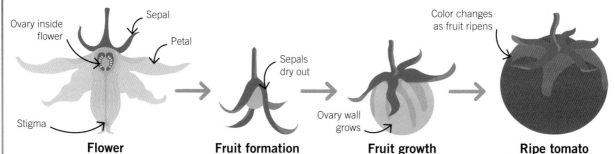

Ovary inside flower

Sepal

Petal

Stigma

Flower

Sepals dry out

Fruit formation

Ovary wall grows

Fruit growth

Color changes as fruit ripens

Ripe tomato

Seed dispersal

Seedlings that grow too close to their parent plant compete with each other and the parent for space, light, water, and nutrients. Most seeds have features that help them travel far from the parent, preventing competition. This scattering of seeds is called dispersal.

Key facts

✓ Seed dispersal helps plants avoid competition for light, space, water, and nutrients.

✓ Plants may use animals, wind, water, or explosive methods to scatter their seeds.

✓ Animals disperse the seeds of inedible fruits in their droppings.

Blowing in the wind
A dandelion flower produces around 150 tiny seeds, each equipped with a parachute of fine hairs that allows it to ride on the wind.

A parachute of feathery hairs makes the seed float through the air.

A hard capsule protects each seed.

⚙ How seeds disperse

Seeds can be dispersed by the wind, animals, water, or explosive seed pods.

Wing

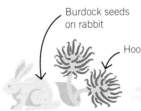

Burdock seeds on rabbit

Hooks

Sycamore seeds have wings that make them spin, slowing their fall as the wind blows them away from the parent tree.

Edible fruits contain seeds. Animals eat the fruits and disperse the seeds in their droppings.

Burdock seeds are covered in tiny hooks that latch onto the fur of animals, which carry the seeds far away.

A coconut floats on water, carrying the single large seed inside it to a distant beach, where it germinates.

Seedpods of some plants burst open violently, flinging seeds far away from the parent plant.

Seeds

A seed is a capsule containing an embryonic plant and its food store inside a protective coat. Seeds can remain dormant for months, waiting for the right conditions to grow.

Key facts

- ✓ A seed is a capsule containing a tiny plant with a food store.
- ✓ Germination is the growth of a seed into a young plant.
- ✓ Seeds need three things to germinate: water, oxygen, and warmth.

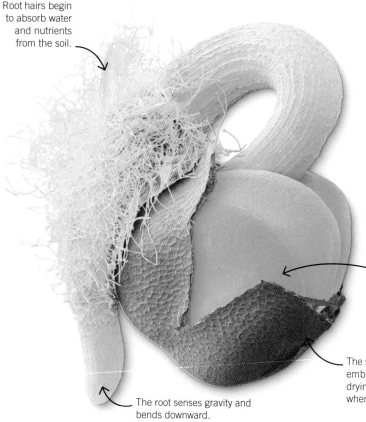

Root hairs begin to absorb water and nutrients from the soil.

Cotyledons (seed leaves) act as a food store inside the seed.

The seed coat protects the embryo and prevents it from drying out. The coat splits when a seed germinates.

The root senses gravity and bends downward.

Germination

Under the right conditions, a seed develops into a new plant through a process called germination. In order to germinate, a seed needs three things: water, oxygen, and warmth. Water helps the seed swell and open. Oxygen allows the cells to respire. Warmth activates the enzymes that break down the seed's food store into simple sugars to feed the young plant.

🔍 Inside a seed

A seed contains a tiny baby plant, known as an embryo, complete with a root and shoot that includes the first true leaves. Seeds also contain a large store of food, often in the form of "seed leaves," or cotyledons.

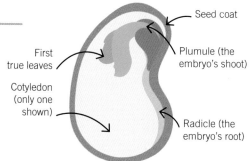

Seed coat

First true leaves

Plumule (the embryo's shoot)

Cotyledon (only one shown)

Radicle (the embryo's root)

Dicotyledons, such as this bean, contain two cotyledons that nearly fill the seed. They are packed with nutrients to help the young plant germinate.

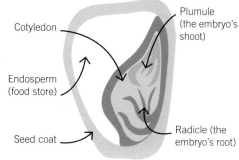

Plumule (the embryo's shoot)

Cotyledon

Endosperm (food store)

Seed coat

Radicle (the embryo's root)

Monocotyledons, such as this corn seed, contain one seed leaf. They get their energy from an additional food store called an endosperm.

Factors that affect germination

Seeds begin to grow (germinate) only when the conditions are just right. This experiment allows you to investigate the effects of three factors—water, oxygen, and warmth—on germination.

Germinating cress
Four test tubes of cress seeds on cotton balls are needed for the experiment. In the first tube, the seeds have water, oxygen, and warmth. In each of the remaining tubes, one of these factors is missing.

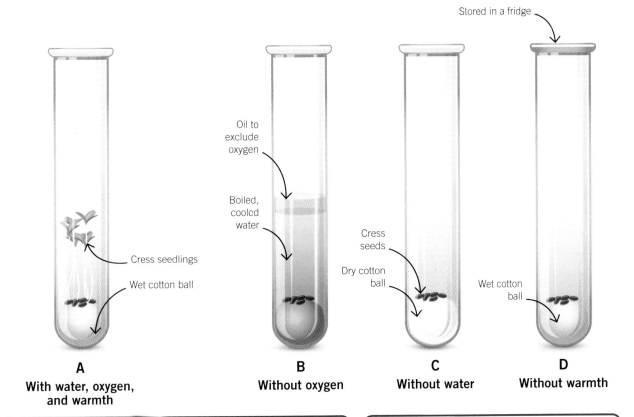

Stored in a fridge

Oil to exclude oxygen

Boiled, cooled water

Cress seeds

Dry cotton ball

Cress seedlings

Wet cotton ball

Wet cotton ball

A
With water, oxygen, and warmth

B
Without oxygen

C
Without water

D
Without warmth

Method

1. Place a cotton ball at the base of four test tubes labeled A, B, C, and D, and add 6 cress seeds to each.

2. Add water to test tubes A and D to make the cotton ball moist.

3. Add boiled, cooled water to test tube B until the tube is half full. Add a thin layer of vegetable oil on top.

4. Keep tubes A, B, and C in a warm room, but place test tube D in a fridge.

5. Observe the test tubes for 3–5 days. If the cotton ball in tubes A or D dries out, add more water to make it moist again.

Results

Seeds will germinate only in test tube A, which has water, oxygen, and warmth—all three conditions are essential for germination. Water is needed to make the seeds swell and open. Oxygen allows the cells to respire. Warmth activates the enzymes needed to break down starch in the seed's food store and turn it into sugar. Test tube B contains boiled water because boiling removes oxygen. The layer of oil on top stops oxygen in the air from getting in.

Asexual reproduction in plants

Many plants can reproduce asexually, which requires only one parent and produces offspring that are genetically identical (clones) to that parent. Reproducing asexually allows plants to multiply in number and spread quickly.

Alligator plant

The alligator plant of Madagascar produces tiny plantlets on the edges of its leaves, each with their own roots and leaves. These drop off the parent and take root to form new plants.

Plantlets grow on the edge of each leaf.

Roots form before the plantlets fall off the parent.

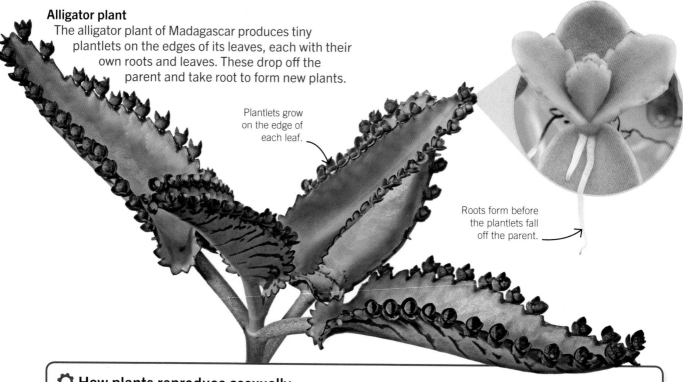

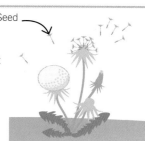

⚙ How plants reproduce asexually

Plants can reproduce asexually in many different ways. These are some of the most common methods.

Runner

Rhizome

Bulblet

Seed

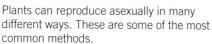

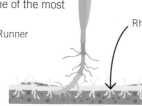

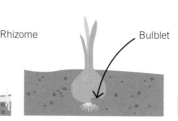

Runners are horizontal stems that grow along the ground and then take root, forming a new plant. Strawberry plants can reproduce this way.

Rhizomes are stems that grow horizontally underground and produce new shoots. Bamboo plants reproduce this way.

Bulbs are underground food stores produced by many plants. They also produce new plants from "bulblets" around the base.

Asexual seeds are made by some flowers, including dandelions. The seeds grow into clones of the parent plant.

Life cycle of insects

Insects begin life as eggs and hatch out as wingless babies. Many insects go through a dramatic change called metamorphosis as they mature into adults.

Key facts

✓ Complete metamorphosis is a dramatic change in an animal's appearance as it matures.

✓ A pupa is a motionless stage in the life cycle of an insect.

✓ Incomplete metamorphosis is a gradual change in an insect's appearance as it develops.

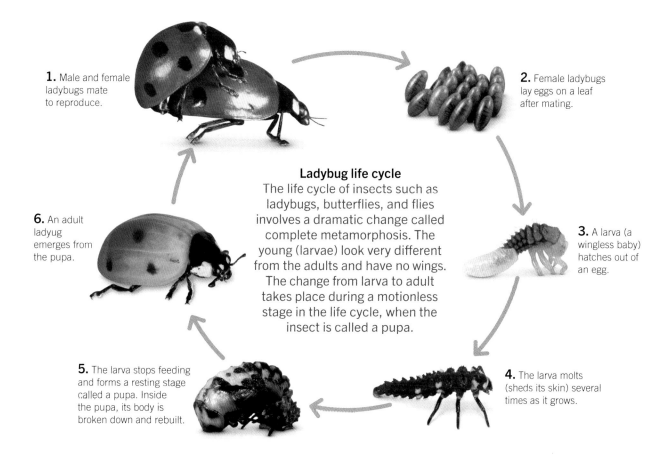

1. Male and female ladybugs mate to reproduce.

2. Female ladybugs lay eggs on a leaf after mating.

3. A larva (a wingless baby) hatches out of an egg.

4. The larva molts (sheds its skin) several times as it grows.

5. The larva stops feeding and forms a resting stage called a pupa. Inside the pupa, its body is broken down and rebuilt.

6. An adult ladyug emerges from the pupa.

Ladybug life cycle
The life cycle of insects such as ladybugs, butterflies, and flies involves a dramatic change called complete metamorphosis. The young (larvae) look very different from the adults and have no wings. The change from larva to adult takes place during a motionless stage in the life cycle, when the insect is called a pupa.

🔍 Incomplete metamorphosis

Insects such as grasshoppers and dragonflies hatch out of their eggs as wingless young called nymphs, which look similar to adults. They molt several times as they grow, acquiring their wings after the final molt. This more gradual change from infant to adult is called incomplete metamorphosis.

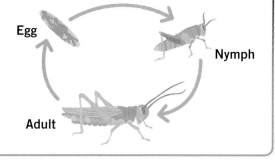

Egg

Nymph

Adult

Life cycle of amphibians

Amphibians are animals that typically spend part of their life cycle in water and part on land. Many amphibians go through a dramatic change called metamorphosis as they prepare for life on land.

Key facts

✓ Amphibians typically spend part of their life in water and part on land.

✓ Many amphibians go through a dramatic change called metamorphosis as they mature.

✓ The aquatic young of amphibians are called tadpoles.

1. A female frog lays eggs in water. Clusters of eggs are called frogspawn.

Common frog life cycle
Frogs live on land but lay their eggs in water, where the eggs hatch into fishlike young called tadpoles. As tadpoles grow, they develop legs, lose their tails, and begin to breathe with lungs instead of gills.

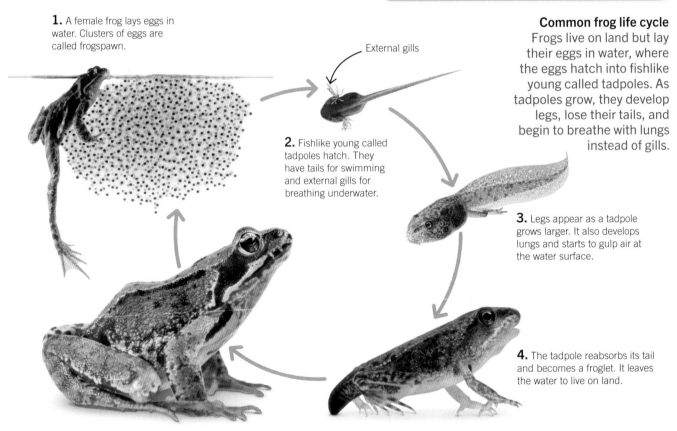

External gills

2. Fishlike young called tadpoles hatch. They have tails for swimming and external gills for breathing underwater.

3. Legs appear as a tadpole grows larger. It also develops lungs and starts to gulp air at the water surface.

4. The tadpole reabsorbs its tail and becomes a froglet. It leaves the water to live on land.

5. An adult frog lives on land but returns to water to mate.

Gills and lungs

Young tadpoles can't obtain oxygen by breathing air. Instead they use gills—feathery organs that absorb oxygen from water and release waste carbon dioxide. When a common frog tadpole is about 10 weeks old, the external gills become internal gills as skin grows over them. Water is taken in through the mouth and forced through the gills. As the tadpole turns into a froglet, the gills are replaced by lungs.

Feathery external gills for breathing underwater

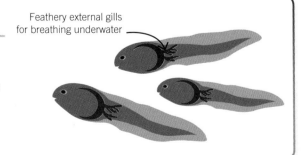

Life cycle of birds

Unlike mammals, which develop inside their mother's body, baby birds develop inside eggs, which are usually laid in a nest. After hatching out, the chicks rely on the parents to look after them.

Key facts

✓ Birds develop inside eggs.

✓ Nearly all chicks rely on parental care after hatching.

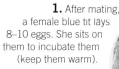

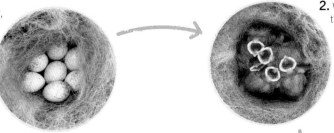

1. After mating, a female blue tit lays 8–10 eggs. She sits on them to incubate them (keep them warm).

2. When the chicks hatch they are helpless, naked, and blind. The parents cooperate to food them, catching hundreds of caterpillars a day.

Blue tit life cycle
Songbirds, such as blue tits, raise their young in a nest in a tree. The babies are born helpless and unable to fly, but they grow quickly and are able to fly at about three weeks old.

4. Adult blue tits find mating partners by singing. The female builds a nest lined with soft material, such as wool, feathers, or spider's webs.

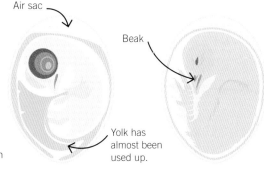

3. The chicks grow quickly and develop feathers within a few days. Eventually, they are big enough to fly and leave the nest.

🔍 Eggs

A bird's egg contains a store of nutrients and water to nourish the embryo developing inside it. Eggs start as a single cell inside the mother's body, where the female egg cell is fertilized by a male sperm cell. After fertilization, the cell absorbs nutrients from the mother's body and swells in size, and a shell develops around it.

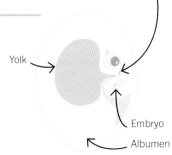

Limb buds

Yolk

Embryo

Albumen

Air sac

Beak

Yolk has almost been used up.

The embryo's limbs begin to form by day 5. The yolk and albumen nourish and cushion the embryo.

By day 12, the bird's limbs, skeleton, and organs are well developed. Soft feathers called down cover the chick.

Around day 21, the chick takes its first breath from the air sac. It wriggles to crack the shell and then breaks out.

Life cycle of mammals

Nearly all mammals spend the first part of their life cycle developing inside their mother's body. After birth, baby mammals feed on milk produced by the mother's body.

Mouse life cycle

About three weeks after mating, a female mouse gives birth to a litter of 5–8 babies. The babies are born hairless and blind but grow quickly and have fur by two weeks old. At eight weeks old, they are fully mature and ready to mate.

1. Newborn mice are blind and hairless and depend on their mother. They feed on milk, a nutritious fluid produced by glands on the mother's belly.

4. Baby mammals develop inside the mother's body in an organ called a uterus. Their blood receives nutrients and oxygen from the mother's blood via an organ called a placenta.

Uterus containing baby

2. As babies grow, their eyes open and they develop fur. They become increasingly active and playful. Playing helps mammals acquire the physical skills they need to survive.

3. When fully grown, mice seek out partners so they can mate and produce their own offspring. Mating in mammals involves internal fertilization, which means the male sperm cell and female egg cell fuse inside the mother's body.

🔍 Marsupials and monotremes

Although most mammals complete the early stage of development inside the mother's body, some mammals develop mostly outside the mother's body. These include marsupials and monotremes. Like all mammals, marsupials and monotremes feed their young with milk.

Marsupials, such as kangaroos, are born when they are very tiny and undeveloped. They complete the early stage of development inside a pouch on the mother's body.

Monotremes are unusual mammals that lay eggs. They include the platypus and hedgehog-like animals called echidnas (above).

Male reproductive system

Sexual reproduction in humans involves a male sex cell (a sperm cell) joining a female sex cell (an egg cell). This is called fertilization and takes place inside the female body. The organs of the male reproductive system produce sperm cells and place them inside the female reproductive system during sex.

📌 **Key facts**

✓ Male sex cells (sperm) are produced inside organs called testes (singular testis).

✓ Sperm are placed in the female's body during sex.

Male organs

Sperm are produced inside two egg-shaped organs called testes. During sex, sperm cells mix with secretions from the prostate gland and seminal vesicles to make a fluid called semen, which helps the sperm cells to swim. The testes hang outside the body in a bag called a scrotum to keep them cooler, since sperm develop better at lower temperatures. During sex, sperm pass out through the penis into the female's body.

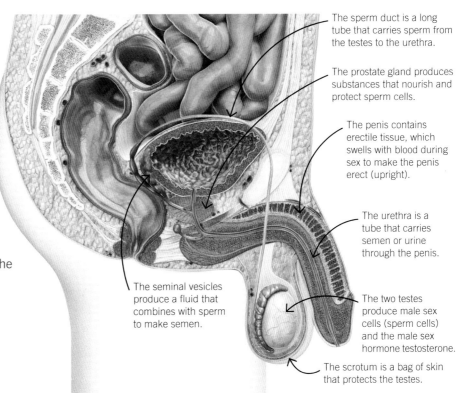

The sperm duct is a long tube that carries sperm from the testes to the urethra.

The prostate gland produces substances that nourish and protect sperm cells.

The penis contains erectile tissue, which swells with blood during sex to make the penis erect (upright).

The urethra is a tube that carries semen or urine through the penis.

The seminal vesicles produce a fluid that combines with sperm to make semen.

The two testes produce male sex cells (sperm cells) and the male sex hormone testosterone.

The scrotum is a bag of skin that protects the testes.

🔍 Human sperm cell

A male's testes produce more than 100 million sperm cells each day. Fueled by the nutrients in semen, each sperm cell swims vigorously in the race to reach an egg cell and fertilize it. At the front of a sperm cell is a sac called the acrosome, which contains a store of digestive enzymes. When a sperm meets an egg, the acrosome bursts and the enzymes make an opening in the egg cell's coat—allowing the sperm cell's nucleus to enter the egg cell and fertilize it.

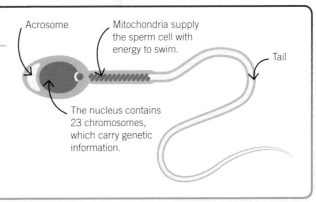

Acrosome

Mitochondria supply the sperm cell with energy to swim.

Tail

The nucleus contains 23 chromosomes, which carry genetic information.

Female reproductive system

The female reproductive system produces sex cells called egg cells. After an egg cell has been fertilized by a sperm cell, it develops inside an organ called a uterus.

Female organs

Once every month between sexual maturity and around the age of 50, an egg cell is released from one of the ovaries in the female body. As it travels toward the uterus, it may be fertilized by a sperm cell. If so, it embeds in the soft inner wall of the uterus and begins to develop into a baby.

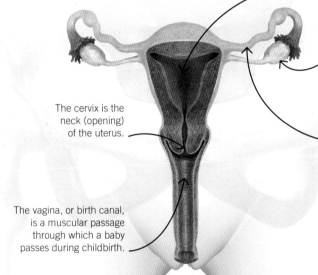

The uterus is a stretchy, muscular organ that holds the developing baby.

The two ovaries produce egg cells (ova). They also produce the female sex hormones estrogen and progesterone.

Egg cells released by an ovary travel through a tube called the oviduct to reach the uterus.

The cervix is the neck (opening) of the uterus.

The vagina, or birth canal, is a muscular passage through which a baby passes during childbirth.

🔍 Human egg cell

At about one-fifth of a millimeter wide, the human egg cell is one of the largest cells in the human body. An egg cell has a large amount of cytoplasm that serves as a store of nutrients for the developing embryo. An outer coat of jelly (called the zona pellucida) surrounds its cell membrane. After a sperm cell has fertilized the egg, the jelly changes to prevent any more sperm from getting through.

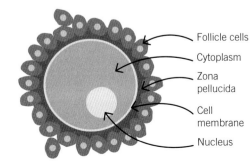

Follicle cells

Cytoplasm

Zona pellucida

Cell membrane

Nucleus

Human fertilization

The joining of a sperm cell and egg cell is called fertilization. When an egg cell is fertilized, it forms a cell called a zygote. The zygote then develops into a ball of cells called an embryo and becomes implanted in the wall of the uterus.

> **Key facts**
>
> ✓ Fertilization is the joining of a sperm cell and an egg cell (ovum) to form a zygote.
>
> ✓ After formation, a zygote divides to form an embryo.
>
> ✓ The embryo implants into the inner lining of the uterus.

In the uterus
After sex, sperm cells swim through fluids in the female's uterus to reach the oviducts in search of an egg cell. To increase the probability of successful fertilization, a male's semen contains millions of sperm cells. However, the female body usually releases only a single egg cell each month. Many sperm cells may meet an egg cell in the oviduct and attempt to fertilize it, but only one can succeed.

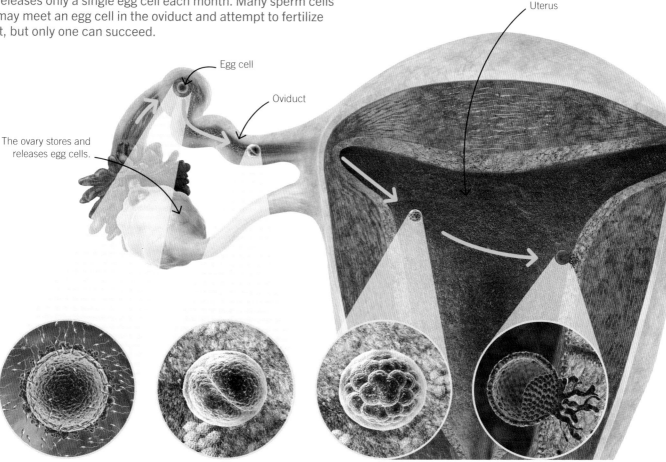

Uterus

Egg cell

Oviduct

The ovary stores and releases egg cells.

1. One of the sperm cells penetrates the egg's outer coat with its head. Their nuclei join, giving the resulting cell (now called a zygote) a full set of 46 chromosomes.

2. As the zygote travels toward the uterus, it divides into two cells. It is now called an embryo.

3. The embryo divides again into four cells, then eight, and so on, forming a ball of cells. After a few hours, the embryo is a hollow ball of cells.

4. After a few days, the embryo reaches the uterus, wafted by tiny beating hairs (cilia) lining the oviduct. It sinks into the soft tissue lining the uterus. This is called implantation.

Pregnancy

It takes around 40 weeks for a fertilized egg cell to develop into a baby ready to be born. This period is known as gestation or pregnancy.

Key facts

✓ The placenta provides the fetus with oxygen and nutrients and removes waste.

✓ The blood of the mother and the fetus do not mix.

✓ Most of the baby's organs develop in the early stages of pregnancy.

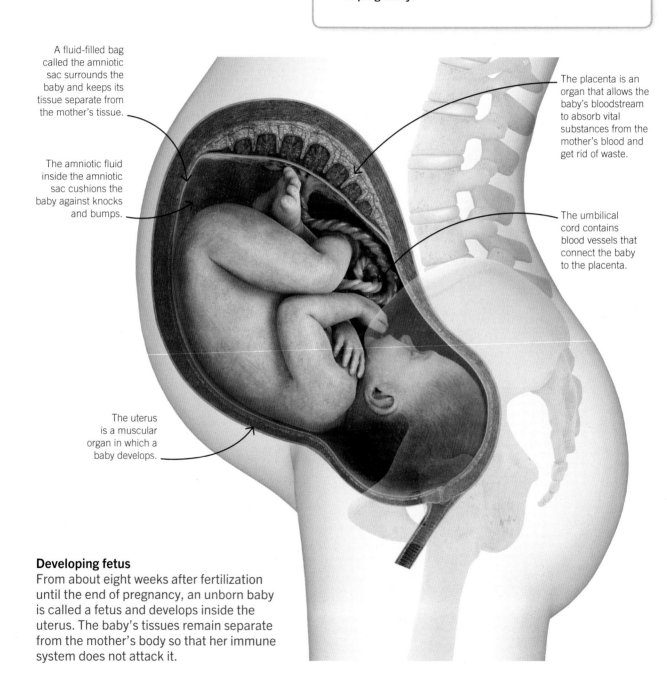

A fluid-filled bag called the amniotic sac surrounds the baby and keeps its tissue separate from the mother's tissue.

The amniotic fluid inside the amniotic sac cushions the baby against knocks and bumps.

The placenta is an organ that allows the baby's bloodstream to absorb vital substances from the mother's blood and get rid of waste.

The umbilical cord contains blood vessels that connect the baby to the placenta.

The uterus is a muscular organ in which a baby develops.

Developing fetus

From about eight weeks after fertilization until the end of pregnancy, an unborn baby is called a fetus and develops inside the uterus. The baby's tissues remain separate from the mother's body so that her immune system does not attack it.

🔍 Stages of growth

Most of the baby's organs develop early in pregnancy. In the later months, when development is mostly complete, the baby grows in size. The developing baby is called an embryo in the first 8 weeks and a fetus after 8 weeks.

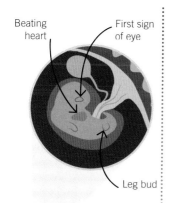

Beating heart — First sign of eye — Leg bud — Uterus

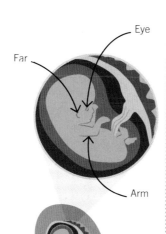

Ear — Eye — Arm — Uterus

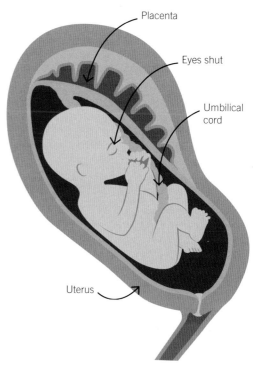

Placenta — Eyes shut — Umbilical cord — Uterus

At 5 weeks after fertilization, the embryo is the size of an apple pip and resembles a tadpole. Its heart has started beating, but its arms and legs are only buds.

At 10 weeks old, the fetus is the size of an olive. Its face, limbs, fingers, toes, and most organs have formed.

At 20 weeks old, the fetus is about as long as a banana. It has eyebrows, body hair, and fingernails, and it can move its muscles. Its development is almost complete, but it will continue to grow much larger.

⚙ The placenta

This temporary organ is the baby's life-support system. It contains tiny blood vessels from the fetus that pass close to the mother's blood vessels, without the blood mixing. Oxygen and nutrients pass from the mother's blood to the baby's blood by diffusion, and waste products such as carbon dioxide and urea diffuse from the baby's blood to the mother's. Although the placenta keeps the baby's blood and the mother's blood separate, some harmful substances can cross it. These include alcohol, nicotine from cigarettes, toxins from certain foods, and some disease-causing pathogens, such as the rubella (German measles) virus.

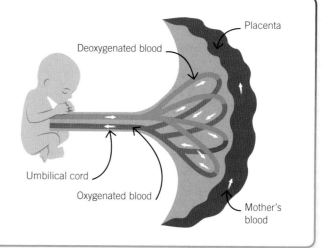

Deoxygenated blood — Placenta — Umbilical cord — Oxygenated blood — Mother's blood

Childbirth

At the end of pregnancy, hormones released by both a baby's body and the mother's body trigger a process called labor, which ends in the birth of the baby.

Newborn baby

After being born, the baby starts to breathe and no longer receives oxygen from the mother. A newborn baby is still attached to the placenta by its umbilical cord. The cord is cut soon after birth, and its remains form the baby's navel (belly button).

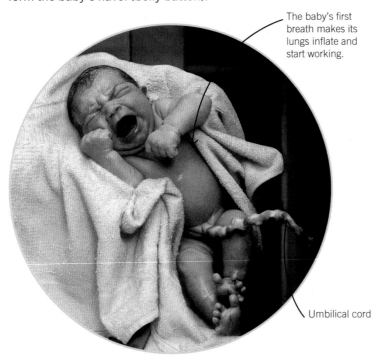

The baby's first breath makes its lungs inflate and start working.

Umbilical cord

Key facts

✓ Labor usually starts with contractions of the uterus's muscular wall.

✓ The muscular contractions grow in strength until they push the baby out of the mother's body.

🔍 Stages of childbirth

The process of childbirth typically follows a sequence of stages.

1. The muscular wall of the uterus begins making brief contractions that the mother can feel. These slowly become stronger and more frequent.

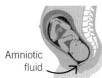

2. The amniotic sac holding the baby opens, causing amniotic fluid to flow out of the mother's vagina.

Amniotic fluid

3. The cervix (the neck of the uterus) dilates (widens).

Cervix

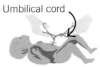

4. The uterus contracts very strongly, pushing the baby out through the cervix and vagina. The baby then takes its first breath.

Umbilical cord

5. The umbilical cord is clamped or tied close to the baby's body to prevent blood loss. It is then cut.

Placenta

6. A few minutes after the baby is born, the placenta (afterbirth) comes out of the mother's body.

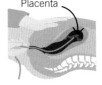

🔍 Breastfeeding and bottle feeding

Breast milk contains antibodies that help protect the baby from disease in early life. Feeding with breast milk also triggers the release of hormones in the mother's body that help her form a close bond with the baby. Breastfeeding mothers may be less likely to develop breast cancer. However, some mothers find breastfeeding uncomfortable and instead use powdered milk called formula. This contains all the nutrients a baby needs, but it lacks antibodies and has to be prepared in sterile conditions with clean water.

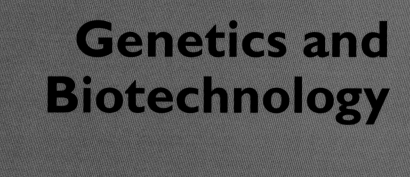

Genetics and Biotechnology

Genome

The genome of an organism is the complete set of all its genes. Genes are biological instructions that control the way an organism grows and develops. They are stored in a molecule called DNA and are passed on from parents to their offspring during reproduction.

Genes and DNA
Each cell in an organism's body carries a complete copy of the genome. In humans, the DNA that makes up the genome is packaged in 46 structures called chromosomes, which are found in the nucleus of each cell.

3. Chromosome
Genes are carried by structures called chromosomes, which often appear X-shaped. Human cells have 46 chromosomes, dog cells have 78, and pea plants have 14.

2. Cell
All organisms are made of tiny building blocks called cells. Each cell carries the organism's genome, usually in its nucleus.

1. Body
Genes control how an organism's body forms, works, and looks. About 20,000 different genes control the human body.

Key facts

- ✓ An organism's genome is a complete set of all its genes.
- ✓ The nucleus in each cell of an organism contains a copy of its genome.
- ✓ Genes are stored in deoxyribonucleic acid (DNA) molecules.

5. Gene
Chemicals called bases link the DNA strands, like rungs in a ladder. Their order forms a code. A gene is a section of DNA with the code for a specific task.

🔍 Protein building

A protein is made of a chain of small units called amino acids.

Protein molecule

Most genes carry instructions for protein molecules to be made. The order of bases in the gene determines the order of amino acids in the protein. Proteins, in turn, control the way cells and bodies function and appear.

4. DNA
A chromosome carries a single, long molecule of deoxyribonucleic acid (DNA). The DNA molecule has two strands that wind around each other to form a twisted, ladderlike shape called a double helix.

⚙ How DNA replicates

DNA can replicate (copy) itself. This allows genes to be copied when cells divide or organisms reproduce.

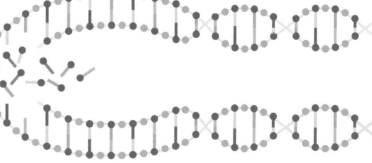

1. The two strands of a DNA molecule unwind and separate. Each has a sequence of bases coding certain genes.

2. Each base links only to a particular partner, so the separate strands act as templates on which new strands form.

3. Two identical molecules of DNA are made, each with the same genes.

Human Genome Project

Completed in 2003, the Human Genome Project was a vast scientific effort to identify and sequence every gene in a typical human genome. The project involved hundreds of scientists and took 13 years to complete. It could lead to great advances in medical science.

Key facts

✓ The Human Genome Project was a project undertaken to identify and sequence every gene in the human genome.

✓ It could lead to many new treatments for disease.

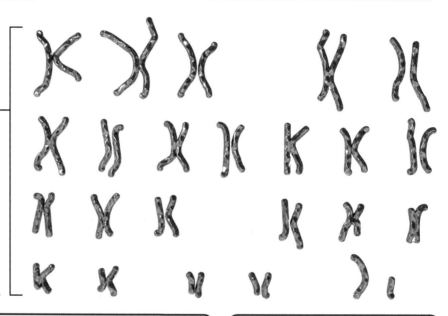

A karyotype is an image of all the chromosomes from one cell, with maternal and paternal chromosomes arranged in pairs.

Human genome
The human genome is made up of around 3 billion DNA base pairs and includes 20,000–25,000 genes. The genome is found in every cell nucleus in the body, stored within 23 pairs of chromosomes.

⚙ Sequencing DNA

To figure out the base sequence in the human genome, scientists split the DNA into fragments of various lengths, each ending in one of the four bases.

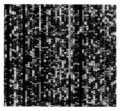

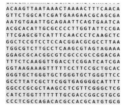

1. The fragments were injected into sheets of gel and then separated by size by pushing them through the gel with an electric current.

2. Fluorescent chemical dyes added to the fragments were used to identify which of the four bases was at the end of each fragment.

3. A camera and computer read off the four colors as the letters A, T, C, and G, representing the four bases in DNA: adenine, thymine, cytosine, and guanine.

🔍 Benefits

● The Human Genome Project could help scientists develop "gene therapy" where faulty genes are replaced with working copies. This could cure genetic diseases such as cystic fibrosis.

● Diseases such as cancer and heart disease are linked to many genes. Identifying them could lead to new ways of preventing or treating disease.

● Doctors could tailor treatments to suit a patient's own genome. Some breast cancer drugs, for instance, work better in women with certain gene variants (alleles).

Structure of DNA

DNA (deoxyribonucleic acid) is the chemical that stores genetic information in living organisms. The information is stored as a code made up of four repeating chemicals called bases, which form the rungs of the molecule.

Key facts

✓ The DNA molecule is made of two complementary strands joined in a double helix.

✓ Each strand is made of repeating units called nucleotides.

✓ Each nucleotide consists of a sugar group, a phosphate group, and a base.

✓ There are four different bases in DNA and their sequence forms the genetic code.

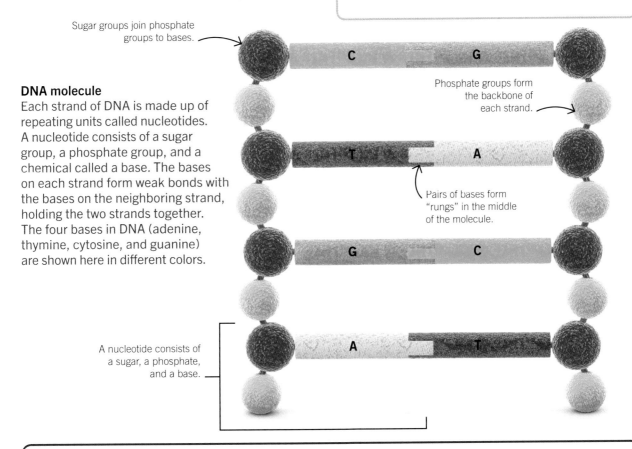

Sugar groups join phosphate groups to bases.

Phosphate groups form the backbone of each strand.

Pairs of bases form "rungs" in the middle of the molecule.

A nucleotide consists of a sugar, a phosphate, and a base.

DNA molecule
Each strand of DNA is made up of repeating units called nucleotides. A nucleotide consists of a sugar group, a phosphate group, and a chemical called a base. The bases on each strand form weak bonds with the bases on the neighboring strand, holding the two strands together. The four bases in DNA (adenine, thymine, cytosine, and guanine) are shown here in different colors.

🔍 Base pairs

DNA contains only four bases, and they always pair up in the same way. Adenine (A) pairs with thymine (T), and cytosine (C) pairs with guanine (G). This means that each strand mirrors the other and can serve as a template to rebuild a new complementary strand. The sequence of letters along each strand forms the code that stores genetic information.

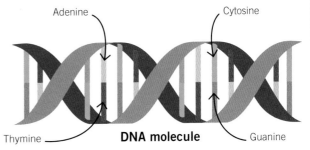

Adenine

Cytosine

Thymine

DNA molecule

Guanine

Protein synthesis 1

Most genes store the genetic information needed to build a particular protein molecule. The sequence of bases in the gene codes for the sequence of amino acids in the protein. When a gene is used to build a protein, we say that the gene is "expressed." The first step in building a protein molecule is called transcription.

Transcription

The DNA molecules stored in a cell nucleus are far too big to leave the nucleus. So when a cell needs to use a gene to build a protein, it makes a copy of that gene. The sequence of bases in the gene is copied by building a molecule called messenger RNA (mRNA). This molecule is very similar to DNA but has the base uracil in place of thymine.

Key facts

✓ The sequence of bases in a gene codes for the sequence of amino acids in a protein.

✓ During transcription, a gene is copied to make a molecule of messenger RNA (mRNA).

✓ mRNA molecules carry copies of genes out of the cell nucleus.

Noncoding DNA

Some of the DNA in the human genome does not code for protein molecules and is called noncoding DNA. Certain stretches of noncoding DNA control other genes by acting as binding sites for the molecules involved in transcription. Other stretches of noncoding DNA do a structural job, forming the ends of chromosomes or other structures needed to help cells divide. And some noncoding DNA sequences are called junk DNA because they may be useless.

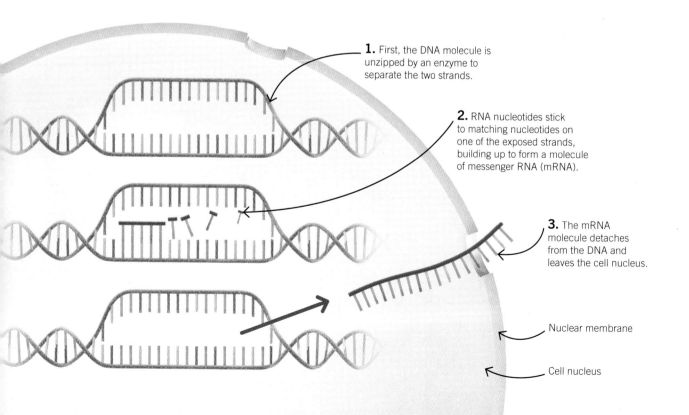

1. First, the DNA molecule is unzipped by an enzyme to separate the two strands.

2. RNA nucleotides stick to matching nucleotides on one of the exposed strands, building up to form a molecule of messenger RNA (mRNA).

3. The mRNA molecule detaches from the DNA and leaves the cell nucleus.

Nuclear membrane

Cell nucleus

Protein synthesis 2

The second stage in protein synthesis is called translation. During translation, organelles called ribosomes read the base sequence on an mRNA molecule three bases at a time. Each triplet of bases is used to attach a particular amino acid to the protein molecule being constructed.

✓ Key facts

✓ Ribosomes read the base sequence of mRNA in groups of three (triplets).

✓ Each triplet (codon) binds to a transfer RNA (tRNA) molecule carrying an amino acid.

✓ During translation, amino acids are added to a growing chain, forming a protein.

Translation

After leaving the cell nucleus, an mRNA molecule binds to an organelle called a ribosome and moves along it. Here, each group of three bases (a triplet or codon) in the RNA binds to a complementary sequence in a small, floating molecule of RNA that carries an amino acid. These floating RNA molecules are called transfer RNA (tRNA). The amino acids stick together and build up to form a chain—a protein molecule.

🔍 Protein shapes

Proteins are chain molecules made from various combinations of about 20 amino acids. After a chain of amino acids has formed, it folds up into a unique shape determined by the sequence of amino acids. The shapes of proteins determine how they interact with other molecules, controlling their function.

Hemoglobin is a protein that folds up into a globular shape to help it transport oxygen in the blood.

Collagen is a protein that forms ropelike fibers ideal for firmly binding different body parts together.

Amylase is a starch-digesting enzyme. Its shape includes an "active site" that binds to target molecules to help catalyze chemical reactions.

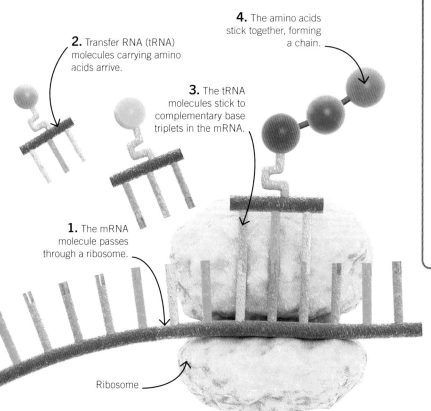

4. The amino acids stick together, forming a chain.

2. Transfer RNA (tRNA) molecules carrying amino acids arrive.

3. The tRNA molecules stick to complementary base triplets in the mRNA.

1. The mRNA molecule passes through a ribosome.

Ribosome

5. Empty tRNA molecules detach from the mRNA molecule.

Mutations

A mutation is a random change in the base sequence of DNA. Mutations in genes that code for proteins can alter the amino acid sequence in the proteins, making the proteins faulty or changing how they work. Mutations in noncoding DNA can switch genes on or off, affecting which proteins are made.

Key facts

✓ Mutations occur naturally. Most do not affect an organism.

✓ Some mutations are harmful, and a small number are beneficial.

✓ Mutations are the source of all new variants of genes (alleles).

✓ Radiation and chemicals that damage DNA can increase the rate of mutation.

Albinism

Albino animals can't produce colored pigments in their skin and are unusually pale. Albinism is usually caused by a mutation in the gene that codes for an enzyme used to make the pigment. Many types of mutations can damage this gene. The one shown here is an insertion mutation—a single extra base has been added to the DNA sequence, changing the amino acids used to build the enzyme.

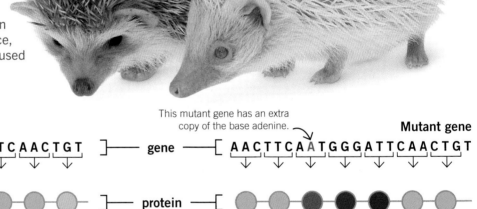

Normal gene

A A C T T C A T G G G A T T C A A C T G T

]— gene —[This mutant gene has an extra copy of the base adenine.

Mutant gene

A A C T T C A A T G G G A T T C A A C T G T

]— protein —[

Correct amino acid sequence

The wrong amino acids are used to build the enzyme, making it useless.

🔍 Types of mutations

There are many different kinds of mutations. Small mutations affect only one or a few bases in DNA. Larger mutations can rearrange long sections of chromosomes.

Original DNA sequence

New base inserted

An insertion mutation occurs when one or more bases are added to a gene. This changes the way triplets of bases are read when proteins are made, altering the amino acid sequence in the protein.

Base deleted

A deletion occurs when one or more bases are deleted. Like an insertion, this changes the sequence of amino acids from the deletion onward when the protein is made.

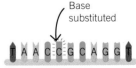

Base substituted

A substitution occurs when a single base in the DNA sequence is changed. This changes a single amino acid in the protein.

Genes and alleles

Organisms that reproduce sexually get a set of genes from their mother and another set from their father. As a result, they have two versions of every gene. Different versions of the same gene are called alleles.

Dominant and recessive alleles

Most leopards have spots, but a few are black. The dark color is caused by an allele of a gene that controls fur pigment. A leopard can have black fur only if it inherits the dark allele from both parents. If it has one dark allele and one normal allele, or two normal alleles, it will have normal spotted fur. The normal allele is described as dominant because it always affects fur color, whereas the dark allele is described as recessive because two copies are needed for it to have an effect.

Key facts

✓ Alleles are variants of the same gene.

✓ An individual with two identical alleles of a gene is called homozygous.

✓ An individual with two different alleles of a gene is called heterozygous.

✓ In heterozygous individuals, one allele of a gene is usually dominant.

🔍 Genotype and phenotype

The combination of alleles a leopard has is its genotype. The observable characteristic controlled by this genotype is called the phenotype. We can write a genotype as two letters: a capital letter for a dominant allele and the same letter in lower case for a recessive allele. For example, a leopard can have any of the genotypes for fur color shown in the table here, but only one produces the black phenotype. When an organism has two identical alleles of a gene, we say it is homozygous for the gene. When it has two different alleles, we say it's heterozygous.

Genotype	Phenotype
DD Homozygous	Typical leopard
Dd Heterozygous	Typical leopard
dd Homozygous	Black leopard

This black leopard has two copies of the recessive dark allele—one from each parent.

This typical leopard has at least one copy of the dominant normal allele.

Genetic crosses

Most characteristics of an organism are influenced by the interaction of multiple genes. However, a few traits are controlled by a single gene. How these characteristics are inherited when organisms breed can be predicted by drawing a genetic cross diagram.

📌 Key facts

✓ A genetic cross diagram shows how organisms inherit characteristics controlled by single genes.

✓ A genetic cross shows the probability of each genotype and phenotype in offspring.

✓ A Punnett square is an alternative to a genetic cross diagram and shows the same information.

Genetic cross diagram
This diagram shows what happens when a leopard with two dominant alleles for spotted fur (DD) breeds with a black leopard, which has two recessive alleles for dark fur (dd). The second row shows the sex cells. The third row shows all the ways the sex cells can combine to form different genotypes. All the offspring are heterozygous—they have two different alleles.

Dominant alleles → **DD**   **dd** ⎤ Genotypes of parents

D **D**   **d** **d** ⎤ Sex cells

Dd **Dd** **Dd** **Dd** ⎤ Genotypes of offspring

All the offspring have the same phenotype (spotted fur).

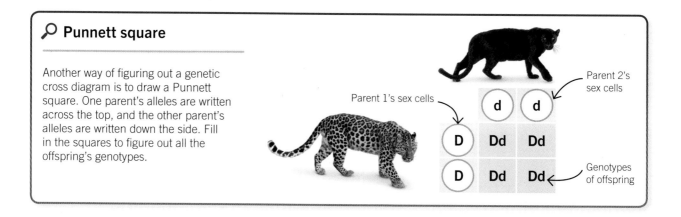

🔍 Punnett square

Another way of figuring out a genetic cross diagram is to draw a Punnett square. One parent's alleles are written across the top, and the other parent's alleles are written down the side. Fill in the squares to figure out all the offspring's genotypes.

Parent 1's sex cells →

Parent 2's sex cells →

	d	**d**
D	**Dd**	**Dd**
D	**Dd**	**Dd**

Genotypes of offspring →

When two heterozygous leopards breed, on average, one in four offspring (25 percent) will be black leopards. The genetic cross tells us the probability of each genotype and phenotype in the next generation.

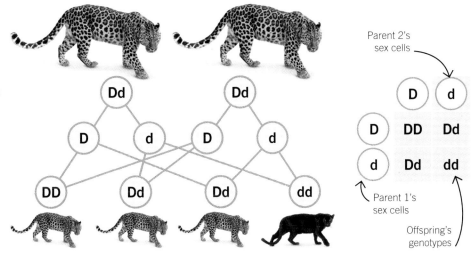

Parent 2's sex cells

Parent 1's sex cells

Offspring's genotypes

When a homozygous spotted leopard breeds with a heterozygous spotted leopard, none of the offspring has the homozygous recessive genotype. So all the babies have normal spotted fur.

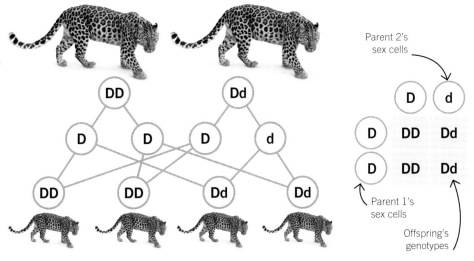

Parent 2's sex cells

Parent 1's sex cells

Offspring's genotypes

When a heterozygous spotted leopard breeds with a black leopard, most of the sex cells carry the recessive gene for black fur. As a result, on average, half of the offspring will be black leopards. So the probability that a baby will be a black leopard is 50 percent.

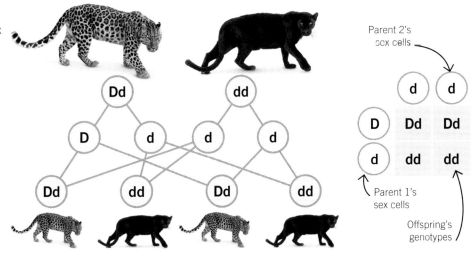

Parent 2's sex cells

Parent 1's sex cells

Offspring's genotypes

Codominance

When an organism has two different alleles of the same gene, one allele is usually dominant and the other recessive. However, sometimes both alleles are expressed. We call these alleles codominant.

Homozygous cross

Flowers of the four o'clock plant can be either red or white. Their color is controlled by a gene with codominant alleles. When the red and white alleles occur together in a heterozygous plant, the flowers are pink—a blend of both colors.

Parental phenotypes

Codominant alleles are written with a capital letter and a superscript letter.

C^RC^R

C^WC^W — Parental genotypes

C^R C^R C^W C^W — Sex cells

C^RC^W C^RC^W C^RC^W C^RC^W — Genotypes of offspring

The phenotype (pink) is a blend of the parental phenotypes (red and white).

Flower of the four o'clock plant

Punnett square

The results of the cross can also be figured out by drawing a Punnett square.

Parent 1's sex cells

Parent 2's sex cells

	C^W	C^W
C^R	C^RC^W	C^RC^W
C^R	C^RC^W	C^RC^W

Offspring's genotypes

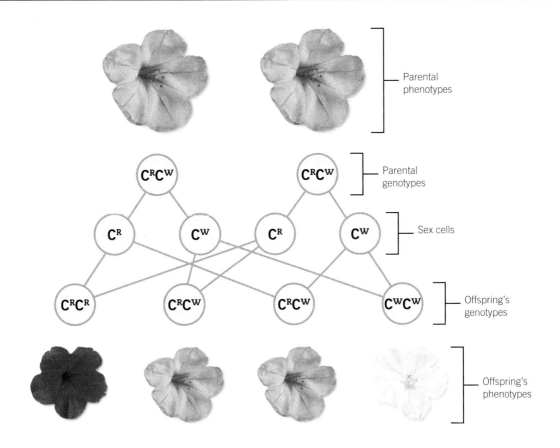

Parental phenotypes

Parental genotypes

Sex cells

Offspring's genotypes

Offspring's phenotypes

Heterozygous cross

If pink flowered plants are bred with each other, their offspring are a mixture of all three colors: red, pink, and white. The ratio of genotypes and the ratio of phenotypes are both 1:2:1. The chance that a plant from the new generation will have red flowers is 25 percent, the chance of pink flowers is 50 percent, and the chance of white flowers is 25 percent.

Punnett square

Parent 1's sex cells

Parent 2's sex cells

Offspring's genotypes

🔍 Roan cattle

The color of a cow's fur is sometimes controlled by codominant genes. If a female cow with a brown coat breeds with a white bull, the brown and white alleles may combine in heterozygous offspring. Both alleles are expressed, giving the offspring a mixture of brown and white hairs in their fur (a color pattern called roan).

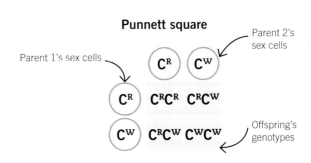

Brown cow

White bull

Roan offspring

Mendel's work

Austrian monk Gregor Mendel (1822–1884) is now recognized as the founder of genetics. By breeding pea plants, he discovered that certain characteristics are controlled by "hereditary units." Today, we call these units genes.

Key facts

✓ Gregor Mendel is the founder of modern genetics.

✓ He discovered "hereditary units" (genes) by breeding pea plants.

✓ He discovered that alleles work in pairs and can be dominant or recessive.

Mendel's peas

Mendel discovered that certain characteristics of pea plants, such as pod color, didn't simply blend together when he bred plants. For instance, when he crossed a plant with green pods and a plant with yellow pods, all the offspring had green pods—the green color appeared to be dominant. But if he then bred these offspring together to create a new generation, not all of them had green pods; about one in four of the second-generation plants had yellow pods.

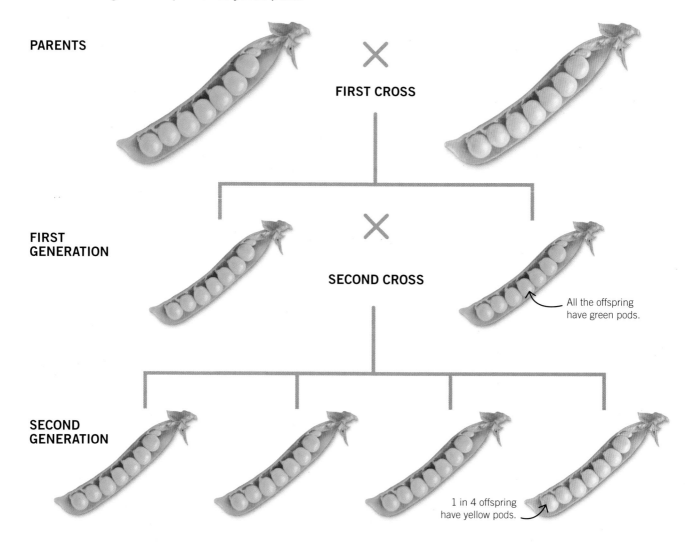

PARENTS

FIRST CROSS

FIRST GENERATION

SECOND CROSS

All the offspring have green pods.

SECOND GENERATION

1 in 4 offspring have yellow pods.

🔍 Explaining Mendel's results

Mendel was struck by the 3:1 ratio that occurred in the second generation of his breeding experiments. He found that this pattern of inheritance also held true for plant height, flower color, pod shape, seed shape, seed color, and even flower position. He theorized that these characteristics were controlled by pairs of "hereditary units" that could separate and recombine during sexual reproduction and that could take two forms: dominant and recessive.

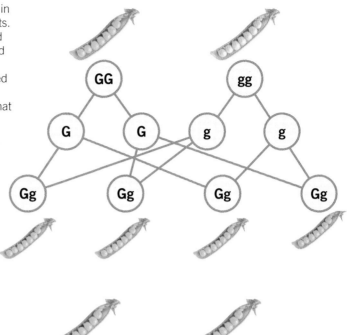

First cross
In the first generation, a pure-bred green pod was crossed with a pure-bred yellow pod. All the offspring were green, so Mendel concluded that the green form of the hereditary unit (G) is dominant.

Second cross
In the second generation, 1 in 4 offspring had yellow pods. Mendel realized that the dominant green form of the hereditary unit must be missing from those plants, leaving two copies of the recessive form (gg).

🔍 Gregor Mendel

Gregor Mendel was a monk who lived in a monastery in Austria. He carried out his experiments in the monastery garden. Although he published the results of his experiments in 1866, his work went largely unnoticed for decades. It wasn't until the 20th century, after chromosomes and DNA were discovered (and long after Mendel had died), that scientists realized the great importance of Mendel's work: Mendel had discovered genes.

Blood groups

Many genes have three or more different alleles. A person's blood group, for example, is controlled by a gene with three alleles. The way these alleles combine creates four different blood groups.

Key facts

✓ Your blood group determines what kind of blood you can receive from a donor.

✓ There are four main blood groups: A, B, AB, and O.

✓ The blood group gene has three alleles.

🔍 Blood group alleles

The blood group gene codes for a protein on the surface of red blood cells. If you receive blood from a nonmatching donor, your body might reject the donor blood cells, causing a dangerous reaction. Two of the blood group alleles (I^A and I^B) are codominant and code for different variants of the protein. The third allele (I^O) is recessive and doesn't produce a protein. The table here shows the different blood groups produced by each combination of the three alleles.

Genotype	$I^A I^A$	$I^A I^O$	$I^B I^B$	$I^B I^O$	$I^A I^B$	$I^O I^O$
Phenotype	A	A	B	B	AB	O

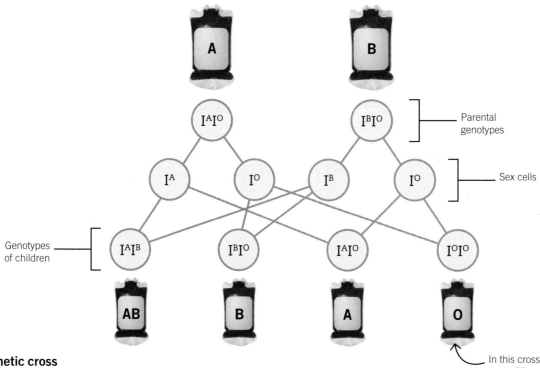

Parental genotypes

Sex cells

Genotypes of children

In this cross, each child has a 25 percent chance of having any of the four main blood groups.

Genetic cross

If you know the genotypes of two parents, you can predict the likelihood of their children's genotypes and blood groups by drawing a genetic cross diagram. This diagram shows the blood groups of the children of parents who have blood groups A and B, but both carry the recessive I^O allele.

Inherited disorders

Some diseases, such as sickle-cell anemia and cystic fibrosis, are caused by a single gene. If the disease is caused by a recessive allele, only people with two copies of the allele will have the disease. Those with only one copy are unaffected "carriers."

Key facts

✓ Inherited disorders can be caused by a single gene.

✓ Some inherited disorders are caused by a recessive allele, whereas others are caused by a dominant allele.

✓ Disorders caused by recessive alleles include sickle-cell anemia and cystic fibrosis.

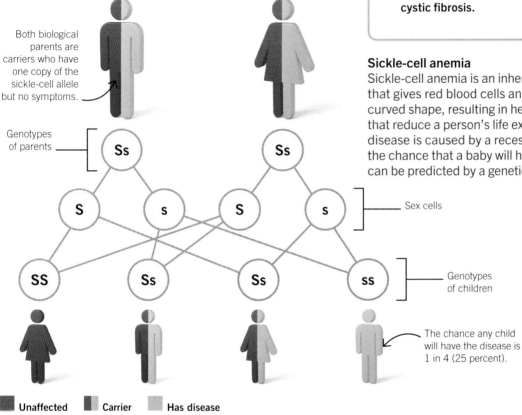

Both biological parents are carriers who have one copy of the sickle-cell allele but no symptoms.

Genotypes of parents

Sex cells

Genotypes of children

The chance any child will have the disease is 1 in 4 (25 percent).

■ Unaffected   ■ Carrier   ■ Has disease

Sickle-cell anemia

Sickle-cell anemia is an inherited disorder that gives red blood cells an abnormal curved shape, resulting in health problems that reduce a person's life expectancy. The disease is caused by a recessive allele, so the chance that a baby will have the disease can be predicted by a genetic cross diagram.

🔎 Family trees

The way inherited disorders pass down through families is sometimes shown using a family tree. In this tree showing inheritance of sickle-cell anemia, squares represent males, circles represent females, and yellow represents the sickle-cell allele. Only one person (Rachel) has inherited two copies of the allele and therefore has the disease.

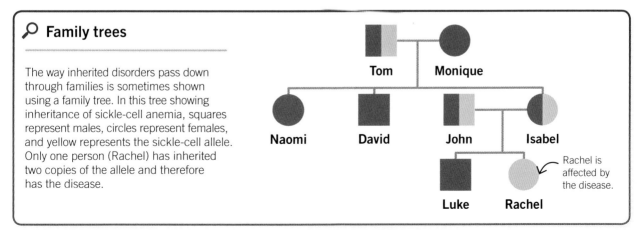

Rachel is affected by the disease.

Genetic testing

A person's DNA can be tested to see whether they have alleles that might cause a genetic disorder. Testing embryos for genetic disorders is known as embryonic screening. Embryonic screening raises ethical questions.

Key facts

✓ Genetic tests check DNA for alleles that cause genetic disorders.

✓ Embryonic screening involves testing human embryos for genetic disorders.

✓ Embryonic screening raises ethical questions.

Testing an embryo

Embryos may be tested for genetic disorders when people use in vitro fertilization (see page 153) to have a baby. Eggs and sperm collected from the parents are used to create embryos in a laboratory. A cell is removed from each embryo and tested for genetic disorders such as cystic fibrosis. Only embryos free of genetic disorders are used for implantation in the mother's body.

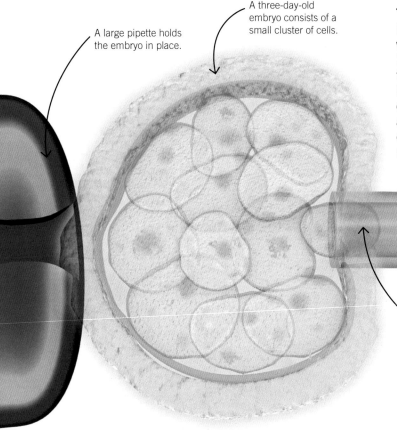

A large pipette holds the embryo in place.

A three-day-old embryo consists of a small cluster of cells.

A small pipette is used to remove a single cell from the embryo. The DNA of this cell is then tested for any abnormalities.

🔍 Pros and cons of embryonic screening

Pros
- Embryonic screening allows couples to raise children free of certain harmful genetic disorders, preventing suffering and ensuring that parents have healthy children.
- Preventing genetic diseases lowers health care costs, reducing the financial burden on the government, taxpayers, and parents.

Cons
- Some people think it is unethical to destroy embryos found to have genetic disorders. For example, some people believe that an embryo has a right to life.
- Screening might one day be abused to select embryos with more desirable traits, such as high IQ, although strict laws currently forbid this.

Sex determination

In humans and other mammals, special chromosomes called the X and Y chromosomes determine sex. Females have two X chromosomes in each cell, and males have one X and one Y chromosome.

Sex chromosomes
The X chromosome is much larger than the Y chromosome and carries up to 1,400 genes. The Y chromosome has only 70–200 genes. Unlike the other 44 chromosomes in a human cell, the sex chromosomes do not pair up to swap genetic material during meiosis (see page 46).

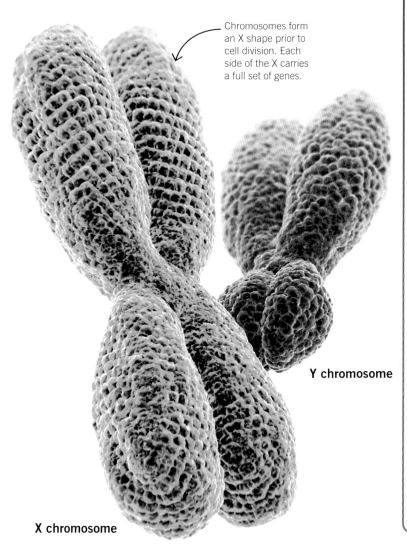

Chromosomes form an X shape prior to cell division. Each side of the X carries a full set of genes.

Y chromosome

X chromosome

Key facts

✓ The X and Y chromosomes determine a person's sex.

✓ While females have two X chromosomes, males have an X and a Y chromosome.

✓ Sex cells (sperm and egg cells) have only one sex chromosome each.

⚙ How sex determination works

When sex cells (sperm and eggs) are made, each cell gets only one sex chromosome. All egg cells carry a single X chromosome, but half of the sperm cells have an X and half have a Y. At fertilization, when the two sex chromosomes combine, the chance that an egg cell is fertilized by a Y-carrying sperm is 50 percent and the chance that it is fertilized by an X-carrying sperm is also 50 percent. So there's a 50 percent chance that any baby is a particular sex.

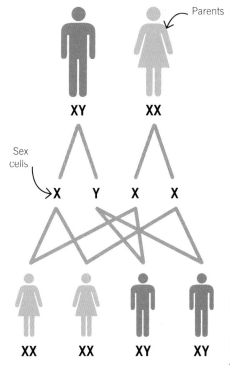

Parents

XY   XX

Sex cells

X   Y   X   X

XX   XX   XY   XY

Sex linkage

Some inherited characteristics are described as sex-linked because the genes that cause them are carried by a sex chromosome. Sex-linked genes follow a pattern of inheritance different from that of normal genes.

Key facts

✓ Sex-linked characteristics are caused by alleles on the X or Y chromosomes (the sex chromosomes).

✓ Disorders caused by sex-linked genes are called sex-linked disorders.

✓ Color blindness is an example of a sex-linked disorder.

Color blindness

Color blindness is a disorder caused by a recessive allele on the X chromosome. It is much more common in males than females because males have only one X chromosome, which means any recessive alleles on that chromosome are expressed. A genetic cross diagram shows how color blindness is inherited. The letters X and Y represent the sex chromosomes, N stands for normal alleles, and a lower-case n represents the faulty allele.

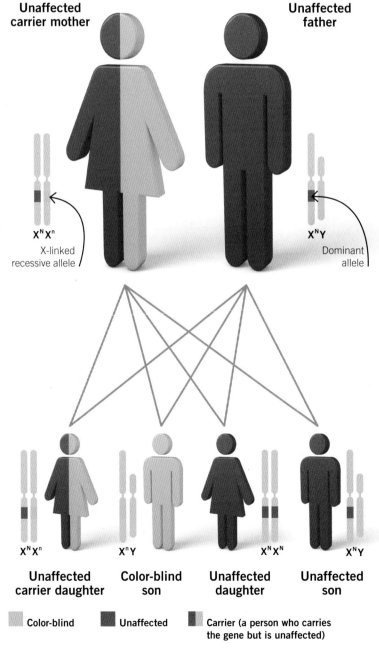

Unaffected carrier mother

$X^N X^n$
X-linked recessive allele

Unaffected father

$X^N Y$
Dominant allele

$X^N X^n$
Unaffected carrier daughter

$X^n Y$
Color-blind son

$X^N X^N$
Unaffected daughter

$X^N Y$
Unaffected son

Color-blind | Unaffected | Carrier (a person who carries the gene but is unaffected)

Red-green color blindness

The most common form of color blindness is called red-green color blindness. It is caused by mutations in the genes that code for light-sensitive proteins in the eye. People with this disorder have difficulty distinguishing certain shades of red and green from each other.

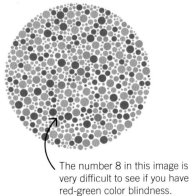

The number 8 in this image is very difficult to see if you have red-green color blindness.

Cloning animals

Cloning involves making genetically identical organisms. Many species produce clones naturally when they reproduce asexually, but large animals such as mammals cannot do this. However, they can be cloned artificially in a laboratory.

Adult cell cloning

In 1996, Dolly the sheep became the first mammal to be cloned from the cell of an adult animal. Adult cell cloning involves taking the nucleus from the cell of an adult animal and fusing it with an egg cell that has had its nucleus removed. The fused cell then grows into an embryo, which is implanted in a surrogate mother.

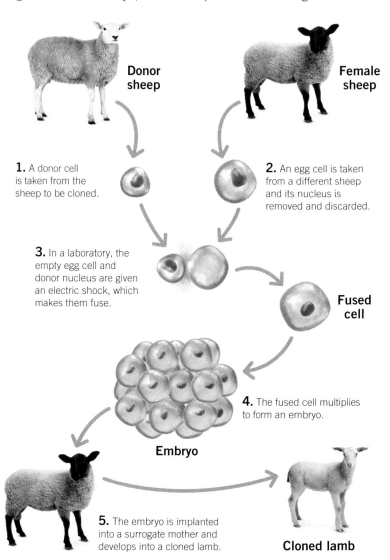

Donor sheep

Female sheep

1. A donor cell is taken from the sheep to be cloned.

2. An egg cell is taken from a different sheep and its nucleus is removed and discarded.

3. In a laboratory, the empty egg cell and donor nucleus are given an electric shock, which makes them fuse.

Fused cell

4. The fused cell multiplies to form an embryo.

Embryo

5. The embryo is implanted into a surrogate mother and develops into a cloned lamb.

Cloned lamb

☝ Key facts

✓ Cloning produces organisms that are genetically identical.

✓ Adult cell cloning involves cloning an animal from the cell of an adult animal.

✓ Farmers sometimes clone animals with desirable characteristics by dividing and transplanting embryos.

🔍 Cloning by embryo transplant

Farm animals are sometimes cloned by dividing an embryo to make several genetically identical embryos, which are then transplanted into surrogate mothers. This allows farmers to rear large numbers of calves from parents with desirable characteristics.

1. Sperm and egg cells are taken from animals with desirable characteristics and combined in a laboratory.

2. The fertilized egg grows into an embryo.

3. Before the embryonic cells begin to specialize, they are divided to make several embryos.

4. The cloned embryos are transplanted into surrogate mothers.

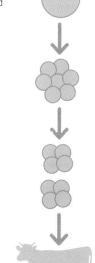

Genetic engineering

Genetic engineering involves the transfer of genes from one species to another. It gives the recipient organism, such as a crop plant, useful characteristics that would be difficult or impossible to achieve by traditional breeding. Organisms that have been changed this way are called genetically modified organisms (GMOs).

Key facts

✓ Genetic engineering involves artificially transferring genes from one species to another.

✓ Benefits include growing food crops more easily and producing drugs.

✓ There are ethical concerns about genetically modifying animals and plants.

Producing insulin

The hormone insulin is used as a drug to treat people with diabetes. Synthetic insulin was the first drug produced from genetically engineered bacteria. The bacteria were created by cutting the insulin gene from human DNA and inserting it into a plasmid—a loop of DNA found in bacteria.

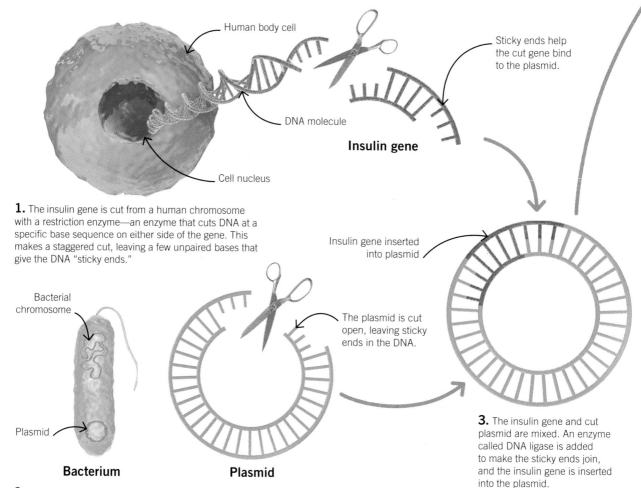

Human body cell

DNA molecule

Insulin gene

Sticky ends help the cut gene bind to the plasmid.

Cell nucleus

1. The insulin gene is cut from a human chromosome with a restriction enzyme—an enzyme that cuts DNA at a specific base sequence on either side of the gene. This makes a staggered cut, leaving a few unpaired bases that give the DNA "sticky ends."

Insulin gene inserted into plasmid

Bacterial chromosome

The plasmid is cut open, leaving sticky ends in the DNA.

Plasmid

Bacterium

Plasmid

2. A plasmid (a loop of DNA from a bacterium) is cut open by the same restriction enzyme, giving it sticky ends that match those on the insulin gene.

3. The insulin gene and cut plasmid are mixed. An enzyme called DNA ligase is added to make the sticky ends join, and the insulin gene is inserted into the plasmid.

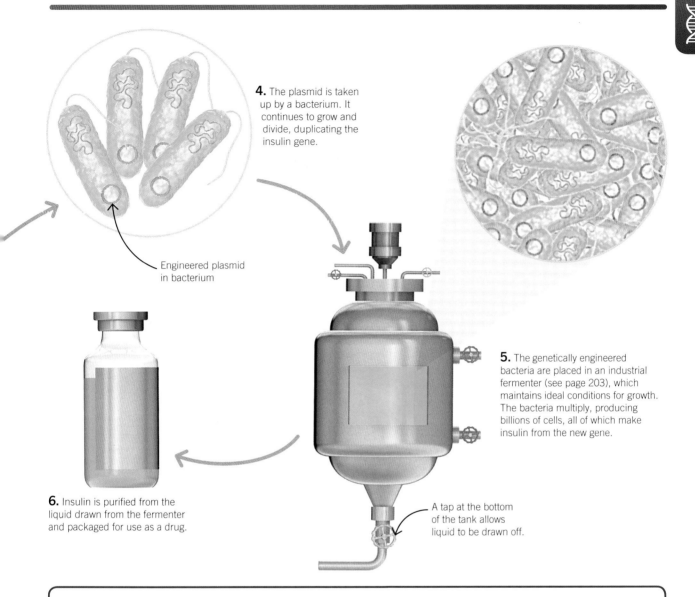

4. The plasmid is taken up by a bacterium. It continues to grow and divide, duplicating the insulin gene.

Engineered plasmid in bacterium

5. The genetically engineered bacteria are placed in an industrial fermenter (see page 203), which maintains ideal conditions for growth. The bacteria multiply, producing billions of cells, all of which make insulin from the new gene.

6. Insulin is purified from the liquid drawn from the fermenter and packaged for use as a drug.

A tap at the bottom of the tank allows liquid to be drawn off.

🔍 Pros and cons of genetic engineering

Pros

- Genetic engineering is a faster and more powerful way of modifying organisms than the traditional method of selective breeding.
- Genetically modified (GM) crops have improved yield, helping reduce hunger in areas without enough food.
- GM crops that resist pests have less need for pesticide sprays, reducing the use of environmentally harmful chemicals.
- Crops genetically modified to contain additional nutrients could help prevent disease.

Cons

- Genetically engineered plants might breed with wild plants, causing transplanted genes to escape into the wild.
- Some people see genetic engineering as interfering with nature.
- There may be as yet undiscovered health problems, such as allergies, caused by eating GM crops.

Cloning plants

Cloning means producing genetically identical organisms. Cloning happens naturally when organisms reproduce asexually. Many organisms, especially plants, are easy to clone artificially. This makes it possible to quickly produce large numbers of plants with desirable properties.

Key facts

✓ Cloning means producing organisms that are genetically identical.

✓ Taking cuttings is a traditional way of cloning that gardeners use.

✓ Micropropagation is a way of cloning plants from tiny samples of tissue.

Micropropagation

Plants that are difficult to grow from seeds or cuttings can be cloned in a lab using a technique called micropropagation. A small sample of cells from the parent plant is placed on an artificial growth medium, such as agar jelly, to form a tissue culture. Plant hormones stimulate the formation of roots and shoots, producing a tiny plantlet. This process can be repeated using cells taken from the plantlet to produce large numbers of clones from a single parent.

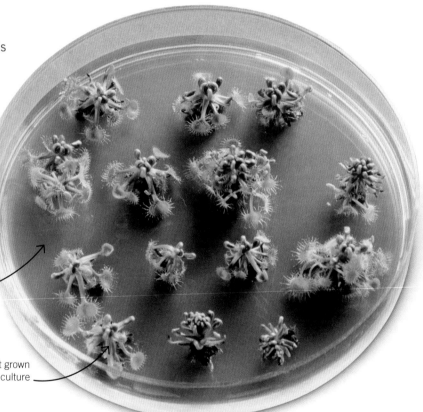

Agar jelly containing nutrients and plant growth hormones

Sundew plantlet grown from tissue culture

⚙ Taking cuttings

Taking cuttings is a traditional way of cloning that gardeners have used for centuries. Unlike most animals, plants have the ability to regenerate from a fragment because they contain numerous stem cells—unspecialized cells that can grow into any kind of tissue.

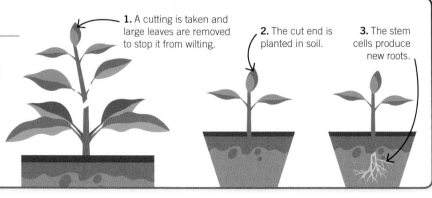

1. A cutting is taken and large leaves are removed to stop it from wilting.

2. The cut end is planted in soil.

3. The stem cells produce new roots.

Industrial fermentation

Industrial fermentation involves the production of microorganisms in vast numbers to manufacture useful products, ranging from wine and yogurt to drugs such as penicillin or insulin. The microorganisms are grown in a nutrient-rich liquid inside steel tanks called fermenters.

Key facts

✓ Industrial fermenters are large steel tanks used to grow useful microorganisms in huge numbers.

✓ Ideal growing conditions are maintained by computer control.

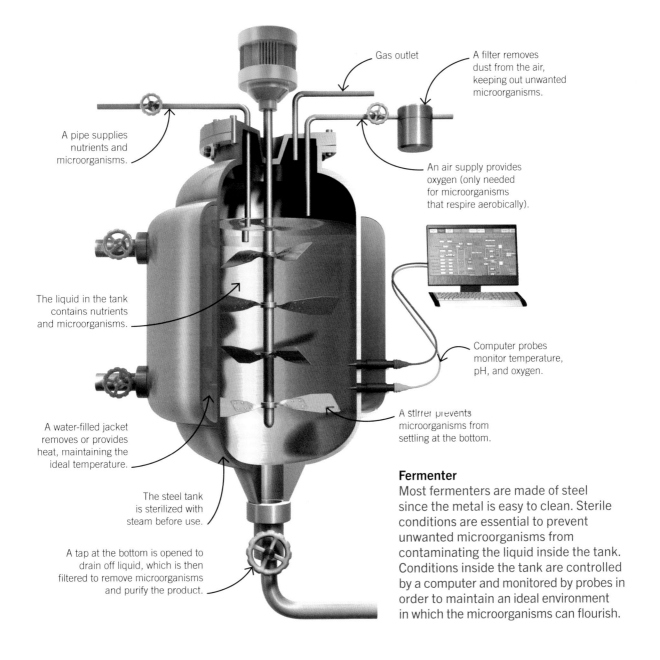

Gas outlet

A filter removes dust from the air, keeping out unwanted microorganisms.

A pipe supplies nutrients and microorganisms.

An air supply provides oxygen (only needed for microorganisms that respire aerobically).

The liquid in the tank contains nutrients and microorganisms.

Computer probes monitor temperature, pH, and oxygen.

A water-filled jacket removes or provides heat, maintaining the ideal temperature.

A stirrer prevents microorganisms from settling at the bottom.

The steel tank is sterilized with steam before use.

A tap at the bottom is opened to drain off liquid, which is then filtered to remove microorganisms and purify the product.

Fermenter

Most fermenters are made of steel since the metal is easy to clean. Sterile conditions are essential to prevent unwanted microorganisms from contaminating the liquid inside the tank. Conditions inside the tank are controlled by a computer and monitored by probes in order to maintain an ideal environment in which the microorganisms can flourish.

Evolution

Variation

All organisms differ slightly, even within the same species or the same family. These differences are known as variation and may be caused by genes, the environment, or a combination of both.

Genetic variation

Much of the variation in a species comes from genetic differences. In organisms that reproduce sexually, each offspring has a unique blend of both parents' genes. Even within the same family, all offspring are slightly different. New variants of genes continuously arise in the population by mutation (see page 186), which is the ultimate source of all genetic variation.

All the kittens are slightly different at birth because each has a unique set of genes.

🔍 Environmental variation

The environment affects the way that organisms develop. Trees that grow in a strong wind, for instance, grow more slowly on the windy side, giving them a lopsided shape as they get larger. Likewise, an animal given insufficient food while growing up will reach a smaller size in adulthood than an animal given plenty of food. Many characteristics of an organism are not determined solely by genes or solely by the environment but by a combination of both.

Continuous and discontinuous variation

Features of an organism that can vary across a range of possibilities show what we call continuous variation. Features with only a limited number of variants show discontinuous variation.

Height
The height that an animal or person grows to is an example of a characteristic that shows continuous variation. An individual can grow to a height with any value between that of the shortest and the tallest individual in the population. Human characteristics that show continuous variation include weight, shoe size, and hand span.

All domestic dogs belong to the same species, but their height varies across a wide range.

🔍 **Variation charts**

When the frequencies of height measurements of many individuals are plotted on a graph, they form a continuous curve called a normal distribution, with a central peak near the average value. In contrast, discontinuous variation— such as blood group in humans—has a limited number of variants with no intermediates. Discontinuous variation is often caused by a single gene. Continuous variation may be caused by genes, the environment, or both.

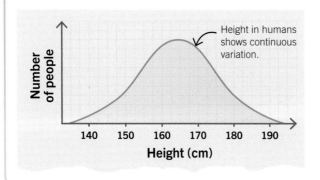

Height in humans shows continuous variation.

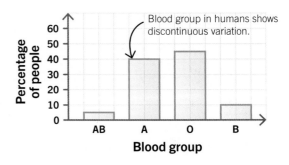

Blood group in humans shows discontinuous variation.

Darwin and Wallace

In the 19th century, British scientists Charles Darwin and Alfred Russel Wallace both traveled around the world, studying wildlife. They independently had the same idea: that species evolve (change over time) by a process known as natural selection.

Key facts

✓ Charles Darwin and Alfred Russel Wallace both proposed the theory that species evolve by natural selection.

✓ The theory was controversial because it clashed with religious beliefs.

Voyage of discovery
In the 1830s, Darwin sailed around the world on HMS *Beagle*. His observations of animals living on islands inspired the idea that species can change. The theory was controversial because it challenged the notion that a god had created every species in its modern form. Darwin amassed a lot of evidence to support the theory, but he could not explain the mechanism of inheritance that made evolution possible, as scientists had yet to discover genes and DNA.

🔍 Founders of evolution

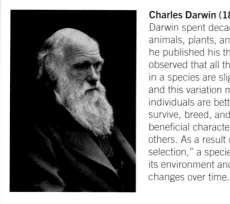

Charles Darwin (1809–1882)
Darwin spent decades studying animals, plants, and fossils before he published his theory. He observed that all the individuals in a species are slightly different, and this variation means some individuals are better able to survive, breed, and pass on their beneficial characteristics than others. As a result of this "natural selection," a species adapts to its environment and gradually changes over time.

Alfred Russel Wallace (1823–1913)
Like Darwin, Wallace traveled widely in tropical countries, studying wildlife. He observed great variation within each species and noticed that closely related species were often found in nearby locations. He proposed that separate populations of the same species can change by natural selection until they are so different that they become separate species.

Evolution

Evolution is the gradual change in the inherited characteristics of organisms that takes place over multiple generations. It is driven mainly by the process of natural selection.

Natural selection
The organisms in a species show variation—they are all slightly different, due to differences in their genes. Those with characteristics better suited to their environment and way of life are more likely to survive and pass on their advantageous genes to the next generation. This difference in the rate of survival is known as natural selection. Over many generations, it causes populations and species to adapt (become better suited) to their environment.

Key facts

✓ Evolution is a change in the characteristics of organisms that takes place over multiple generations.

✓ Evolution is driven by the process of natural selection.

✓ Natural selection causes populations to adapt to (become more suited to) their environment.

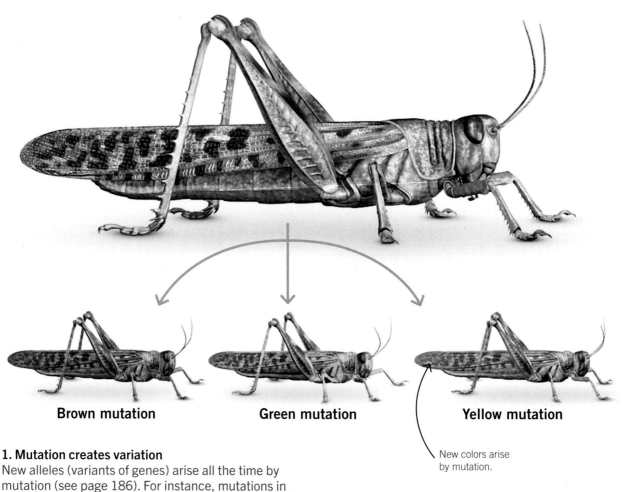

Brown mutation   **Green mutation**   **Yellow mutation**

New colors arise by mutation.

1. Mutation creates variation
New alleles (variants of genes) arise all the time by mutation (see page 186). For instance, mutations in a gene that affect the exoskeleton of grasshoppers might result in a population with varying colors.

🔍 The struggle to survive

The theory of evolution by natural selection was first proposed by British scientists Charles Darwin and Alfred Russel Wallace (see page 207). Darwin noticed that many animals produce far more offspring than will survive to reach adulthood. A female common frog, for instance, can lay 2,000 eggs a year, but the vast majority of her offspring will fail to survive. The struggle to survive results in a continual process of natural selection that favors individuals with the best genes.

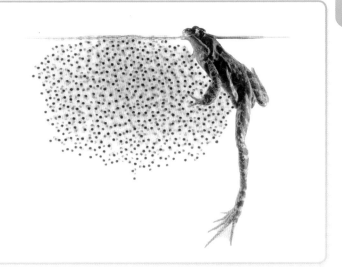

The green grasshoppers are well camouflaged.

Birds can see yellow and brown grasshoppers most easily.

Natural selection causes the population to change color.

Brown and yellow grasshoppers are well camouflaged.

2. Survival of the fittest
Green grasshoppers are hard to see among lush vegetation, but brown and yellow ones stand out and are more likely to get eaten. The green grasshoppers survive and pass on their genes, making green grasshoppers increasingly common. This process is known as natural selection or survival of the fittest.

3. A changing environment
Over time, environments change. For instance, the climate might become drier, making the vegetation less lush. Now green grasshoppers are easy to see, and the yellow or brown grasshoppers are more likely to survive. The gene for yellow skin becomes more common, and the whole population adapts to the change in the environment.

Fossils

Fossils are the preserved remains or impressions of organisms that lived in the distant past. Earth's fossil record supports the theory of evolution, showing that species have changed over time and that the species of the past were related to today's species.

Evidence from the past

Although the fossil record is incomplete, many fossils show the path that evolution has taken. Fossils of the 122-million-year-old dinosaur *Sinornithosaurus* were discovered in China in 1999. This small ground-dwelling animal was covered in birdlike feathers, but unlike a modern bird, it had teeth, a bony tail, and claws. The mixture of dinosaur and bird features supports the theory that birds evolved from dinosaurs.

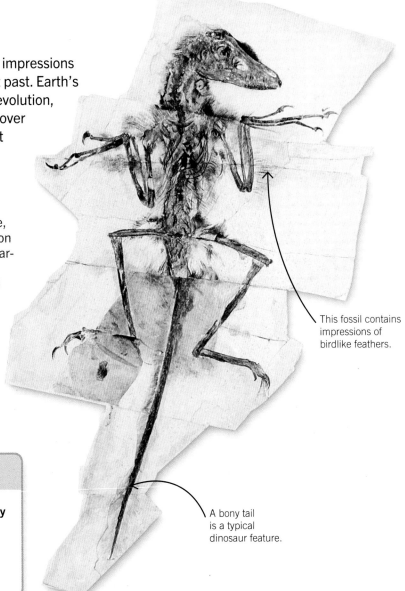

This fossil contains impressions of birdlike feathers.

A bony tail is a typical dinosaur feature.

Key facts

✓ **The fossil record supports the theory of evolution.**

✓ **Extinct species from the past were related to today's species.**

How fossils form

Most fossils form from hard body parts that don't easily decay, such as bones and shells. Buried in mud for millions of years, they are eventually replaced by minerals and turn to rock. Fossils can also form from casts (impressions) or footprints of an organism. A few rare fossils fully preserve an organism's body in substances such as amber or tar.

1. An animal dies and its body settles in the mud on the sea floor.

2. Sediment buries the body. Over time, the animal's remains and sediments turn to rock.

3. Millions of years later, movements in Earth's crust bring the fossil to the surface.

Antibiotic-resistant bacteria

Because evolution takes place over generations, it is difficult to observe in species with a long lifespan, such as humans. However, many bacteria have a generation time of less than 30 minutes and can evolve very quickly. The widespread use of antibiotic drugs has led to the evolution of antibiotic-resistant bacteria that now pose a serious health risk.

Evolving resistance

Like any species, bacteria can change over time by the process of natural selection. The use of antibiotics creates a "selection pressure" that favors mutants with a gene for antibiotic resistance. One example of an antibiotic-resistant strain is the superbug MRSA (methicillin-resistant *Staphylococcus aureus*). MRSA infections are common in hospitals and can be fatal.

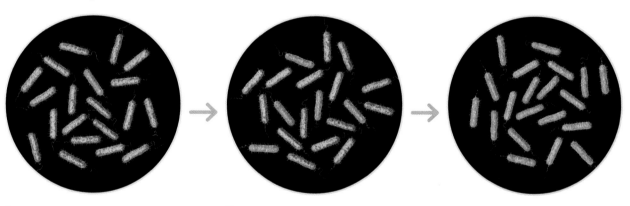

1. A random mutation gives a bacterium antibiotic resistance.

2. When the bacteria are exposed to the antibiotic, natural selection takes place. Nonresistant cells die, but the mutant bacteria keep dividing.

3. Eventually the whole population is resistant to the antibiotic.

🔍 Fighting superbugs

The rise of antibiotic-resistant superbugs poses a significant risk to health. New antibiotics are being developed, but this is a very slow and expensive process. In the meantime, there are several measures that can help prevent or slow down the evolution of resistant strains.

1. Doctors should not prescribe antibiotics inappropriately, such as for viral illnesses like flu and colds. Antibiotics cannot kill viruses.

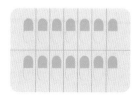

2. Patients prescribed antibiotics should complete their whole course so that all the bacteria are killed and there are none left to mutate into resistant forms.

3. The use of antibiotics in farming to make animals grow more quickly is now restricted in some countries.

Selective breeding

The characteristics of domestic animals and plants can be changed by selective breeding. Also called artificial selection, this works in a similar way to natural selection but is faster and is controlled by humans.

Breeding plants

Humans have been practicing selective breeding ever since they started growing crops and domesticating animals thousands of years ago. Selective breeding involves choosing parents with the best characteristics and using them to create offspring. Repeated over many generations, this enhances desirable characteristics. For instance, many of the vegetable crops we eat are derived from different parts of a single plant species (the wild cabbage) that were altered by selective breeding.

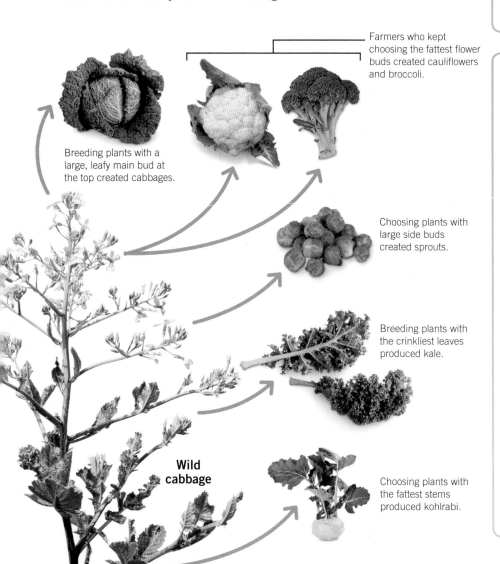

Farmers who kept choosing the fattest flower buds created cauliflowers and broccoli.

Breeding plants with a large, leafy main bud at the top created cabbages.

Choosing plants with large side buds created sprouts.

Breeding plants with the crinkliest leaves produced kale.

Wild cabbage

Choosing plants with the fattest stems produced kohlrabi.

Key facts

✓ Selective breeding involves choosing parents with desirable characteristics and using those to produce offspring.

✓ Also called artificial selection, selective breeding works in a similar way to natural selection.

✓ Humans have been using selective breeding for thousands of years to produce crop plants and domestic animal breeds.

Pros and cons of selective breeding

Pros
- Farm animals produced by selective breeding produce more meat, milk, wool, or eggs.
- Crop plants grow faster and have a higher yield.
- Garden plants have bigger, more colorful flowers.
- Pets such as dogs have a gentle temperament.

Cons
- Selective breeding makes crops less genetically varied and therefore more susceptible to disease.
- It can lead to inbreeding (breeding between closely related organisms), which can cause health problems due to genetic defects.
- Selective breeding is much slower than genetic engineering.

Speciation

A species is a group of similar organisms that can breed with each other to produce fertile offspring. Evolution can lead to the formation of new species (speciation) if a species splits into separate populations that change so much they can no longer interbreed.

Key facts

✓ If a species splits into separate populations, they may evolve into new species.

✓ Geographic isolation is one of the main ways in which new species form.

Geographic isolation

When a species splits into separate populations that become geographically isolated, the populations may evolve into different species. The Galápagos Islands in the Pacific Ocean were colonized by an ancestral tortoise species several million years ago. Isolated on each island, separate populations adapted to local conditions and evolved into new species. On arid Española Island, the tortoises fed on shrubs and evolved long necks and saddle-shaped shells that helped them reach higher. On rainy Isabela Island, however, the tortoises fed on ground plants and evolved short necks and dome-shaped shells.

On the driest islands, the tortoises have long necks and saddle-shaped shells.

On wetter, greener islands, the tortoises have shorter necks and dome-shaped shells.

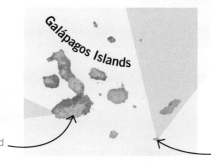

Galápagos Islands

Isabela Island

Española Island

🔍 Isolating mechanisms

When closely related species come into contact, there is a possibility that they might breed and produce offspring called hybrids. Hybrids are usually infertile (unable to produce offspring). For the parents, producing hybrids is a waste of time and resources, so it pays to recognize members of their own species when seeking mates. Many animal species use signals such as color and sound to identify their own species. For example, butterflies recognize members of their own species by their wing colors, and birds use distinctive songs. These signals, which keep species distinct, are called isolating mechanisms.

Extinction

If all the members of a species die, the species disappears and can never be restored—it has become extinct. Nearly all the species that have existed on Earth are now extinct.

Death of the dodo

The dodo was a large flightless bird that lived on the island of Mauritius. It was first seen by humans in 1598, when sailors landed on the island. Over the following years, its population went into decline. Sailors cut down the forest in which it lived, hunted the birds for meat, and introduced new predators to the island, including pigs, monkeys, dogs, cats, and rats. Around 1662, the last dodo died and the species became extinct.

Like many birds living on isolated islands, dodos had lost the power of flight and so could not escape from introduced predators.

Reconstruction of a dodo

Causes of extinction

Extinctions have happened throughout history and have many causes, including those listed here. In recent years, human activity has become a major cause of extinction.

The appearance of new predators, including human hunters	A natural disaster such as an asteroid impact or a massive volcanic eruption
The appearance of a new species that competes for the same resources and habitats	The loss of natural habitat such as forest
The spread of a deadly new disease	The gradual change of a species into a new species
A change in climate	

Ecology

Ecology

Ecology is the study of organisms and how they interact with each other and their environment. The organisms and the environment they live in make up an ecosystem.

Key facts

✓ An ecosystem is made up of a community of living organisms and the environment in which they live.

✓ A population is a group of organisms of the same species living in the same area.

✓ A community consists of all the populations of all the organisms that live in an ecosystem.

✓ A habitat is a place in an ecosystem where a particular organism lives.

A grassland ecosystem in Africa

This ecosystem includes many animal and plant species. The living things that shape an ecosystem are sometimes called biotic components or biotic factors. Ecosystems are also affected by environmental factors such as water, temperature, light, and wind (abiotic factors).

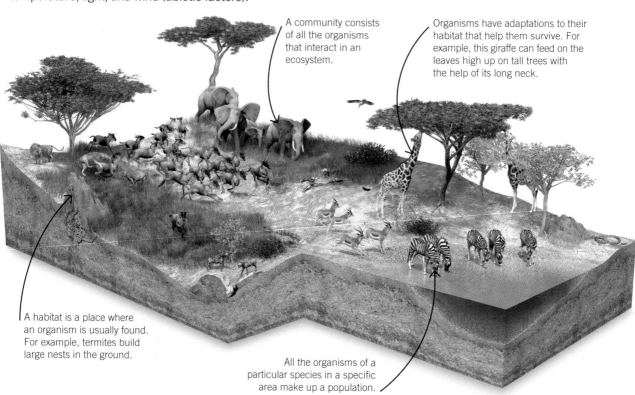

A community consists of all the organisms that interact in an ecosystem.

Organisms have adaptations to their habitat that help them survive. For example, this giraffe can feed on the leaves high up on tall trees with the help of its long neck.

A habitat is a place where an organism is usually found. For example, termites build large nests in the ground.

All the organisms of a particular species in a specific area make up a population.

Ecosystems

There are many different ecosystems around the world, including coral reefs, deserts, rain forests, grasslands, and tundra.

Coral reef

Desert

Rain forest

Interdependence

The organisms in a community are dependent on each other for many things, such as food and shelter. This means that a change in the population of one species in an ecosystem can affect many other species in the same community.

Depending on animals and plants
This adult blue tit bird needs to find a safe place in a tree to build its nest. It also needs to find food for its chicks.

Key facts

✓ Organisms in a community depend on each other—this is called interdependence.

✓ Animals may depend on plants for shelter and food.

✓ Animals may depend on other animals for food.

✓ Some plants depend on animals for pollination or seed dispersal.

Blue tit chicks prefer certain moth caterpillars, which are most common in oak woodland. An adult needs to collect around 100 caterpillars a day to feed one chick.

The blue tit depends on oak, ash, and alder trees, which have suitable holes that make good sites for nesting.

🔍 Dependence of plants on animals

Plants also depend on animals for several things. For example, many flowering plants depend on insects for pollination, and some depend on animals to disperse their seeds to other places where they can grow.

Bee pollinating a flower

Squirrel burying a seed

Classifying feeding

There are many different ways to describe the feeding relationships between organisms. The term used to describe an organism depends on the relationship that is being discussed.

Predator, prey, scavenger	A predator is an animal that hunts and kills other animals to eat. The animal that is killed by a predator is its prey. Scavengers eat animals that are already dead.	  Predator Prey Scavenger
Carnivore, herbivore, and omnivore	Carnivore, herbivore, and omnivore describe an animal's diet. A carnivore eats only meat, an herbivore eats only plants, and an omnivore eats both plants and meat.	 Carnivore Herbivore Omnivore
Producer and consumer	Producer and consumer describe trophic (feeding) levels in a food chain or web. A producer makes its own food by capturing energy from the environment—for example, plants and algae photosynthesize. A consumer gets its food by eating other animals. All animals are consumers.	  Producer Consumer

Decomposers

Organisms that feed on dead or waste material are called decomposers because they help to break down organic matter as they digest it. Many fungi and bacteria are decomposers. Some animals, such as earthworms and wood lice, help decomposition by eating detritus—decomposing fragments of dead plants and animals.

Fungi are decomposers.

Worms eat detritus.

Food webs

The feeding levels, also known as trophic levels, in a community are shown in a food web. Food webs start at the producer level—usually plants or algae that produce their own food through photosynthesis.

Hedgerow food web

The arrows in a food web show what each organism is eaten by. For example, blackbirds are the predators of slugs and the prey of hawks. The arrows also indicate the transfer of energy along a food chain.

Secondary and tertiary consumers

Carnivores that feed on herbivores (primary consumers) are called secondary consumers. Those that feed on secondary consumers are called tertiary consumers.

Primary consumers

Animals that eat plant material are called primary consumers. They are the first consumers in a food web. All consumers get their food by eating other living organisms.

Producers

The first stage of a food web includes the producers. These are typically plants that make their own food by capturing energy from light.

A fox can be either a primary consumer (eats berries), a secondary consumer (eats field mice), or a tertiary consumer (eats blackbirds).

Hawk

Fox

The blackbird is both a primary consumer, because it feeds on berries, and a secondary consumer, because it feeds on slugs.

Blackbird

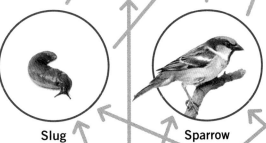

Slug

Sparrow

Field mouse

Rabbit

Grass seeds are eaten by many animals.

Berries on plants

Grass

Decomposers

Decomposers are organisms that feed on the dead remains of other organisms. They play an important role in recycling the carbon, nitrogen, and other materials found in the organic matter in an ecosystem.

Key facts

✓ Decomposers are organisms such as bacteria and fungi that break down dead animals and plants or their waste.

✓ Decomposers are important for recycling materials such as minerals in ecosystems.

✓ Decomposition can produce useful products such as compost and biogas.

Fungus

Decomposition by fungi

When fungi or other decomposers feed on dead organisms, they break down the nutrients into simpler molecules that they can absorb. In doing so, they also release useful materials such as mineral ions into the soil. Plants can then absorb these minerals, which helps them grow. Useful materials are continually recycled through ecosystems by the processes of growth, death, and decomposition.

The main body of a fungus is the white mycelium, made up of threads called hyphae. These penetrate and grow through dead matter, such as this rotting tree. Mushrooms and toadstools form only to release spores, which help fungi reproduce.

🔍 Examples of decomposition

Useful decomposition
Decomposition by fungi and bacteria can be helpful, such as when we make compost from dead plant material to fertilize garden soil. Decomposition can also be used to make biogas from plant and animal waste.

Unhelpful decomposition
Food is quickly decomposed by fungi and bacteria unless it is stored in conditions that slow their respiration and growth, such as cold or dry conditions, or those lacking oxygen.

The fluffy growth on decaying food is caused by fungi called molds.

Abiotic factors

Abiotic (nonliving) factors are environmental conditions that affect the organisms in an ecosystem. They include rainfall, temperature, light levels, and the pH and mineral content of soil.

Key facts

✓ Abiotic factors are nonliving factors caused by the environment that affect the organisms in an ecosystem.

✓ Examples of abiotic factors include rainfall, temperature, light levels, and the pH and mineral content of soil.

✓ Many species are adapted to particular abiotic conditions.

✓ If abiotic conditions in an ecosystem change, some organisms in the community may die out.

Abiotic factors at work

Abiotic factors affect organisms in many ways. In some ecosystems, extreme conditions such as lack of water mean that animals and plants need special adaptations to survive. All ecosystems can be affected by sudden changes in abiotic factors.

Reaching the light

Epiphytic plants (plants that grow on another plant without drawing nourishment from it) are adapted to grow high up on rain forest trees so that they can get enough light for photosynthesis. Below the trees there is too little light for most plants to grow.

The epiphytic plant shown here is an orchid.

Temperature extremes

Very few plants and animals can cope with the heat and drought (lack of water) in deserts. Those plants that do survive have very few leaves to reduce water loss, while animals usually come out only at night when it is cooler.

Desert plants have very deep roots that collect as much water as possible when it rains.

Tree trunks snap if the wind speed is too high.

High winds

These can damage large numbers of trees in a forest. This will increase the amount of light that gets to the forest floor and will affect which plants grow well there, which in turn affects the animals that feed on them.

These cows will struggle to find enough grass to eat from the flooded fields.

Flooding

Too much rain can cause problems for animals and plants. Plants may die from having waterlogged roots. Animals may find it difficult to move around in flooded areas.

Biotic factors

Ecosystems are shaped by a wide range of influences. Anything biological that affects an ecosystem—from living organisms to ecological relationships—is called a biotic factor.

Changing biotic factors
Biotic factors include food availability, diseases, the presence of humans, and relationships such as predation and competition. A change in any of these can have a powerful effect on an ecosystem.

Key facts

✓ Biotic factors include all the organisms in an ecosystem.

✓ Food availability and the presence of humans or diseases are examples of biotic factors.

✓ Ecological relationships such as predation and competition are biotic factors.

✓ A change in a biotic factor can alter the abundance or distribution of species in an ecosystem.

Food availability
The number of animals an ecosystem can support is limited by the amount of food available. If food availability falls—for example, because of a drought—animal populations will fall, too. This kind of biotic factor is also known as a limiting factor.

The number of wildebeest is limited by the amount of grass.

Predation
A predator is an animal that hunts and kills other animals, called prey. The number of predators in an ecosystem affects the number of prey. If the predator population falls, the prey population is likely to rise. In a healthy ecosystem, predator and prey numbers are usually in balance.

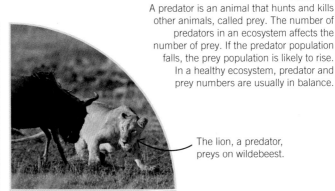

The lion, a predator, preys on wildebeest.

Blood-sucking insects such as mosquitoes can spread diseases.

Diseases
Many diseases are caused by infectious microorganisms, such as bacteria, viruses, or parasites carried by biting insects. If a new disease appears in an ecosystem, the outbreak can spread rapidly, causing the population of affected animals or plants to fall dramatically.

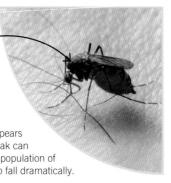

Hyenas and vultures compete for food at a carcass.

Competition
When different species need the same resource, such as food, they are described as competitors. For instance, scavengers at a carcass compete for meat, and plants growing in the same space compete for light. If the population of one species in an ecosystem falls, its competitors are likely to rise in number.

🔍 Types of competitions

There are two types of competitions. Interspecific competition happens between members of different species—such as a vulture and a hyena competing over meat. Intraspecific competition happens between members of the same species—such as when two male elephant seals compete over females: the winner of this fight gets to mate.

Southern elephant seals

Predator–prey cycles

Predators reduce prey numbers by eating the prey, but if prey numbers are too low, then competition for food between members of the same predator species will mean some predators will starve and die. This relationship between the number of predators and their prey is known as a predator–prey cycle.

Key facts

✓ The number of predators in an ecosystem affects the number of prey and vice versa.

✓ The changing number of predators and prey in an ecosystem make up a predator–prey cycle and can be shown on a graph.

✓ Simple predator–prey cycles can happen only in very simple food chains, where predators cannot move away to feed elsewhere.

Lynx–snowshoe hare cycle

In parts of the Arctic tundra, lynxes mainly eat snowshoe hares. The graph below shows how the lynx and hare populations rise and fall over time, with changes in one population affecting the other. In more complex ecosystems, the cycle is less clear as predators feed on many different kinds of prey.

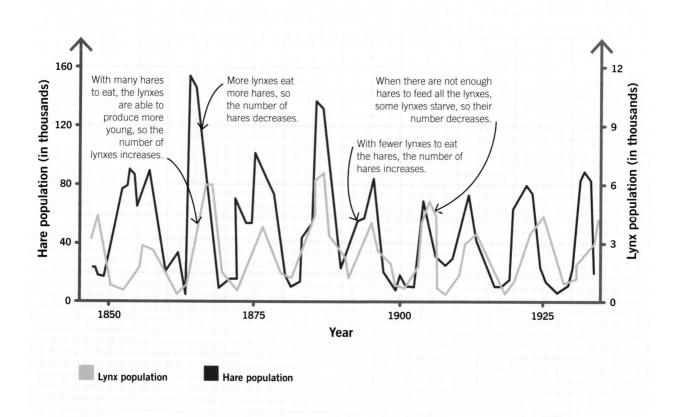

With many hares to eat, the lynxes are able to produce more young, so the number of lynxes increases.

More lynxes eat more hares, so the number of hares decreases.

When there are not enough hares to feed all the lynxes, some lynxes starve, so their number decreases.

With fewer lynxes to eat the hares, the number of hares increases.

Lynx population   Hare population

Social behavior

Many animals lead solitary lives, but others live in social groups. Living together and cooperating can help increase the animals' chance of survival.

Advantages of social behavior
Social behavior can help protect against attack by predators, make it easier to get food, or protect individuals from the environment.

Honey bees
When a honey bee finds food, it lets the other bees in the hive know by performing a waggle dance. The dance indicates the direction and distance of food, saving other bees time and energy spent on collecting food.

There can be up to 60,000 honey bees in a hive.

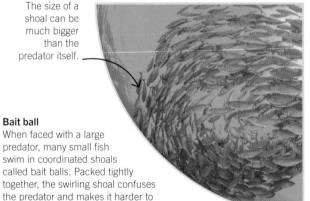

The size of a shoal can be much bigger than the predator itself.

Bait ball
When faced with a large predator, many small fish swim in coordinated shoals called bait balls. Packed tightly together, the swirling shoal confuses the predator and makes it harder to isolate and catch an individual fish.

Wolves
Wolves live together in a pack of up to 20 individuals. Living together is safer since there are more eyes to watch for predators. They also hunt as a team, which makes it possible for them to bring down much larger prey than they could on their own.

When close to prey, the pack splits to attack from different directions, making a kill more likely.

Emperor penguins form vast colonies (groups) that consist of hundreds of thousands of penguins.

Emperor penguins
To survive the bitterly cold Antarctic winter, male emperor penguins huddle tightly together for warmth. They constantly shuffle around so that they all get some warmth by moving to the center.

🔍 Genetics and social behavior

Animals that live and work together in groups are often closely related. For instance, in many ant colonies the workers are all sisters that share up to three-quarters of their genes with each other. The workers cannot breed themselves, but by helping the queen produce more workers, they ensure their own genes are passed on to many offspring.

Fire ants work together to build huge nests.

Energy transfers

Every organism needs energy to power the chemical reactions that take place in living cells. Plants get their energy from light during photosynthesis and store it in starch in their tissues, while animals get their energy by breaking down substances in their food.

Key facts

✓ Animals obtain energy from food.

✓ Plants obtain energy from sunlight by the process of photosynthesis.

✓ Organisms lose energy to the environment in the form of heat released by chemical reactions.

✓ Animals also lose energy to the environment in their urine and feces.

✓ Only a small proportion of the energy gained can be passed on to the next trophic level.

Energy transfers to and from a rabbit

Only some of the energy that a growing animal gets from its food is stored in its tissues (the sum of which make up its biomass). The rest escapes to the animal's surroundings while being used or is released as waste.

The rabbit gains energy from the plants that it eats.

A lot of energy is lost from the rabbit as heat released during chemical reactions, such as respiration.

Only a little of the energy a rabbit gains from eating is stored in new tissues. This is the only energy from the plants that is transferred to the fox when it eats the rabbit.

Some energy is lost from the rabbit in substances in its urine and feces.

🖺 Calculating energy transfer efficiency

As energy is passed along a food chain, much of it escapes. Energy transfer efficiency is the percentage of energy that is captured between one trophic level and the next.

$$\text{energy transfer efficiency} = \frac{\text{energy stored in biomass in a trophic level}}{\text{energy available to trophic level}}$$

Energy transfer efficiency varies a great deal between different organisms. For example, animals that live in cold habitats lose far more energy to their surroundings as heat than animals living in warm habitats.

Example: In an aquatic ecosystem, the energy stored in the biomass of primary consumers in a particular area was estimated to be 6,184 kJ/m². For secondary consumers, it was 280 kJ/m². To calculate the energy transfer efficiency for secondary consumers:

1. Substitute numbers in the formula:

$$\text{energy transfer efficiency} = \frac{280}{6{,}184}$$

2. Use a calculator to find the answer:

$$\frac{280}{6{,}184} = 0.045$$

3. You can change the answer to a percentage:

$$0.045 \times 100\% = 4.5\%$$

Pyramids of biomass

A pyramid of biomass shows the biomass of living organisms in each trophic level of a food chain or an ecosystem (see page 219). The biomass in each trophic level is usually less than in the level below because all organisms lose a great deal of energy to their surroundings.

Key facts

✓ Pyramids of biomass show the biomass in each trophic level of a food chain.

✓ The lowest level of a pyramid of biomass is always the producers.

✓ Pyramids of biomass explain why food chains are limited in length.

Terrestrial pyramid of biomass
Pyramids of biomass typically show how biomass falls along a food chain. As a result, top predators such as hawks are far less common than producer organisms. There isn't enough biomass in the top level to support a higher trophic level, so the food chain is limited in length.

Pyramids of biomass are always drawn with the producer level at the bottom of the pyramid.

Tertiary consumers:
hawks eat songbirds

Secondary consumers:
songbirds eat caterpillars

Primary consumers:
caterpillars eat leaves

Producers:
plants

 Calculating the percentage of biomass transfer

The percentage of biomass transferred from one trophic level to the level above it is calculated using the following equation:

$$\text{percentage biomass transfer} = \frac{\text{biomass in higher trophic level}}{\text{biomass in lower trophic level}} \times 100$$

Example: Scientists studying an ecosystem estimated the biomass of primary consumers (higher trophic level) at 89 kg/m² and the biomass of all producers (lower trophic level) at 615 kg/m². To calculate the percentage of biomass transfer between these trophic levels:

1. Substitute numbers in the formula.

$$\text{percentage biomass transfer} = \frac{89}{615}$$

2. Use a calculator to find the answer.

$$\frac{89}{615} = 0.145$$

3. Change the answer to a percentage.

$$0.145 \times 100\% = 14.5\%$$

Drawing pyramids of biomass

Pyramids of biomass should be drawn to scale. They also need to be drawn in a particular way. Use a sharp pencil and a ruler to make sure your diagram is neat and clear.

Example
Draw a pyramid of biomass for the food chain data in the table.

| Plant | Caterpillar | Bird |

Trophic level	Biomass (kg/m²)
Birds	20
Caterpillars	90
Plants	600

1. Choose a suitable scale for the largest biomass value (in this case, 600 kg/m² for plants) to fit the graph paper you are using—for example, 15 cm. This gives the scale of 15 cm = 600 kg/m².

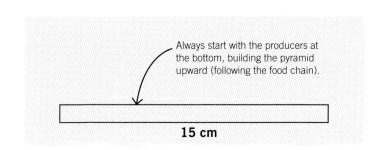

Always start with the producers at the bottom, building the pyramid upward (following the food chain).

15 cm

2. Adjust the other values to the same scale.

$$\frac{15}{600} \times 20 = 0.5$$

$$\frac{15}{600} \times 90 = 2.25$$

Trophic level	Biomass (kg/m²)	Width of bar (cm)
Birds	20	0.5
Caterpillars	90	2.25
Plants	600	15

3. Draw the bars using the scaled values you have calculated. The bars should all be the same height (it doesn't matter what that height is as long as it is sensible) and should be centered. Label your diagram using the information you have been given.

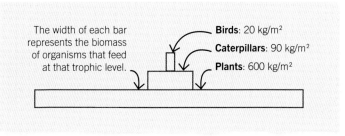

The width of each bar represents the biomass of organisms that feed at that trophic level.

Birds: 20 kg/m²
Caterpillars: 90 kg/m²
Plants: 600 kg/m²

Abundance

Abundance is the number of organisms of a particular species in a certain area. Ecologists often measure the abundance of species to see if numbers change. For instance, they might want to find out if a species is at risk of dying out, or they might want to study the changing numbers of predators and prey.

Key facts

✓ Abundance is the number of organisms of a particular species in a certain area.

✓ A quadrat is a square frame used to sample species that do not move.

✓ Quadrat samples taken randomly can be used to estimate abundance in an area.

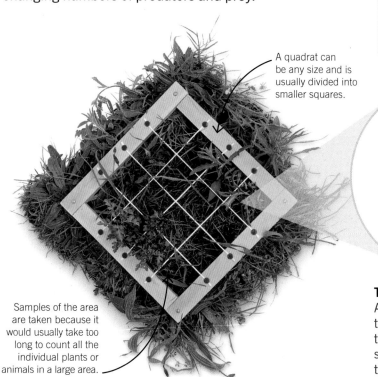

A quadrat can be any size and is usually divided into smaller squares.

Samples of the area are taken because it would usually take too long to count all the individual plants or animals in a large area.

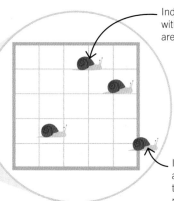

Individuals within the quadrat are recorded.

Individuals that are half outside the quadrat are not counted.

Taking quadrat samples

A quadrat is a square frame that is used to take samples of plants or animals that don't move much. The more samples that are taken, the better the estimate of the population size.

 Quadrat sampling

1. Figure out where to place the quadrats in the study area—quadrats should be placed randomly over a wide area of the habitat so that the sampling is representative of the whole area.

2. Count the number of individuals of the study species within each quadrat that you have placed.

3. Use your values to calculate abundance for the whole area using the equation:

$$\text{population size} = \frac{\text{total number of organisms in all quadrats}}{1} \times \frac{\text{total study area}}{\text{total area of quadrats}}$$

Example:

Quadrat number	1	2	3	4	5	6
Number of snails in quadrat	0	2	1	0	3	0

Total number of snails = 6
Total area of quadrats = 6 m²
Total study area = 150 m²

$$\text{population size} = 6 \times \frac{150}{6} = 150$$

Carrying capacity

The number of organisms that can survive in an ecosystem is limited by how much food, water, and other resources are available. The maximum population of a species that an ecosystem can sustain is called the carrying capacity.

Limiting factors

Ecosystems with very little food and water have a small carrying capacity. The Arctic tundra where caribou (reindeer) live, for example, has a limited amount of the grass and lichen that they feed on, especially in winter. This ecosystem has a low carrying capacity, so caribou herds must travel great distances to find the food they need.

Key facts

✓ The carrying capacity is the maximum population of a species that can be sustained by a habitat over a period of time.

✓ Carrying capacity is limited by the amount of resources (for example, food) in a habitat.

Caribou migrate huge distances in search of food.

🔍 High-nutrient ecosystems

Despite being very cold, the waters around Antarctica have a high carrying capacity for many whale, seal, and penguin species. This is because the water contains a high level of nutrients, supporting vast populations of krill and fish that the larger animals feed on.

Baleen whales, such as Bryde's whales, are among the largest mammals on Earth but feed on small, shrimplike krill.

🔍 Low-nutrient adaptations

This sundew plant will slowly digest the fly and absorb the nutrients so that it can grow faster.

Some plants that grow in soil with low nutrient levels have adapted to get more nutrients by catching small animals.

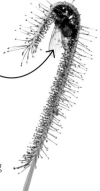

Distribution of organisms

Distribution is the way in which organisms are spread out in an area. For example, they may be clumped in groups or scattered randomly. Distribution can be linked to changes in abiotic living factors (see page 221).

(see page 221)

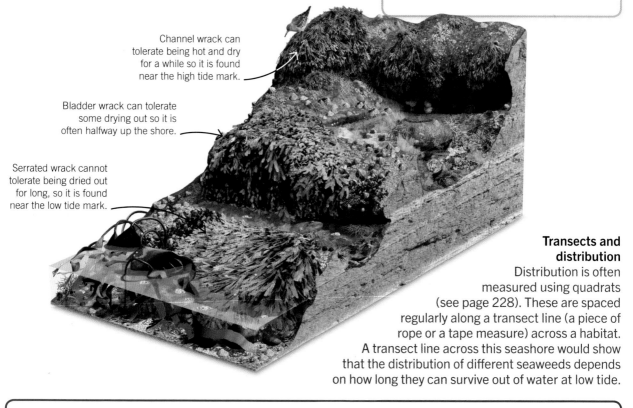

Channel wrack can tolerate being hot and dry for a while so it is found near the high tide mark.

Bladder wrack can tolerate some drying out so it is often halfway up the shore.

Serrated wrack cannot tolerate being dried out for long, so it is found near the low tide mark.

> ### Key facts
>
> ✓ Distribution is how organisms are spread out in an area.
>
> ✓ Quadrats placed at regular intervals along a transect line are used to measure distribution.
>
> ✓ The distribution of a population may be linked to changes in abiotic factors.

Transects and distribution

Distribution is often measured using quadrats (see page 228). These are spaced regularly along a transect line (a piece of rope or a tape measure) across a habitat. A transect line across this seashore would show that the distribution of different seaweeds depends on how long they can survive out of water at low tide.

(see page 228)

⚙ Carrying out a transect study

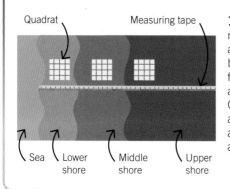

Quadrat   Measuring tape

Sea   Lower shore   Middle shore   Upper shore

1. A transect line is marked out using a measuring tape between two points—for example, high and low tide marks. Quadrats are placed at regular distances along the line, such as every 2 meters.

2. The species inside each quadrat are recorded. Abiotic factors (such as temperature and time out of sea water) are also recorded for each quadrat point.

3. The distribution of species is compared with the change in abiotic measurements along the transect. If they show a similar pattern of change, then the species may be affected by that factor.

The water cycle

Materials such as water, carbon, and nitrogen are constantly cycled between the biotic (living) and abiotic (nonliving) parts of ecosystems. All living things depend on water because their cells are largely made of it.

Processes in the water cycle

The water cycle depends on the abiotic processes of evaporation and condensation and the biotic process of transpiration. These processes return water to the land and sea as precipitation (rain, snow, and hail).

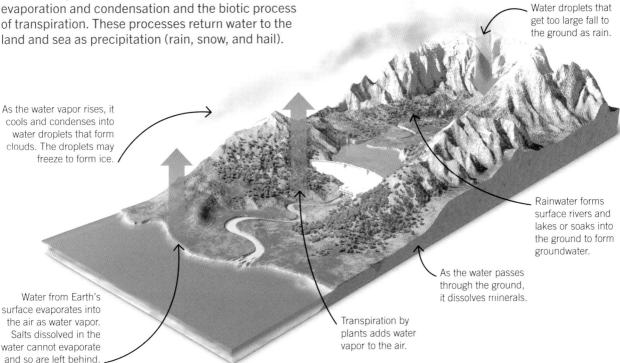

Water droplets that get too large fall to the ground as rain.

As the water vapor rises, it cools and condenses into water droplets that form clouds. The droplets may freeze to form ice.

Rainwater forms surface rivers and lakes or soaks into the ground to form groundwater.

As the water passes through the ground, it dissolves minerals.

Water from Earth's surface evaporates into the air as water vapor. Salts dissolved in the water cannot evaporate and so are left behind.

Transpiration by plants adds water vapor to the air.

🔍 Too little rain

Conserving water

Plants and animals that live where there is little rain have adaptations that keep as much water as possible inside them. The kidneys of a desert rat, for example, extract most of the water that is usually lost in urine, keeping it in the rat's body.

Desert rat

Drinking water for people

Sea water is undrinkable because of the salt content. People who live where there is too little rain, such as in desert regions, can make drinking water by removing salt from sea water using the process of desalination.

Desalination plant

The carbon cycle

Carbon is continually cycled between the living (biotic) and nonliving (abiotic) parts of ecosystems. Biotic forms of carbon include complex carbon compounds such as proteins, sugars, and fats, while abiotic forms include carbon dioxide in the atmosphere.

Key facts

✓ Carbon cycles between complex carbon compounds in living organisms and carbon dioxide in the air.

✓ Photosynthesis is the biotic process that removes carbon dioxide from the air.

✓ Respiration is the biotic process that adds carbon dioxide to the air.

Processes in the carbon cycle

Carbon is cycled from the air, through food chains, and back into the air again as a result of several key processes. These include the biotic processes of respiration and photosynthesis and the abiotic processes of rock and fossil fuel formation, weathering, and combustion.

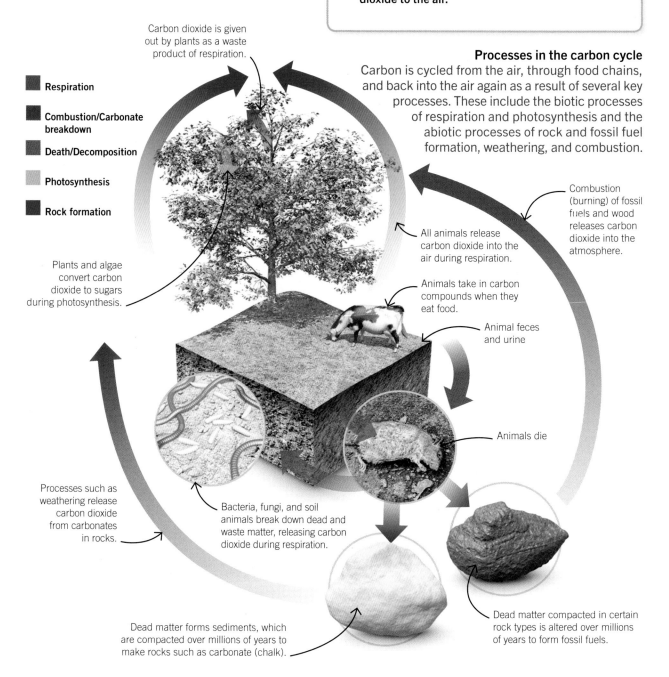

Carbon dioxide is given out by plants as a waste product of respiration.

Respiration

Combustion/Carbonate breakdown

Death/Decomposition

Photosynthesis

Rock formation

Plants and algae convert carbon dioxide to sugars during photosynthesis.

Combustion (burning) of fossil fuels and wood releases carbon dioxide into the atmosphere.

All animals release carbon dioxide into the air during respiration.

Animals take in carbon compounds when they eat food.

Animal feces and urine

Animals die

Processes such as weathering release carbon dioxide from carbonates in rocks.

Bacteria, fungi, and soil animals break down dead and waste matter, releasing carbon dioxide during respiration.

Dead matter forms sediments, which are compacted over millions of years to make rocks such as carbonate (chalk).

Dead matter compacted in certain rock types is altered over millions of years to form fossil fuels.

The nitrogen cycle

Nitrogen is an essential part of proteins and DNA, which all living organisms need. Although 78 percent of the air is nitrogen gas, most organisms cannot use this. Plants get nitrogen compounds from the soil, and animals get nitrogen compounds from food.

Key facts

✓ Nitrogen is an essential part of proteins and DNA, which all organisms need.

✓ Plants get their nitrogen as simple inorganic compounds from the soil.

✓ Animals get their nitrogen as complex nitrogen compounds in their food.

✓ Bacteria are essential to the nitrogen cycle.

How the nitrogen cycle works

Bacteria are an essential part of the nitrogen cycle. As well as breaking down dead matter, which releases nitrogen compounds into the soil, they convert nitrogen from the air into a soluble form that plants can absorb.

Lightning can turn nitrogen gas in air into nitrogen compounds that dissolve in rain.

Plants combine sugars made by photosynthesis with nitrogen compounds from soil to create proteins and nucleic acids.

Soil and the roots of some plants contain nitrogen-fixing bacteria— they convert nitrogen from the air into simple nitrogen compounds.

Animals get nitrogen as proteins and nucleic acids in their food. They digest these to form smaller units and use those to make new proteins and nucleic acids.

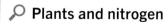

Plants absorb simple, inorganic nitrogen compounds called nitrates from soil through their roots.

Soil contains decomposers such as bacteria that digest dead organic matter and release inorganic nitrogen compounds.

Dead plants and animals and animal waste contain proteins and nucleic acids.

🔍 Plants and nitrogen

Legume plants, such as peas, beans, and clover, have root nodules that contain nitrogen-fixing bacteria. The plants obtain nitrogen compounds from the bacteria, which they need for making proteins, and the bacteria obtain sugars from the plants, which they need for respiration. This is a mutualistic relationship—a relationship that benefits both partners.

Root nodules

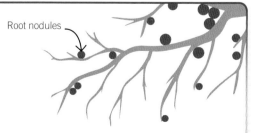

Humans and the Environment

Human population growth

The human population has grown rapidly as a result of industrialization and improvements in agriculture, hygiene, and health care.

World human population growth since 1750
The world population has increased rapidly since around 1750, when industrialization began. Evidence from birth rates suggests that the growth rate of the human population is now beginning to slow down.

🔍 Predicting future growth

Predictions of future population growth vary due to assumptions about how birth rate will change in different countries, based on changes in health, industrialization of developing areas, and birth control.

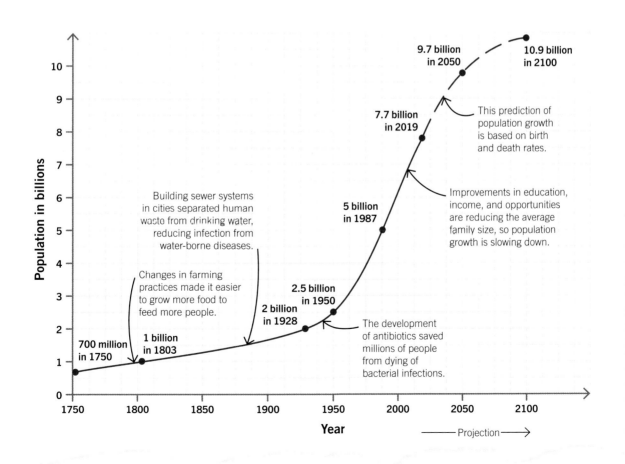

9.7 billion in 2050

10.9 billion in 2100

This prediction of population growth is based on birth and death rates.

7.7 billion in 2019

Improvements in education, income, and opportunities are reducing the average family size, so population growth is slowing down.

Building sewer systems in cities separated human waste from drinking water, reducing infection from water-borne diseases.

5 billion in 1987

Changes in farming practices made it easier to grow more food to feed more people.

2.5 billion in 1950

2 billion in 1928

The development of antibiotics saved millions of people from dying of bacterial infections.

700 million in 1750

1 billion in 1803

Population in billions

1750 1800 1850 1900 1950 2000 2050 2100

Year

Projection →

Need for resources

Humans need resources from the environment to live and thrive. These resources include food, water, and all the materials we need for buildings, clothing, and everything that we use.

Conflict with nature

As the human population grows, we need more and more resources. This leaves fewer resources for other living species, including space, water, and nutrients. We also produce more pollution from human activities, which damages the environment.

Clearing land for humans to use destroys habitats for other species.

🔍 Threats to wildlife

More than a million species are now endangered or at risk due to human activity. Our need for land has encroached on the habitats of many species. Our ever-increasing consumption of resources and disposal of waste has also spread pollution to the most remote habitats, including oceans.

Habitat loss
Wild Asian elephants live in forests and natural grassland. These habitats are shrinking as people build more railroads, roads, and buildings. Elephants are at risk of being killed by trains and traffic as they migrate across different parts of their range.

Plastic pollution
Every year tons of plastic litter is washed into the ocean. Large marine animals may mistake plastic items for food, while small marine animals may swallow tiny plastic granules. The plastic fills their stomach, leaving less space for food and increasing the risk of starvation.

Biodiversity

Biodiversity is the variety of different species living in a particular area. Some ecosystems are more biodiverse than others. For example, coral reefs cover less than 1 percent of the sea floor but are home to an estimated 25 percent of all marine organisms.

Key facts

✓ Biodiversity is the variety of species in an area.

✓ Coral reefs and rain forests are ecosystems with high biodiversity.

✓ Reducing biodiversity could damage ecosystems permanently.

Coral reef biodiversity

The high biodiversity of a coral reef depends on the warmth and light received by algae that live in the water and inside the corals. Algae photosynthesize and provide food for the coral animals. This is the base of the food web of a reef community. The coral structures also provide different habitats for animals.

Coral reefs form in warm, shallow water, where the temperature is between 20 and 28°C.

Coral reefs are built by tiny coral polyps, which are animals.

These tiny green specks are algae living in the coral polyp tissues.

The huge variety of coral provides food and shelter for numerous animals. These, in turn, provide food for many preditors.

🔍 Why biodiversity matters

Protecting areas of high biodiversity is important because they benefit humans in many ways. Ecosystems such as rain forests provide us with clean air and water as well as sources of new medicines and materials. Human activity can damage such natural ecosystems, reducing their diversity. If species become extinct, an ecosystem can be permanently damaged.

Global warming

Global warming is the long-term increase in Earth's air and surface temperatures. Most people accept that this warming has been caused by the rise in atmospheric carbon dioxide resulting from human activities, such as burning fossil fuels.

Key facts

✓ Global warming is the long-term warming of Earth's surface and atmosphere.

✓ Global warming is caused by the increasing concentrations of carbon dioxide and other greenhouse gases in the atmosphere.

✓ If atmospheric carbon dioxide continues to increase, global temperatures will continue to rise.

Sun

Energy from the sun passes through the atmosphere.

Some of the heat escapes into space.

Some of the heat is trapped by greenhouse gases in the atmosphere.

A blanket of greenhouse gases encircles Earth.

The atmosphere

Earth

Greenhouse gases
Greenhouse gases in Earth's atmosphere act like a greenhouse—they trap some of the heat from the sun, warming the Earth. Carbon dioxide and methane are known as greenhouse gases. Without the greenhouse effect, Earth's surface would be too cold to sustain life. However, too much carbon dioxide causes global warming.

🔍 Global temperature and atmospheric carbon dioxide

This graph shows that atmospheric carbon dioxide and mean global temperature have both increased over the last 50 years. If atmospheric carbon dioxide continues to rise, then global warming is likely to continue.

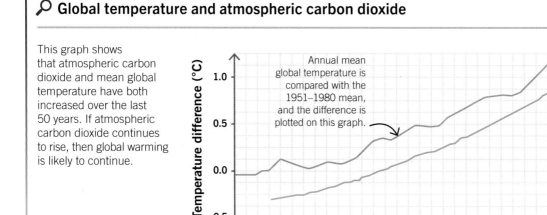

Annual mean global temperature is compared with the 1951–1980 mean, and the difference is plotted on this graph.

■ Temperature difference

■ Carbon dioxide

Climate change

Global warming doesn't just increase Earth's surface temperature. It also changes weather patterns, affecting which places get rain or not and how windy it is.

Key facts

✓ Global warming changes weather patterns.

✓ Changing weather patterns can cause more or less rain to fall in a region and create more storms.

✓ Climate change is causing more extreme weather events today than 30 years ago.

Extreme effects

This chart shows that extreme events that harm humans and wildlife are becoming more common. The increase in frequency is probably due to climate change.

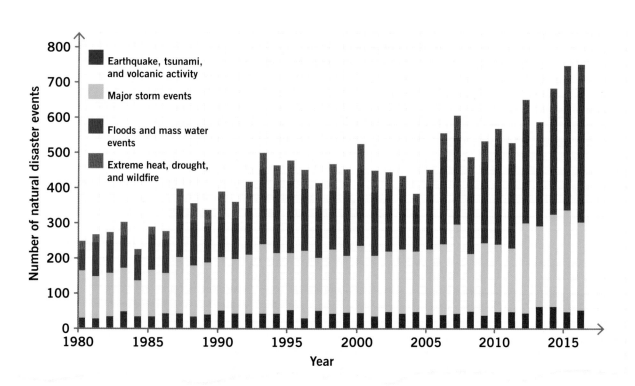

Legend:
- Earthquake, tsunami, and volcanic activity
- Major storm events
- Floods and mass water events
- Extreme heat, drought, and wildfire

Y-axis: Number of natural disaster events (0–800)
X-axis: Year (1980–2015)

🔍 Changing planet

Climate change is causing some regions of the world to get drier and suffer more drought and others to get wetter. Melting of glaciers and ice caps adds more water to oceans, increasing sea levels and flooding low-lying regions.

Drought
Lack of rainfall means droughts are more common. Rivers dry up, and there is less fresh water for animals and plants.

Rising sea levels
As sea levels rise, more low-lying land is flooded, destroying habitats for wildlife and places where people live.

Changing ecosystems

A change in the amount of heat and water in an ecosystem affects the organisms living there. Organisms are adapted to particular conditions, so if those conditions change too much, the organisms may die out.

Key facts

✓ Climate change is changing the conditions in many ecosystems.

✓ Organisms are adapted to particular conditions and may die out if conditions change too much.

✓ Interdependence of organisms in communities means that if one species dies out, it could cause the extinction of many others.

Coral bleaching

If seawater temperature rises by more than about 1°C, the algae living inside corals are pushed out into the water. This makes the corals turn white, which is called coral bleaching. Without algae to provide food, the bleached coral may starve and die. It is also more susceptible to disease.

Many fish depend on the living corals for food—if corals die, many species find it difficult to survive. The reef will quickly change from an area of high biodiversity to one of low biodiversity.

A change in temperature or water pollution can cause algae to leave the coral. The coral will eventually die.

Bleached coral

Dead coral animals leave behind the hard coral structure, although this may eventually crumble, leaving few places for other animals to hide.

Healthy coral

🔍 Habitat change

Many species are decreasing in number due to habitat change as Earth warms up. The interdependence of species in communities means that the extinction of one species could cause many other species in the community to become extinct.

Melting Arctic ice
Polar bears catch much of their food (seals) by lying in wait on the ice. Melting Arctic ice means less food for polar bears and even possible starvation.

Deforestation
Orangutans play an important role in dispersing the seeds of rain forest plants, but they are endangered due to habitat change and deforestation. If the orangutans die out, the plants also die out.

Changing distributions

Environmental changes can cause some species to move to new areas, changing their distribution. These changes may be caused by natural processes, such as the cycle of seasons, or by human activities that lead to habitat destruction or climate change.

Key facts

✓ Environmental changes can affect the distribution of organisms.

✓ Changing distributions can be caused by natural changes in the environment or by human activity.

✓ Climate change could cause some species to spread beyond their current range and others to die out as habitats change.

Climate change and distribution

Climate change could alter the distribution of the two bird species shown here. A warming climate would allow the hoopoe to spread north, extending its range. The Scottish crossbill, however, could become extinct as a result of habitat loss.

 Scottish crossbill ▨ Hoopoe

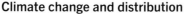

Scottish crossbill
The Scottish crossbill lives only in the cool pine forests of northern Scotland, where it feeds on the seeds of the Scots pine. These forests will disappear if the climate becomes too warm, causing the crossbill to die out.

European hoopoe
This bird lives in warm, dry habitats but is occasionally seen as far north as southern England. A warming climate would allow it to spread further north.

🔍 Migration

Some animals respond to seasonal changes in the environment by making long trips called migrations. Monarch butterflies migrate thousands of kilometers each year between their breeding sites in North America and their winter roosting sites in tropical Mexico.

🔍 Spreading disease

Climate change might also result in a change in the distribution of organisms that spread disease, such as malaria-carrying mosquitoes. Normally found in warm countries, these may bring malaria to northern Europe as temperatures rise.

Carbon sinks

Plants absorb carbon dioxide from the atmosphere by photosynthesis. Growing trees use a lot of this carbon to make their leaves and the wood of their trunks, and because they absorb more carbon than they release as carbon dioxide in respiration, they are described as carbon sinks.

Effects of deforestation

When trees are cut down, much of the carbon locked inside them ends up in the atmosphere. If they are left to decay or are burned, this carbon is released as carbon dioxide, which adds to global warming (see page 238). More than 18 million acres of forest are cleared each year to grow crops or build houses, or for mining.

Key facts

✓ Carbon sinks absorb more carbon from the atmosphere than they release and store it over long periods of time.

✓ Forests and peatland are important carbon sinks.

✓ Clearing and burning forests and peat releases their carbon, raising carbon dioxide levels in the atmosphere.

Large areas of rain forest in southern Asia are destroyed and replanted with oil palm to provide oil for many products. This not only contributes to global warming but also destroys habitats and reduces biodiversity.

🔍 Peat bog destruction

Peat cutting
Peat forms from the remains of plants that grow in cool, waterlogged soil. Like forests, peat bogs are carbon sinks. In some countries, peat is cut and burned as fuel, which releases its locked carbon into the atmosphere.

Peat covers about 3 percent of Earth's surface.

Peatland fires
If peat dries out, it is much more likely to burn. Large areas of burning peat bog can release vast quantities of carbon dioxide into the air.

Peatland fires in Indonesia are often started deliberately to clear land for farming.

Introduced species

When people travel they may take animals or plants with them, sometimes by accident. Introducing new species to an area can cause problems. The new species might outcompete native species and become "invasive," or it might become parasites of native species.

Key facts

✓ Species may be introduced to a new region by accident or by intention.

✓ Some introduced species are invasive, surviving well and reproducing rapidly.

Rosy wolf snail
The rosy wolf snail is a predator that was introduced to Tahiti from southeastern US to eat the giant African land snails. However, it prefers small prey and so has caused the extinction of many *Partula* species.

Extinction of Tahiti tree snails
The island of Tahiti and the surrounding islands were home to around 75 species of Polynesian tree snails (*Partula* species). However, the introduction of snails from other parts of the world led to the loss of all but 12 native species, which were saved by being bred in captivity.

Partula snails
These snails are endemic species—they are found only on the island of Tahiti and nearby islands. *Partula* snails are particularly at risk due to introduced species.

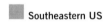

██ Tahiti   ██ Southeastern US   ██ East Africa

Giant African land snail
This snail was accidentally introduced to Tahiti from East Africa. It breeds rapidly and eats plants that *Partula* snails eat.

🔍 Invasive plants

Water hyacinth
Water hyacinth has been introduced from the Amazon to many parts of the world as an ornamental pond plant, but it has escaped into the wild. It grows up to 5 m per day, outcompeting native aquatic plants and blocking waterways, as can be seen in this lake in Africa.

Kudzu vine
A fast-growing climbing vine originally found in Southeast Asia, the kudzu vine has spread to parts of the US and New Zealand. It grows up to 26 cm a day, smothering trees and preventing light from getting through to the plants below.

Water pollution

The release of harmful substances into the natural environment is known as pollution. Water can become polluted by accident when chemicals escape from factories or fertilizers get into rivers and lakes.

Key facts

✓ Water pollution occurs when substances harmful to wildlife get into rivers and lakes.

✓ Eutrophication is a form of water pollution caused by nutrients that stimulate the growth of algae.

✓ Eutrophication can kill animals such as fish.

✓ Sewage treatment removes nutrients from waste so the water is safe to return to the environment.

Eutrophication

Eutrophication is a form of pollution caused by nutrients entering water, such as when fertilizers from farmland wash into rivers. The added nutrients help the plants and algae in the water grow faster but can lead to the death of aquatic animals such as fish.

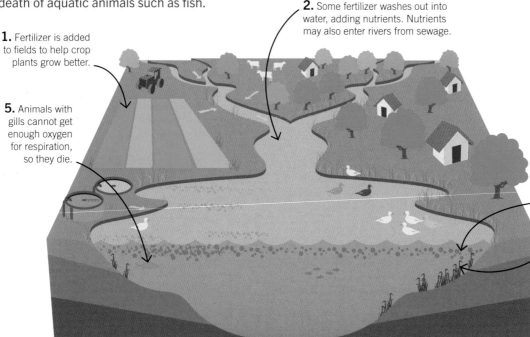

2. Some fertilizer washes out into water, adding nutrients. Nutrients may also enter rivers from sewage.

1. Fertilizer is added to fields to help crop plants grow better.

5. Animals with gills cannot get enough oxygen for respiration, so they die.

3. Extra nutrients cause plants and algae to grow faster. The growth of algae on the surface of the water prevents light from reaching plants deeper down, which then die.

4. Decaying plants stimulate the growth of decomposers, such as bacteria. They use up oxygen in the water.

🔍 Sewage treatment plants

Human waste (feces and urine) contains high levels of nutrients such as nitrogen compounds. Sewage treatment plants collect the waste and use bacteria and biological processes to remove the nutrients from the water so it is safe to return to the environment.

Bubbling air through sewage encourages bacteria to grow quickly and remove nutrients from the liquid.

Land pollution

Land pollution is caused by the release of harmful substances into the soil. These substances may come from mining waste, refuse in landfill sites, or chemical wastes from factories.

Landfill sites

The world's population produces more than 3 million tons of trash every day. One way of getting rid of this waste is to dump it in large holes—landfill sites. But this takes up a lot of land, causing loss of natural habitat. Hazardous chemicals may also seep into the ground from the waste for many years.

Key facts

✓ Land pollution is caused when harmful substances get into the soil.

✓ These substances include mining waste, refuse in landfill sites, and chemical waste from factories.

✓ Landfill sites take up a lot of space and destroy habitats.

✓ Recycling as much waste as possible reduces the amount of refuse needing disposal.

🔍 Other solutions to waste disposal

There are other ways to get rid of waste, such as incineration (burning). This can also cause problems, such as releasing carbon dioxide and other pollutants into the air. A better solution is to limit consumption and to recycle as much as we can. The more we recycle, the less refuse there is to dispose of by landfill or incineration.

Food waste **Metal** **Paper** **Plastics**

Decaying refuse releases toxic compounds that seep into the ground, harming wildlife nearby.

Air pollution

Air pollution occurs when harmful substances are released into the air. Most air pollution is caused by the combustion (burning) of fossil fuels such as coal, oil, and natural gas.

Acid rain

Combustion of fossil fuels releases acidic gases such as sulfur dioxide and nitrogen oxides. When these gases dissolve in water droplets in clouds, they can produce acid rain, which is harmful to living organisms.

Key facts

✓ Air pollution is caused by harmful substances in the air.

✓ Acid rain is caused by acidic gases, such as sulfur dioxide and nitrogen oxides, dissolving in rainwater.

✓ In some countries, legislation to reduce sulfur in fuels and from emissions has reduced acid rain.

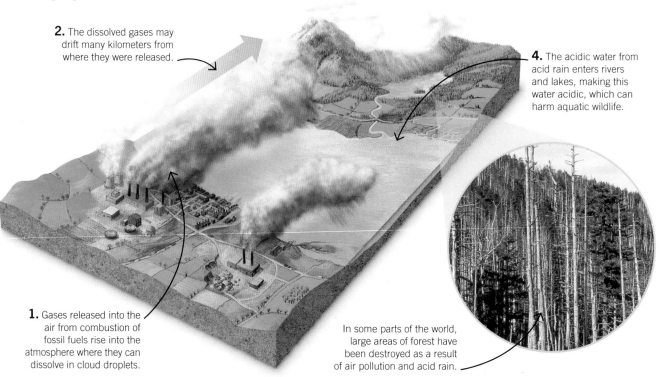

3. The dissolved gases fall as acid rain. This can harm living organisms over large areas.

2. The dissolved gases may drift many kilometers from where they were released.

4. The acidic water from acid rain enters rivers and lakes, making this water acidic, which can harm aquatic wildlife.

1. Gases released into the air from combustion of fossil fuels rise into the atmosphere where they can dissolve in cloud droplets.

In some parts of the world, large areas of forest have been destroyed as a result of air pollution and acid rain.

🔍 Particles in the air

Particulates are tiny solid particles in the air. The smallest of these can be damaging when breathed in, making respiratory diseases and heart disease more likely, or triggering asthma attacks. Burning diesel fuel in vehicle engines is a major source of particulates.

Concentrations of particulates in the air are usually higher around busy roads.

Conservation

Conservation is the protection of species and natural habitats. It may involve breeding animals in zoos or growing plants in botanic gargens to increase their numbers. Protecting habitats can increase population numbers in the wild.

✓ Conservation is the protection of species and their habitats.

✓ Conservation includes measures such as creating reserves.

✓ Educating people who live close to important natural habitats can support conservation efforts by reducing conflict between humans and wildlife.

✓ Conservation of a keystone species can help protect many species in the same ecosystem.

Tiger conservation in India

An estimated 80,000 tigers were killed by hunters in India between 1875 and 1925. By 2006, there were about 1,400 tigers left in India. Conservation measures increased that number to about 3,000 by 2018, but a lack of suitable habitat will limit further recovery. Conservation of tigers involves protecting large areas of habitat, which benefits the other species in the area.

🔍 Keystone species

Keystone species are species that play an important part in how an ecosystem functions. Conservation of keystone species helps protect many other species in the same community. For example, beavers are keystone species because they build dams to create pools for their homes. This changes the surroundings, creating new wet habitats and increasing biodiversity.

🔍 Measures for conserving animals

● Create reserves to protect habitats and species

● Educate local people to reduce damage to habitats and species

● Introduce measures to improve habitats, such as reforestation

● Monitor populations of endangered species

Food security

Providing enough food for people to eat is known as food security. Although the world grows enough to feed everyone, some people are at risk of malnutrition or starvation due to poor local harvests, low incomes, or the impact of war.

Key facts

✓ Food security means providing enough food for everyone to eat.

✓ Food security will become more challenging as the human population grows.

✓ Food security could be affected by climate change and change in diets.

Threats to food security

Producing enough food for everyone could become more difficult in the future. This is because factors such as population growth, climate, diet, and pests and diseases could reduce the amount of food we can grow or need.

Population growth
As countries develop and human populations grow, the demand for food will increase, so we will need to produce a lot more food than we are currently doing. Population growth will also increase the need for more energy and water as well as other resources.

With more people in the world, the demand for food increases.

Cattle graze on land that was once covered with rain forest trees.

Diet
As people earn more money, they tend to eat more meat than food from plants. However, raising livestock rather than growing plants for food uses more resources, including more land, water, and nutrients. So less food is produced in total.

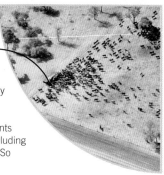

Climate change
Fluctuating weather patterns due to climate change will have an effect on the amount of rain a region gets. They may also lead to an increase in extreme weather events, such as floods and droughts, making it more difficult to grow crops and raise food animals.

Climate change makes seasonal rain less dependable so crops fail more often.

Locusts can strip crops in just a few hours.

Pests and diseases
Climate change helps pests and diseases spread to more regions. These affect crops and animals. For example, locusts are found in tropical regions but could spread to crops in cooler regions as the climate warms.

🔍 Why does a plant-based diet help the environment?

Using land to produce plant foods rather than meat is much more efficient. Because energy is lost as it passes from one trophic level to the next (see page 225), much more land and water is required to produce 1 kg of beef than the same mass of plant protein, such as soy. Livestock farming also produces greater emissions of greenhouse gases.

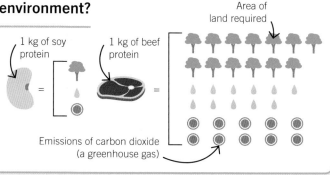

1 kg of soy protein

1 kg of beef protein

Area of land required

Emissions of carbon dioxide (a greenhouse gas)

Food production and sustainability

Sustainable food production means producing food in a way that can continue for the long term without harming the environment or using up valuable resources.

Key facts

✓ Sustainable resources can be used indefinitely without harming the environment.

✓ Sustainable food production means producing food without harming the environment.

✓ Fishing is made more sustainable by fishing quotas, larger mesh sizes, marine reserves, and fish farming.

Sustainability in fishing

Increased fishing has led to the collapse of many fish populations in the oceans, damaging marine ecosystems. To make fishing sustainable, we need to improve the way we fish.

Fishing quotas

A number of countries have now imposed fishing quotas (limits). These restrict how many fish can be caught and at what time of the year. The quotas are carefully planned to protect the most vulnerable fish species, especially during the breeding season.

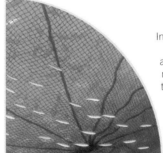

Mesh size

Increasing the mesh size (making the gaps in the nets bigger) allows smaller fish to swim out of nets and escape. These fish can then grow and reproduce, which ensures that their populations are maintained.

Fish pens ——

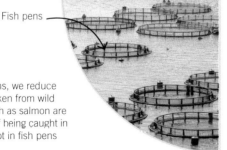

Marine wildlife flourishes in areas where fishing is not allowed.

Farming fish

By farming fish in pens, we reduce the number of fish taken from wild populations. Fish such as salmon are now farmed instead of being caught in the wild. They are kept in fish pens in rivers or the sea.

Marine reserves

Fishing is banned in marine reserves (no-fishing zones) so that fish there can grow to breeding size. This allows fish to multiply and spread into nearby waters, helping improve both the diversity and number of fish.

🔍 Problems with farming fish

Although fish farms help reduce overfishing in the wild, they can also cause problems. Uneaten fish food and fish droppings add nutrients to the water, which can cause eutrophication (see page 244). Pests and diseases can spread in the crowded pens. Parasites called sea lice, for instance, are common in fish farms and can spread to wild populations.

Sea lice are parasites that feed on the skin and blood of fish.

Farming methods

Intensive farming and organic farming are two different methods of farming. Intensive farming uses modern techniques to maximize yield (the amount of food produced). Organic farming aims to minimize harm to the environment.

Effects of farming methods

Conservation of the environment is easier on organic farms, where fewer chemicals are used and some land is left to grow wild. In contrast, intensive farming involves the use of chemicals to fertilize crops and to control pests, weeds, and diseases as well as machinery to work the land.

Key facts

✓ Intensive farming and organic farming are two contrasting types of farming methods.

✓ Organic farming uses fewer chemicals than intensive farming and so causes less damage to the environment.

✓ Very large areas of crops in intensive farming are easier to manage but provide little space for other species.

✓ Organically produced food may cost more than food produced intensively.

Organic rice farm

Intensive crop farming

Organic farming				Intensive farming		
Features	**Pros**	**Cons**		**Features**	**Pros**	**Cons**
Smaller fields surrounded by more hedges and trees	Higher biodiversity	Higher maintenance, food is more expensive		Very large fields	Easier to work with large machinery	Monocultures (one crop) susceptible to pests and disease
More wildflowers	Better pollination of crops	Wildflowers compete with crop for resources		High use of artificial fertilizers	Rapid crop growth, increased yield	High risk of pollution of waterways
Few chemicals used	Less harm to wildlife and less pollution of waterways	More damage to crops by pests		High use of chemicals for pest and disease control	Less damage to crops by pests, greater yield	High risk of harm to wildlife species

Biofuels

Biofuels are fuels made from waste plant and animal material (biomass) and can be used instead of fossil fuels. Bioethanol comes from the fermentation (breakdown) of sugar-rich plant matter, such as sugar cane. Biodiesel comes from vegetable or animal fats.

Key facts

✓ Biofuels are made from waste plant and animal material (biomass).

✓ Biofuels may contribute less to global warming than fossil fuels because biofuel crops absorb carbon from the air as they grow.

✓ Production of biofuels has led to deforestation in tropical areas.

Using and producing bioethanol

When bioethanol is burned in car engines, the amount of carbon released into the air is the same as the amount absorbed when the fuel was made. However, biofuels are not carbon neutral. Forests may be cut down to make room for the biofuel crops, and machinery is needed to make and transport the fuels.

1. Crops for biomass
Sugar cane grows fast and absorbs carbon dioxide from the atmosphere, turning the carbon into sugar by photosynthesis.

5. Releasing carbon dioxide
When bioethanol is burned, it releases as much carbon dioxide into the air as the growing sugar cane originally absorbed.

2. Harvesting crops
The sugar cane is harvested and processed to release its sugar, which is used as a source of food by yeast.

4. Using biofuel
The ethanol produced in this way is called bioethanol. It can be burned as fuel in car engines or used as heating fuel.

3. Making biofuel
The yeast feeds on the sugar by fermentation (see page 203), producing ethanol as a waste product.

🔍 Pros and cons of growing biofuel crops

Pros

● Unlike fossil fuels, biofuels are a renewable source of energy—the crops that generate the biofuel can be grown over and over again.

● If biofuel crops are continually grown to offset the carbon released by burning the fuels, biofuels may contribute less to global warming than fossil fuels.

Cons

● Biofuel production has led to deforestation in tropical areas, contributing to global warming.

● Most engines have to be modified to run on biofuels.

● Biofuel crops may use up land that could be used for other purposes, such as growing food.

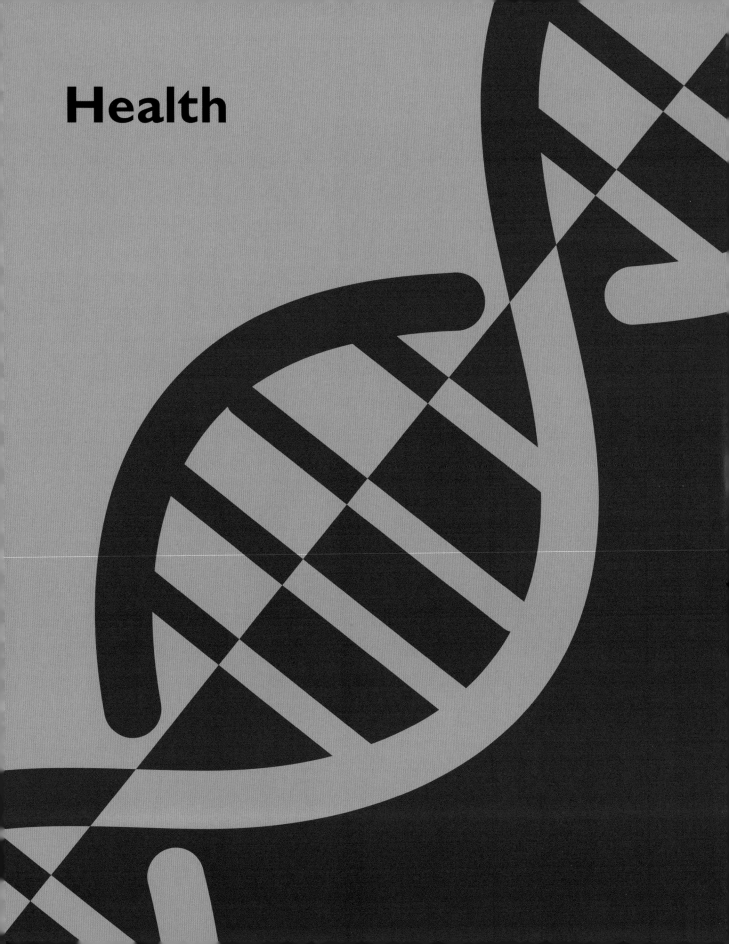

Health

Health and disease

A healthy body is one that works properly and is free of disease. A disease is any condition that stops the body from working properly or makes a person feel unwell. There are hundreds of different diseases, and their causes vary widely.

Causes of disease

Some diseases are caused by microorganisms that spread from one person to another (pathogens). These diseases are described as transmissible or communicable. Other diseases, such as heart disease and diabetes, are not transmissible. The risk of nontransmissible diseases is affected by a person's lifestyle and their genes.

Key facts

✓ A disease is any condition that stops part of the body from working properly or makes a person feel unwell.

✓ Diseases caused by infectious microorganisms (pathogens) are called communicable or transmissible diseases.

✓ Diseases that are not caused by infectious microorganisms are called noncommunicable or nontransmissible diseases.

Providing clean water for entire communities protects people from serious diseases such as cholera, which is caused by contaminated water or food.

🔍 Causes of disease worldwide

The major causes of diseases vary in different parts of the world. In poorer countries, many of the diseases are caused by food or infections transmitted by poor sanitation. The deadly disease malaria mainly affects tropical countries. In wealthier countries, infectious diseases are less common, but diseases caused by a rich diet and lack of exercise have a considerable impact on health.

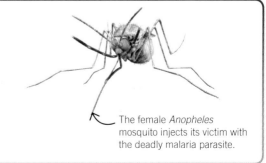

The female *Anopheles* mosquito injects its victim with the deadly malaria parasite.

Effects of lifestyle on disease

Our bodies need the right balance of nutrients and a good supply of oxygen to stay healthy. By ensuring that we eat sensibly, get regular exercise, and avoid harmful substances such as tobacco and alcohol, we can reduce the risk of certain diseases as we grow older.

Key facts

✓ Regular exercise strengthens the heart and muscles, making the body fitter and healthier.

✓ Because vaccines and antibiotics have reduced infectious diseases, people are now more likely to die from nontransmissible diseases.

✓ Obesity increases the risk of type 2 diabetes.

✓ Alcohol increases risk of liver disease.

Healthy workout

Whether you are playing a sport, such as soccer, or walking regularly, your heart, lungs, and muscles all work harder and become stronger in the process.

Regular walking or running is good for the heart and lungs.

Physical games and sports are both fun and good for the body.

🔍 Lifestyle diseases

As improvements in health care have reduced the likelihood of transmissible diseases in many parts of the world, the number of people dying from nontransmissible diseases has risen. Many of these diseases are affected by a person's lifestyle. Smoking, lack of exercise, and a rich diet all increase the risk of diseases such as cancer, diabetes, and cardiovascular disease.

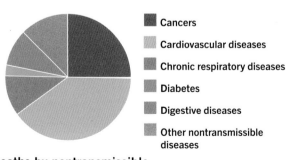

■ Cancers
■ Cardiovascular diseases
■ Chronic respiratory diseases
■ Diabetes
■ Digestive diseases
■ Other nontransmissible diseases

Deaths by nontransmissible diseases in people under the age of 70

Heart disease

The heart is the organ responsible for pumping oxygenated, nutrient-rich blood around the body. But an unhealthy lifestyle can stop it from functioning effectively. Diseases of the heart and blood vessels are known as cardiovascular diseases, and they are nontransmissible—they cannot be transferred between people.

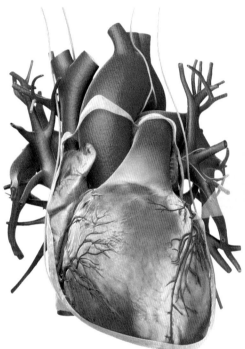

Normal blood flow

Fatty material

Abnormal blood flow

Healthy artery

Blocked artery

Blocked arteries

Fatty material (such as cholesterol) flowing through the blood can stick to the walls of the coronary arteries, which supply the heart muscle with oxygenated blood. This forms a hard lump, which can rupture and completely block the artery, causing a heart attack. If this happens to the arteries in the brain, it can starve the brain of oxygen, causing a stroke.

How stents work

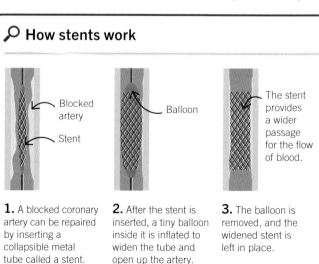

Blocked artery

Stent

Balloon

The stent provides a wider passage for the flow of blood.

1. A blocked coronary artery can be repaired by inserting a collapsible metal tube called a stent.

2. After the stent is inserted, a tiny balloon inside it is inflated to widen the tube and open up the artery.

3. The balloon is removed, and the widened stent is left in place.

How statins work

Taking drugs called statins can reduce the level of cholesterol in the blood. Statins work by slowing down the rate of fatty deposit buildup. However, they can cause liver and kidney problems.

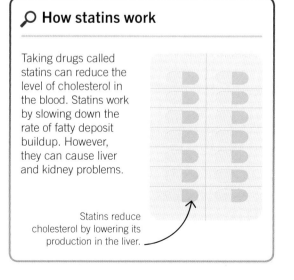

Statins reduce cholesterol by lowering its production in the liver.

Heart surgery

Some types of heart diseases can be effectively treated only with surgery. Old age or a heart attack can prevent the heart from working properly, depriving the body's tissues of the blood they need. If a heart is beyond repair, it may need to be replaced with a donor organ (a heart transplant).

Key facts

- ✓ Some types of heart diseases must be treated by surgery.
- ✓ Faulty valves can be corrected with biological or artificial replacements.
- ✓ If a heart is beyond repair, a heart transplant from a donor is needed.
- ✓ Artificial hearts can keep patients alive while they wait for a heart transplant.

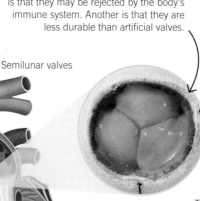

Semilunar valves

Bicuspid valve

Tricuspid valve

Biological valve
One disadvantage of using biological valves is that they may be rejected by the body's immune system. Another is that they are less durable than artificial valves.

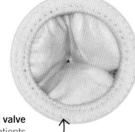

Artificial valve
These are longer lasting, but patients receiving them may need long-term medication to prevent blood clots.

Valves
Valves are flaps between the chambers of the heart that keep blood flowing in one direction. A patient with heart valve disease may receive a valve transplant from a human donor or an animal. These are called biological valves. Artificial valves made from durable materials, such as plastic, can also be used.

🔍 Heart transplant

Donor heart
Sometimes a heart transplant is the only long-term option for a patient with heart disease. After such an operation, the patient is given immunosuppressant (anti-rejection) drugs for the rest of their life. These drugs stop their immune system from rejecting the transplant.

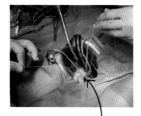

A team of surgeons perform open-heart surgery.

Artificial heart
Patients often have to wait for a donor heart and so artificial hearts are used as a temporary measure. Sometimes they are used to allow the heart to recover after major surgery or replace the heart completely if the patient is not suitable for a donor heart.

This X-ray shows an artificial heart. Two plastic tubes deliver blood around the body.

Pathogens

Some types of diseases are caused by microorganisms called pathogens (germs), which can spread from one person to another as they reproduce. We say an affected person is "infected." Diseases caused by pathogens are known as infectious diseases, communicable diseases, or transmissible diseases.

Types of pathogens
The simplest pathogens that consist of cells are bacteria (see page 39). More complex pathogens include protoctists (see page 38) and fungi. Viruses are smaller, simpler particles not made of cells. All viruses must invade host cells to reproduce.

Key facts

✓ Pathogens are disease-causing organisms that feed and reproduce in an organism called a host.

✓ Pathogens are usually microscopic and single-celled.

✓ Pathogens include various kinds of bacteria, protoctists, fungi, and viruses.

✓ Different kinds of pathogens affect either animals (including humans) or plants.

✓ Pathogens such as bacteria may produce toxins that damage tissues and make us feel ill.

Viruses
A virus invades a host cell and hijacks the cell's controls to make copies of the virus. The cell eventually bursts, releasing hundreds of new viruses and making the host ill. The influenza virus can cause flu symptoms in less than a day.

***Salmonella* bacterium**

Bacteria
Once inside a host, bacteria reproduce, releasing toxins that cause illness. *Salmonella* bacteria can multiply millions of times in a few hours, causing food poisoning.

Influenza virus

Protoctists
These simple, single-celled organisms live as parasites on or inside organisms that they invade, causing damage that makes the host ill. Infection by the malaria parasite can be fatal.

Malaria parasites in a blood cell

Rose black spot fungus

Fungi
Some fungi live on plants and animals as parasites. The rose black spot fungus, for example, invades the leaves of rose plants, which then wither and fall off. This limits photosynthesis.

🔍 Monitoring diseases

Scientists monitor an outbreak of a disease in a country by studying the rate of new cases (the incidence of the disease) over a period of time. By recording new cases, they can see how effective disease-preventing measures have been. This graph shows how the introduction of the polio vaccine in the US affected the rate of new cases and the rate of polio-related deaths between 1950 and 2010.

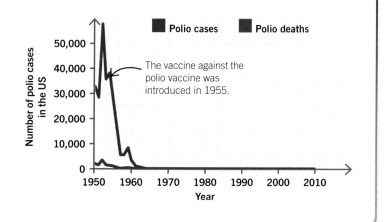

The vaccine against the polio vaccine was introduced in 1955.

Transmissible diseases

A disease caused by pathogens that pass from one living thing (host) to another is called a transmissible or communicable disease. Pathogens obtain nourishment from their host so that they can reproduce.

Transmission routes for human pathogens

The method of transmission from host to host depends on the kind of pathogen involved. Shown below are the main ways in which pathogens are transmitted from one person to another, causing disease.

Water
Drinking or even bathing in water that is contaminated by a pathogen can spread disease—pathogens enter your digestive system when swallowed and some can penetrate the skin.

Food and drinks
If food and drinks are not stored, cooked, or prepared properly, they may contain pathogens that cause food poisoning when consumed.

Vectors
These are organisms that transmit pathogens to other species, including humans. Some insects are vectors. *Anopheles* mosquitoes, for example, can transmit the malaria pathogen to humans in their bites.

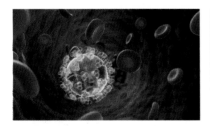

Body fluids
Some pathogens spread in body fluids such as blood and semen. The HIV virus, for example, is transmitted by unprotected sex, through contaminated blood transfusions, or through sharing needles to inject drugs.

Air
If you have a cold and sneeze, thousands of tiny droplets containing the cold virus are sprayed into the air that other people then breathe in.

Contact
Touching something, such as a dirty kitchen surface or floor, or even shaking hands with someone, can transfer pathogens.

Viruses

Viruses are not cells—they are much smaller particles made of a protein coat surrounding genetic material. They lack the cellular machinery needed to use the information stored in their genes, so they can reproduce only by invading cells.

How a virus reproduces
Once inside the body, a virus reproduces rapidly, damaging cells in the process and making a person feel ill. There are two ways in which a virus can reproduce: the lytic pathway and the lysogenic pathway.

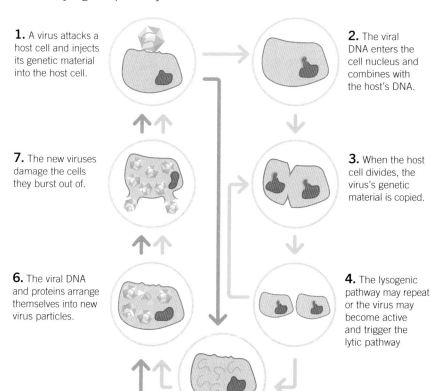

1. A virus attacks a host cell and injects its genetic material into the host cell.

2. The viral DNA enters the cell nucleus and combines with the host's DNA.

7. The new viruses damage the cells they burst out of.

3. When the host cell divides, the virus's genetic material is copied.

6. The viral DNA and proteins arrange themselves into new virus particles.

4. The lysogenic pathway may repeat or the virus may become active and trigger the lytic pathway

5. The viral genes instruct the cell to produce copies of the virus's DNA and proteins.

Lytic pathway
Many viruses end up destroying the cells they infect, making these cells split to release new viruses. This process is called the lytic pathway and takes only a few minutes to complete.

Lysogenic pathway
Some viruses insert their genetic material into the host's DNA, so the information for building new viruses is passed on to new cells. This process is called the lysogenic pathway and can cause infections that last for years.

Virus structure

Simple viruses
Most viruses have a simple structure, with a protein coat surrounding genetic material. The genetic material may take the form of DNA or the related molecule RNA. The genetic material carries the instructions for making more viral genetic material and proteins.

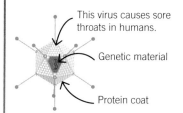

This virus causes sore throats in humans.

Genetic material

Protein coat

HIV
Unlike other viruses, the human immunodeficiency virus (HIV) is surrounded by an oily membrane that helps disguise it from the immune system. It also contains an enzyme to help it infect the host's DNA with its own genetic material.

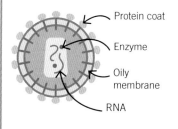

Protein coat

Enzyme

Oily membrane

RNA

Viral diseases

Many diseases are caused by viruses. Examples include HIV/AIDS, measles, and ebola in humans, and tobacco mosaic disease in plants.

HIV

HIV (human immunodeficiency virus) is transmitted by bodily fluids during unprotected sex or when needles are shared to inject drugs. The virus invades white blood cells, weakening the immune system. The infection may only cause flu-like symptoms at first, but without treatment it can progress to a life-threatening condition called AIDS (acquired immunodeficiency syndrome). Antiviral drugs slow down or even stop the disease from progressing to AIDS by preventing the virus from replicating.

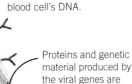

The virus's genes combine with the white blood cell's DNA.

Proteins and genetic material produced by the viral genes are assembled to make new viruses.

The virus fuses with white blood cells and inserts its genes.

HIV

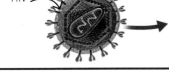

New viruses are released and invade more white blood cells.

🔍 Examples of viral infections

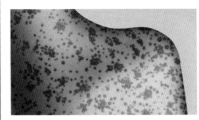

Measles
The measles virus is released into the air when someone infected with it sneezes. It may then be inhaled by another person. Symptoms include a fever and a rash. Measles can be prevented with vaccination.

Ebola
The deadly ebola virus is spread by contact with the bodily fluids of an infected person. Symptoms include a fever and internal bleeding from the eyes, nose, and mouth. The spread of the virus can be limited by isolating people infected by it.

Tobacco mosaic virus
Plants infected with the tobacco mosaic virus have a mosaic of patchy colors on the leaves, which also become crinkly. The virus is transmitted when infected plants touch. It reduces chlorophyll production, impairing photosynthesis and stunting growth.

Bacterial diseases

Bacteria can be useful. Gut bacteria, for example, aid digestion, and bacteria in the soil break down organic matter, releasing nutrients that help plants grow. Many bacteria, however, can cause serious illnesses.

Salmonella

The acidic conditions in the human stomach destroy most bacteria in food. But some harmful bacteria, such as *Salmonella*, survive and infect the intestine. Their toxins cause food poisoning, with symptoms such as vomiting, abdominal cramps, and diarrhea.

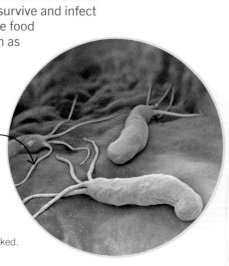

Salmonella bacteria use their hairlike strands (flagella) to move.

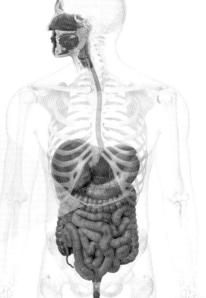

Salmonella bacteria
Shown here are the rod-shaped *Salmonella* bacteria that cause food poisoning. You can get *Salmonella* by eating contaminated food, such as chicken that hasn't been thoroughly cooked.

🔍 Examples of bacterial infections

Gonorrhea
Like other sexually transmitted infections (STIs), gonorrhea is passed on through sexual contact. Symptoms include burning pain when urinating. It is treated with antibiotics. Using condoms helps protect people from STIs.

Tuberculosis
Tuberculosis (TB) bacteria infect the lungs and are spread by coughing and sneezing. The disease can be prevented with a vaccination and treated with antibiotics. If left untreated, it can cause lung damage and ultimately death.

Crown gall disease
This disease affects plants, including fruit trees. The bacterium *Agrobacterium tumefaciens* enters the plant through a wound in a stem or roots, causing large, wartlike tumors called galls, which damage the plant.

Protoctist and fungal diseases

Most disease-causing protoctists and fungi are single-celled organisms. They invade other organisms and live on or inside them as parasites, feeding on their flesh. This can make the host ill and may even kill the host.

Key facts

✓ Most disease-causing protoctists and fungi are single-celled organisms.

✓ The malaria pathogen is a protoctist transmitted by a mosquito vector.

✓ A vector is an organism that carries and transmits pathogens to other species.

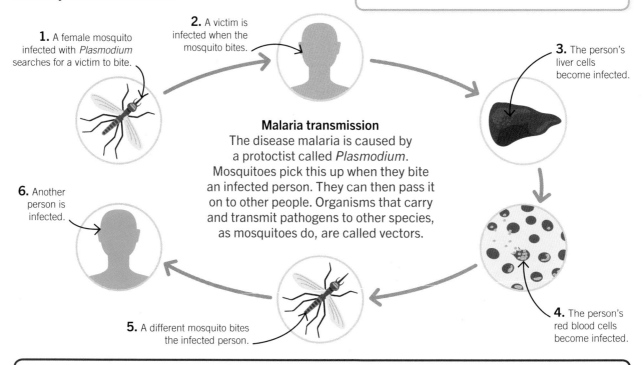

1. A female mosquito infected with *Plasmodium* searches for a victim to bite.

2. A victim is infected when the mosquito bites.

3. The person's liver cells become infected.

6. Another person is infected.

5. A different mosquito bites the infected person.

4. The person's red blood cells become infected.

Malaria transmission

The disease malaria is caused by a protoctist called *Plasmodium*. Mosquitoes pick this up when they bite an infected person. They can then pass it on to other people. Organisms that carry and transmit pathogens to other species, as mosquitoes do, are called vectors.

Fungal infections

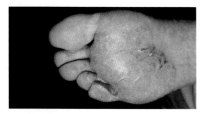

Athlete's foot
The parasitic fungus that causes athlete's foot thrives in warm, moist conditions. It spreads through direct contact with contaminated objects. Symptoms include cracked, flaking, and itchy skin. An antifungal cream can treat it.

Powdery mildew
Erysiphales fungi infect a wide range of plants. White, powdery patches appear on leaves and stems. The fungi limits photosynthesis and uses up the plant's nutrients. Affected plants can be treated with fungicides.

Ash dieback
Ash trees are affected by the deadly fungus *Hymenoscyphus fraxineus*. The spores are spread through air, infecting other ash trees. The fungus causes shoots and bark to die. Replanting with another species slows the spread of the disease.

Body barriers

Every day, the human body is bombarded with disease-causing pathogens—the air that you breathe, the objects that you touch, and the food that you eat have pathogens that can make you feel ill. But the body has a number of ways to keep it free from pathogens.

First line of defense

Some of your body's defense barriers are physical, such as your skin and the hairs in your nose; others are chemical, including stomach acid and the enzymes in mucus.

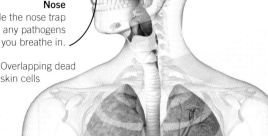

Eyes
Tears are a chemical defense against pathogens—they contain enzymes that destroy them. Every time you blink, bacteria and dust particles are washed away from the surface of your eyes.

Nose
Tiny hairs inside the nose trap dust particles and any pathogens that you breathe in.

Cilia in airways

Overlapping dead skin cells

Airways
Cells lining the airways leading to the lungs secrete mucus—a sticky fluid that traps pathogens. Tiny hairs called cilia sweep the pathogen laden mucus up to the throat, where it is swallowed.

Skin
The tough outer layer of your skin is made up of overlapping dead cells packed tightly together. Pathogens can't get through unless the skin is cut open by an injury. If your skin does get cut, a scab forms to stop pathogens from entering the body.

Stomach acid
Hydrochloric acid secreted in the stomach kills pathogens in food as well as microbes in any mucus swallowed from the throat.

⚙ How scabs form

Sticky fibrin thread

Platelet

Cut

1. When skin bleeds, tiny cell fragments called platelets are activated in the blood. They stick to the wound and release chemicals that cause a soluble blood protein, fibrinogen, to turn into fibrin, which is insoluble and forms sticky threads.

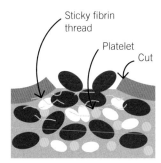

2. Red blood cells are trapped in the network of fibrin threads, forming a plug, while white blood cells attack any invading pathogens. The clot dries and hardens to form a protective scab, giving your skin time to heal.

Scab

White blood cell

Fibrin mesh

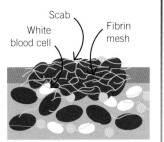

Phagocytes

Despite the effectiveness of your body's natural defense barriers, such as your skin, some pathogens still get into your body. When this happens, your body has a second line of defense—the immune system, which produces millions of white blood cells to attack pathogens such as bacteria.

Key facts

✓ The immune system involves the activity of white blood cells that fight infection.

✓ Phagocytes are white blood cells that engulf (surround and swallow) pathogens.

✓ The process of engulfing and digesting a pathogen is called phagocytosis.

✓ Unlike some other kinds of white blood cells, phagocytes are nonspecific—a phagocyte will attack any kind of pathogen.

Pathogen-eating phagocytes

Within minutes of pathogens entering your body, white blood cells called phagocytes multiply rapidly. Phagocytes are nonspecific—they target all types of pathogens. They squeeze out of your blood capillaries to get to the site of infection. Once there, phagocytes change shape to engulf (surround and swallow) and destroy pathogens. This process is called phagocytosis.

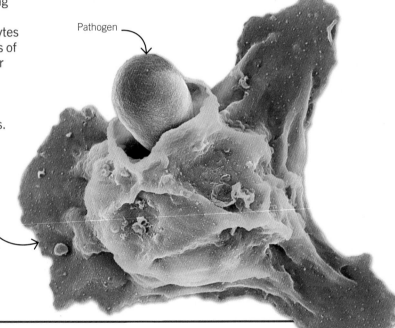

Pathogen

The phagocyte engulfs the pathogen.

⚙ How phagocytosis works

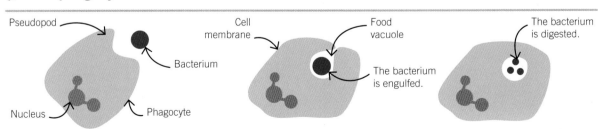

Pseudopod

Cell membrane

Food vacuole

The bacterium is digested.

Bacterium

The bacterium is engulfed.

Nucleus

Phagocyte

1. The phagocyte changes shape by stretching out parts of its cell into pseudopods (false feet) that can surround the bacterium.

2. As the pseudopods completely envelop the bacterium, the cell membrane joins, trapping the target inside a fluid-filled sac called a food vacuole. The bacterium is used to help feed the phagocyte.

3. Digestive enzymes are poured into the food vacuole to kill and break down the bacterium into tiny, harmless parts. The phagocyte is then ready to attack again.

Lymphocytes

Phagocytes and lymphocytes are the two main types of white blood cells that help defend the body against disease. Phagocytes start killing pathogens very quickly after an infection. But the infection also spurs lymphocytes into action. They produce defensive chemicals called antibodies that help give the body immunity over a longer period of time.

Targeting pathogens

Lymphocytes produce proteins called antibodies that target specific pathogens. Lymphocytes also remember the same pathogens in case they enter the body again months or years later. Pathogen cells have surface chemicals called antigens that antibodies stick to, flagging the invading cells for destruction by phagocytes. Your body's own cells also have antigens, but your immune system recognizes them as your own and so normally does not attack them.

Key facts

- ✓ Lymphocytes are white blood cells that produce chemicals called antibodies.
- ✓ The immune system recognizes pathogen cells as foreign and attempts to destroy them.
- ✓ The immune system recognizes the body's own cells and does not normally attack them.
- ✓ Antigens are cell surface proteins found on pathogens and on the body's own cells.
- ✓ Antibodies bind to antigens that have matching shapes.

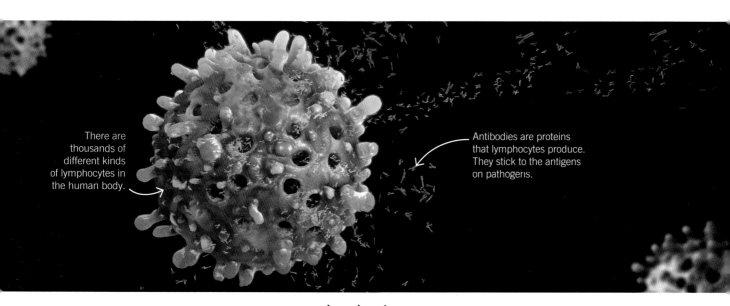

There are thousands of different kinds of lymphocytes in the human body.

Antibodies are proteins that lymphocytes produce. They stick to the antigens on pathogens.

Lymphocyte

🔍 Antibodies and antigens

Every type of pathogen has antigens with a specific shape. Lymphocytes produce a huge range of antibodies, ensuring that some will match and stick to every pathogen. When an antibody sticks to a pathogen, it attracts phagocytes, which destroy the invading cell.

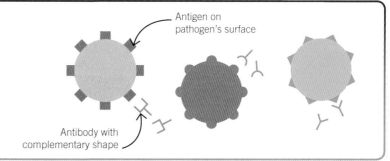

Antigen on pathogen's surface

Antibody with complementary shape

Long-term immunity

When your body is first infected by a pathogen, it takes a while for it to produce the right kind of antibody to fight that infection. But if this same pathogen attacks you later in life, your immune system remembers the first attack and will respond so well that you may not suffer any symptoms at all—your body has developed immunity to the disease.

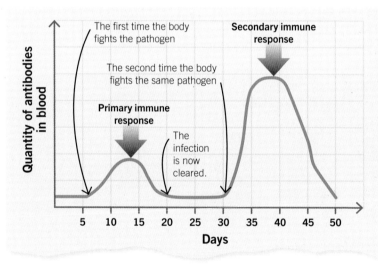

Primary and secondary immune responses

Lymphocytes play a vital role in defending your body against pathogens by producing chemicals called antibodies. This is called the immune response. The second exposure to the pathogen causes a faster secondary immune response because some of the memory cells produced in the first encounter stay in your bloodstream ready to fight the infection again.

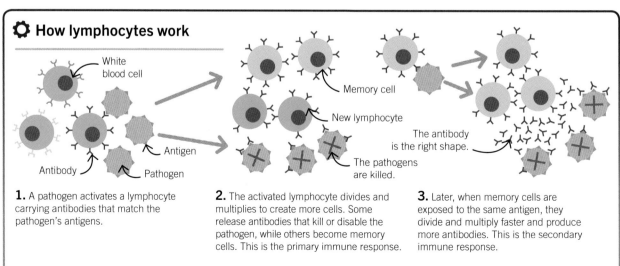

⚙ **How lymphocytes work**

1. A pathogen activates a lymphocyte carrying antibodies that match the pathogen's antigens.

2. The activated lymphocyte divides and multiplies to create more cells. Some release antibodies that kill or disable the pathogen, while others become memory cells. This is the primary immune response.

3. Later, when memory cells are exposed to the same antigen, they divide and multiply faster and produce more antibodies. This is the secondary immune response.

Vaccination

Scientific understanding of how the body's immune system works has led to the development of drugs called vaccines that protect individuals from infectious diseases. Injecting the body with vaccines containing weakened or dead pathogens stimulates the body to produce memory cells, making it immune to a disease.

Controlling infectious diseases

Vaccines are important not just to help stop individuals from getting harmful infectious diseases, but also to prevent these diseases from spreading through a population. Some vaccines give lifelong immunity, but others require periodic boosters.

Key facts

✓ A vaccine contains antigens, usually in the form of small amounts of dead or inactive pathogens.

✓ The antigen in the vaccine triggers production of antibodies and memory cells—the primary immune response.

✓ If the pathogen infects the body in the future, its antigens trigger memory cells to produce more antibodies faster—the secondary immune response.

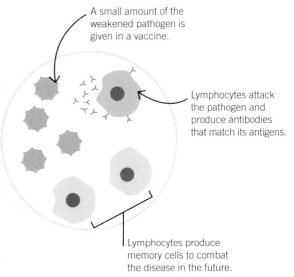

A small amount of the weakened pathogen is given in a vaccine.

Lymphocytes attack the pathogen and produce antibodies that match its antigens.

Lymphocytes produce memory cells to combat the disease in the future.

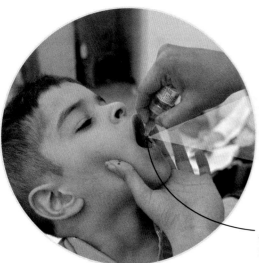

Instead of an injection, the vaccine for polio is given orally.

🔍 Pros and cons of vaccination

Pros

● Vaccination has helped control the spread of dangerous infectious diseases. For instance, polio infections throughout the world have fallen by 99 percent.

● Vaccination has reduced the number of deaths from infectious diseases, especially in children.

● Protecting a person from a disease by using vaccination can be cheaper than treating them if they contract the disease.

Cons

● Some people may develop reactions or side-effects to vaccines.

● Vaccines that are administered as injections can be painful, and some people develop needle phobias.

● People may take fewer precautions to avoid disease after vaccination, but not all vaccines are 100 percent effective.

Monoclonal antibodies

Antibodies are very specific and bind only to particular types of molecules. This allows us to use them to diagnose disease, test for pregnancy, or deliver drugs to cancer cells. Antibodies used in these ways are called monoclonal antibodies and are made by cloning antibody-making cells artificially.

Key facts

✓ Monoclonal antibodies are antibodies made artificially in a laboratory by cloning antibody-making cells.

✓ They are produced by fusing lymphocytes with fast-growing tumor cells to make hybridoma cells.

✓ They bind to particular targets, which are their antigens.

✓ Monoclonal antibodies can be used to diagnose disease, test for pregnancy, or deliver drugs to cancer cells.

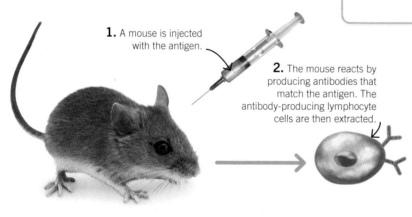

1. A mouse is injected with the antigen.

2. The mouse reacts by producing antibodies that match the antigen. The antibody-producing lymphocyte cells are then extracted.

3. The lymphocytes are fused with fast-dividing Tumor cells in a lab to produce hybrid cells called hybridomas.

Tumor cell

Making monoclonal antibodies
The lymphocyte cells that make antibodies in an animal's body are difficult to grow in a laboratory, so scientists fuse them with fast-dividing tumor cells, which are much easier to grow. This produces hybrid cells called hybridomas. These have features of both cells: they divide quickly and they make antibodies.

Monoclonal antibodies ready to be used.

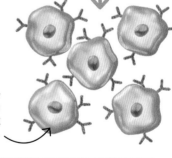

4. Hybridoma cells multiply quickly and easily, which makes them ideal for producing large quantities of the antibodies.

🔍 How monoclonal antibodies are used

Because monoclonal antibodies bind only to a specific target (their antigen), they can be used in tests that detect when this target is present. One kind of antibody is used in pregnancy tests—it binds to a hormone called HCG (human chorionic gonadotrophin), which is produced by pregnant women and detected by placing a urine sample on a testing device.

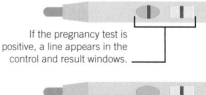

If the pregnancy test is positive, a line appears in the control and result windows.

If the test is negative, a line appears in the control window.

Cancer

Normal body cells grow and divide at a controlled rate. But if something goes wrong with this process, cells may multiply uncontrollably, producing growths called tumors. The most dangerous tumors are called malignant and can spread to other parts of the body, causing cancer. Other tumors do not spread and are described as benign.

Causes and treatment of cancer

A number of factors can increase the risk of cancer, including genes, diet, and exposure to chemicals called carcinogens, such as those in cigarette smoke. Treatment for cancer includes radiotherapy and chemotherapy, both of which attack fast-dividing cells in the body but can cause unpleasant side effects.

Key facts

✓ Cancer occurs when changes inside cells cause them to grow and divide uncontrollably.

✓ Malignant tumors are tumors that can invade other parts of the body, causing cancer.

✓ Cells from malignant tumors can break away and start growing elsewhere to form secondary tumors.

✓ Benign tumors do not invade other parts of the body.

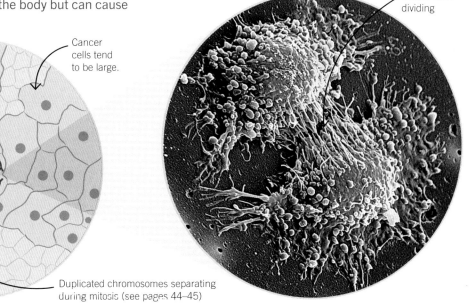

Cancer cells tend to be large.

Cancer cells dividing

Healthy cells

Duplicated chromosomes separating during mitosis (see pages 44–45)

🔍 Targeting cancer cells

Modern cancer treatments make use of the immune system to target cancer cells directly. One technique is to create monoclonal antibodies (see page 268) that bind to the antigens on cancer cells. The antibodies kill the cells by delivering cancer-fighting drugs to them (shown here), by making them clump so they are easier to remove, or by triggering attack by the body's immune system.

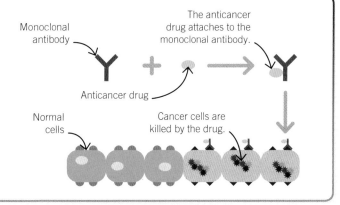

Monoclonal antibody

The anticancer drug attaches to the monoclonal antibody.

Anticancer drug

Normal cells

Cancer cells are killed by the drug.

Drugs

Drugs are chemicals that change the workings of the body, either physically or mentally. Some drugs, such as alcohol, caffeine, and nicotine, are used recreationally. However, most drugs are taken to treat, prevent, or diagnose diseases.

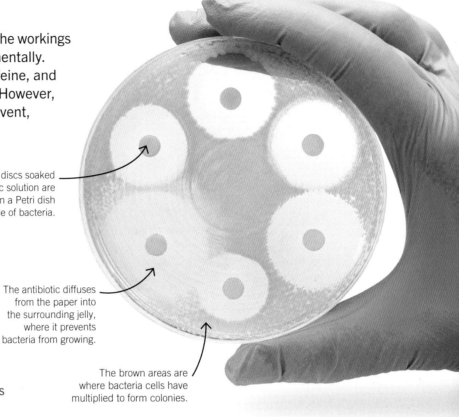

Small paper discs soaked in antibiotic solution are placed in a Petri dish with a sample of bacteria.

The antibiotic diffuses from the paper into the surrounding jelly, where it prevents bacteria from growing.

The brown areas are where bacteria cells have multiplied to form colonies.

How drugs work

Most drugs work by changing the chemical processes that happen inside the cells. For example, penicillin is an antibiotic that is used to treat bacterial infections. It works by interfering with an enzyme that bacteria use to build their cell walls. This stops bacteria from growing, which helps cure infection. Antibiotics can be tested in a laboratory by seeing how they affect the growth of bacteria in a Petri dish.

Key facts

✓ Drugs are chemicals that change the workings of the body either physically or mentally.

✓ Antibiotics are drugs used to kill or slow the growth of bacteria inside the body.

✓ Different kinds of bacteria are sensitive to different kinds of antibiotic.

✓ Antibiotics have no effect on viruses. Instead, antiviral drugs stop them from replicating inside the body.

✓ Drug resistance has evolved in some pathogens; antibiotic-resistant strains of bacteria are a growing problem.

🔍 Drug resistance

Infectious diseases can become difficult to treat with drugs if the pathogens that cause them become resistant. Some pathogens acquire resistance to an antibiotic because of a change in their DNA called a mutation (see page 186). When this antibiotic is then used to treat an infection, only the sensitive bacteria die, leaving the resistant ones to multiply.

3. Only the resistant bacteria survive, and they divide over and over again—resistance rapidly spreads.

1. Nonresistant bacteria

2. One cell mutates, giving it a gene that makes it resistant to the antibiotic.

Testing drugs

New drugs are continually being developed to help improve the treatment of disease. The process of development may take many years as each drug must be carefully tested to ensure it is both effective and safe to use.

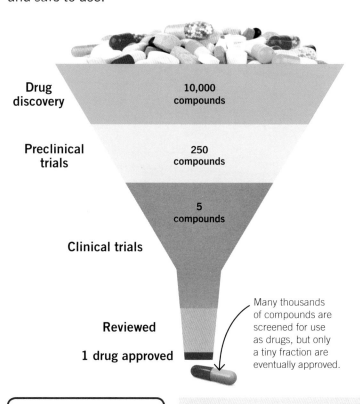

Drug discovery — 10,000 compounds

Preclinical trials — 250 compounds

5 compounds

Clinical trials

Reviewed

1 drug approved

Many thousands of compounds are screened for use as drugs, but only a tiny fraction are eventually approved.

Drug development

Drug development may involve modifying existing drugs so they work better, synthesizing new drugs chemically, or screening natural compounds extracted from plants or microorganisms. For example, the heart drug digitalis comes from the foxglove plant, and the antibiotic penicillin comes from *Penicillium* mold. New drugs may have harmful side-effects, so scientists may spend 10–15 years testing them before they are approved.

🔍 Clinical trials

Drug trials are usually performed on two groups of volunteers: one group, the test group, receives the drug, while the other, the control group, might receive a placebo (a tablet or injection with no drug). Researchers look for differences in responses of the two groups to figure out if the drug is working.

	Types of trial		
	Blind trial	**Double-blind trial**	**Open trial**
The volunteer knows if they are getting the drug or the placebo.	No This is to prevent the volunteer from being influenced by any prior knowledge.	No This is to prevent the volunteer from being influenced by any prior knowledge.	Yes This happens as a last resort when a blind or double-blind trial is not possible.
The researcher knows if the volunteer is getting the drug or the placebo.	Yes	No This is to prevent the researcher from sending out any signals about the nature of the treatment.	Yes

Pests and plants

Plants suffer from a wide range of diseases and pests, from fungal and viral infections to sap-sucking insects and leaf-eating caterpillars. Some plant pests also act as vectors, spreading diseases to plants just as mosquitoes transmit diseases to humans.

Spreading disease

Aphids are slow-moving insects that breed rapidly. They cause considerable damage to plants, weakening them by feeding off the sugary sap and infecting plant tissues with potentially fatal viruses. Aphid control on commercial crops—such as by using chemical pesticides or natural aphid predator—is an important factor in helping keep yields high.

Key facts

✓ By feeding on leaves and sap, pests weaken or even kill plants.

✓ Some pests are vectors of pathogens, spreading infectious diseases from plant to plant.

✓ Plant diseases can be identified by looking at symptoms such as stunted growth, spots on leaves, and the presence of pests, or by doing tests in a laboratory.

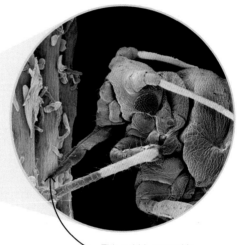

This aphid, seen with a scanning electron microscope, feeds on plant sap by inserting its sharp tubelike mouthpart (called a stylet) into the plant.

Aphids suck up to several times their own weight of sap every day.

Aphids

🔍 Diagnosing plant diseases

Plant diseases can often be identified by looking at symptoms, which include stunted growth, spots on leaves, discoloration, and the presence of pests. Scientists can also identify plant pathogens in the laboratory by looking at tissue under a microscope, by culturing microbes, or by using testing kits that contain monoclonal antibodies (see page 268). Shown here is the rod-shaped tobacco mosaic virus, which can damage a wide range of plants, including tomatoes, peppers, and tobacco.

Tobacco mosaic virus

Plant defenses

Plants lack the types of immune systems that are found in animals. Instead, they have their own ways of fighting harmful organisms. Many of these defenses are physical barriers, such as the protective bark of trees. Plants also have chemical defenses that deter plant eaters and help kill pests.

Key facts

- ✓ Bark on trees forms an effective defense barrier.
- ✓ Cellulose cell walls are made from tough fibers that are very difficult for animals to digest.
- ✓ Waxy cuticles on leaves protect plants from pathogens.
- ✓ Some plants produce distasteful or poisonous chemicals that deter plant-eating animals.

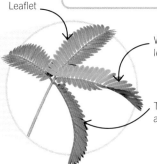

Leaflet

When touched, the leaflets start to fold.

The leaf droops and looks wilted.

Sensitive plant

One plant has evolved a way of avoiding attack by plant-eating animals. *Mimosa pudica*, also known as the sensitive plant, has leaflets that fold when they are touched. It takes only a few seconds for the entire leaf to fold. This helps dislodge plant-eating insects and makes the plant look less appetizing.

🔍 Nature's defenses

Bark
Plants with thick bark (an outer layer of dead cells) have an effective first line of defense against pathogens. Like your skin, bark acts as a physical barrier against harmful pathogens.

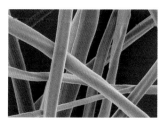

Cell walls
Plant cell walls are made from a tough carbohydrate called cellulose, which is very difficult for animals to digest. Plant eaters need special microorganisms in their stomachs or intestines to break down cellulose.

Cuticle and spines
The outermost layer (epidermis) of a plant has a waxy waterproof layer known as the cuticle. This covering makes it harder for pathogens to infect the plant. Many desert plants also have spines that deter animals.

Distasteful leaves
Some plants have bitter-tasting or poisonous chemicals and animals soon learn not to eat these plants again. For example, some clover plants release small amounts of cyanide that deter plant-eating animals.

Glossary

Abiotic factors The environmental conditions that affect an ecosystem, such as temperature, light level, and availability of water. Abiotic means nonliving.

Accurate A measurement taken in a science experiment is accurate if it is close to the true value being measured.

Acrosome A sac of digestive enzymes in the head of a sperm cell.

Active site The part of an enzyme molecule that substrate molecules bind to.

Active transport The transport of molecules across a cell membrane against the concentration gradient. Active transport requires energy from respiration.

Adaptation A feature of an organism that makes it better suited to its way of life. The streamlined shape of a dolphin, for instance, is an adaptation to living in water.

Adrenal gland A hormone-producing gland located on the kidney. The two adrenal glands produce the hormone adrenaline, which prepares the body for action.

Adrenaline A hormone that prepares the body for action during times of danger or excitement.

Aerobic respiration The transfer of energy from food molecules to living cells in the presence of oxygen.

Albumen The white of an egg, consisting of water and proteins that nourish the developing embryo.

Algae Simple, plantlike organisms that live in water and make their food by photosynthesis.

Allele One version of a gene that comes in several different variants.

Alveoli Tiny air pockets in the lungs where gases are exchanged between the air and bloodstream.

Amino acids The building blocks of protein molecules.

Amphibian A cold-blooded animal, such as a frog or newt, that spends part of its life in water and part on land.

Amylase An enzyme that digests the carbohydrate starch.

Anaerobic respiration The transfer of energy from food molecules to living cells in the absence of oxygen.

Antennae Sensitive feelers on the heads of insects or other invertebrates.

Antibiotic A drug that kills bacteria.

Antibodies Chemicals produced by the body's immune system that bind to specific target molecules (antigens) on bacteria or other foreign cells, helping the body destroy them.

Antidiuretic hormone (ADH) A hormone that helps the body conserve water by making the kidneys reabsorb water from the fluid that forms urine.

Antigen A cell surface molecule that an antibody binds to.

Antiseptic A chemical that kills pathogens such as bacteria but is not harmful to the human body.

Aquatic organism An organism that lives in water.

Arachnid An arthropod with eight legs, such as a spider or scorpion.

Artery A large, thick-walled blood vessel that carries blood away from the heart.

Arthropod An animal with an external skeleton and jointed legs. Insects, spiders, scorpions, and millipedes are all types of arthropods.

Aseptic technique A technique that helps prevent samples of microorganisms from becoming contaminated with unwanted microorganisms.

Asexual reproduction Reproduction by a single parent, resulting in offspring that are genetically identical to the parent.

Atrium (plural atria) One of the two upper chambers in the heart.

Auxin A plant hormone that controls the way shoots and roots grow in response to light or gravity.

Axis One of the two perpendicular lines showing measurements plotted on a graph.

Axon A long, thin fiber that carries outgoing nerve impulses in a neuron (nerve cell).

Bacteria Microscopic, single-celled organisms that are found in almost every kind of habitat on Earth, including on and inside the human body. Many bacteria are helpful but some cause disease.

Bill The jaws of a bird, also called a beak.

Biodiversity A measure of the variety of different species in a particular area (or a measure of the amount of genetic variation within a species).

Biomass The total mass of living organisms in a particular area or any biological material used as fuel.

Biome A major division of the living world, such as rain forest, desert, or temperate grassland. Each biome has its own distinctive climate, vegetation, and animal life.

Biotic factor Any biological influence on an ecosystem. Biotic factors include disease, food availability, the presence of predators and parasites, and relationships such as competition and mutualism.

Blind trial A clinical trial, such as a drug test, in which patients don't know whether they've received the real treatment or an ineffective substance (a placebo).

Blood A fluid that circulates through the bodies of animals delivering vital substances to cells and removing waste chemicals.

Bowman's capsule A cup-shaped sac that forms part of one of the million or so filtering units (nephrons) in a kidney.

Cancer A disease in which body cells divide and multiply abnormally, forming malignant growths called tumors.

Capillary The smallest type of blood vessel in the human body.

Carbohydrate An energy-rich substance found in food. Sugar and starch are types of carbohydrates.

Carbon dioxide A gas found in air. Animals and plants release carbon dioxide as a waste product, but plants also use it in photosynthesis.

Cardiac output The total volume of blood pumped by the left side of the heart per minute.

Cardiovascular disease A disease that affects the heart or blood vessels.

Carnivore A meat-eating animal with teeth shaped for tearing flesh.

Carrier A person who carries a gene for a genetic disorder but has no symptoms.

Cartilage A tough but flexible tissue found on the bones of animals. Cartilaginous fish have a skeleton made almost entirely of cartilage.

Catalyst A chemical that speeds up a chemical reaction without being changed itself.

Cell A tiny unit of living matter. Cells are the building blocks of all living things.

Cell division The process by which one cell splits to produce two cells, called daughter cells.

Cell membrane A very thin layer of molecules that forms an outer barrier around a cell's cytoplasm, controlling which substances enter or leave the cell.

Cell sap The liquid that fills a vacuole in a plant cell. Cell sap consists of water and various dissolved substances, such as sugars.

Cell wall A thick outer wall that surrounds and supports a plant cell. Microorganisms and fungi also have cell walls, but animals do not.

Cellulose A fibrous carbohydrate that forms the walls of plant cells.

Celsius A temperature scale based on the melting point of ice (0°C) and the boiling point of water (100°C), with 100 equal divisions, called degrees, between them.

Central nervous system (CNS) The control center of the nervous system, consisting of the brain and spinal cord.

Cerebral cortex The outer layer of the human brain.

Cerebral hemisphere One of the two roughly symmetrical left and right halves into which the outer part of the human brain (the cerebral cortex) is divided.

Cerebrum The main part of the human brain, responsible for voluntary actions, senses, body movement, personality, language, and other functions.

Chemical A pure element or compound. Water, iron, salt, and oxygen are all chemicals.

Chlorophyll A green substance in plants that absorbs energy from sunlight, allowing plants to make food by photosynthesis.

Chloroplasts Tiny structures in plant cells that contain the green pigment chlorophyll. Photosynthesis takes place in chloroplasts.

Chromosome A structure in the nucleus of a cell, made from coiled DNA strands, that carries genetic information.

Circulatory system The heart and blood vessels of an animal, which together form a transport system serving the whole body.

Climate The pattern of weather and seasons a place experiences in a typical year.

Climate change Long-term changes in Earth's weather patterns.

Clone An organism with exactly the same genes as its parent.

Clinical trial A scientific experiment carried out to test whether a medical treatment, such as a new drug, is effective in humans.

Codominance When two alleles of a gene are codominant, both affect the organism and neither is dominant or recessive.

Color blindness A visual disorder that makes it difficult for a person to tell the difference between certain colors.

Communicable disease A disease that can spread from one person to another. *See also* transmissible disease.

Community All the organisms that share an environment. An ecosystem is made up of a community of organisms and their shared physical environment.

Competition An interaction between organisms or species that need the same resource, resulting in conflict or harm.

Compound A chemical consisting of two or more elements whose atoms have bonded.

Concentration A measure of the amount of solute dissolved in a solution.

Concentration gradient The difference between the concentration of a substance in one area and its concentration in another area. A large (steep) concentration gradient results in a fast rate of diffusion.

Condensation The change of a gas into a liquid.

Conservation Protection of wildlife or habitats.

Continuous data Numerical data that can include any value within a range. Examples of continuous measurements include the height or weight of people. *See also* discrete data.

Contraceptive A device or drug that prevents a woman from becoming pregnant.

Control variable A variable that is kept constant in an experiment.

Coral A small marine animal that catches food with stinging tentacles. Coral reefs form from the skeletons of corals that live in colonies.

Cornea The curved, transparent front part of the eye. The cornea helps focus light entering the eye.

Crustacean An invertebrate with a hard exoskeleton, gills, and usually more than 10 pairs of limbs, such as a shrimp or lobster. Most crustaceans live in water.

Cuticle A waxy, waterproof layer on a leaf that reduces water loss.

Cytoplasm The jellylike interior of a cell.

Data A collection of information, such as facts and statistics.

Decompose Break down into simpler chemicals. Dead organisms decompose (decay) because smaller organisms feed on their remains, digesting their tissue.

Decomposer An organism that feeds on dead organic matter, causing it to decompose.

Denature Change the shape of a protein. When enzymes are denatured by heat or acidity, they no longer function.

Deoxygenated blood Blood that is low in oxygen.

Dependent variable The variable in an experiment that is measured to obtain the experiment's results.

Desalination Removal of salt from water.

Diabetes A medical condition in which the body's systems for controlling glucose in the blood stop working properly.

Dialysis An artificial way of cleaning the blood of a person whose kidneys have stopped working.

Diffusion The gradual mixing of two or more substances as a result of the random movement of their particles.

Digestion Breaking down food into small molecules so that it can be absorbed by cells.

Dilate Widen.

Diploid Containing two sets of chromosomes. Most human body cells are diploid because they contain a set of chromosomes inherited from the person's mother and a set from the father.

Discrete data Numerical data that can take only certain values, such as whole numbers. An example of discrete data is the number of chicks in a nest. *See also* continuous data.

Diversity A term to describe the variety of different species.

DNA Deoxyribonucleic acid, the chemical that stores genetic information inside living cells.

Dominant An allele (version of a gene) that is always expressed.

Double-blind trial A clinical trial in which neither the patients nor the researchers know who has received the real drug and who has received an ineffective substance (a placebo).

Drought A long period of low rainfall resulting in a lack of water and very dry conditions.

Drug A chemical taken into the body in order to alter the way the body works. Most drugs are taken to treat or prevent disease.

Ecology The scientific study of interactions between organisms and between organisms and their environment.

Ecosystem A community of animals and plants and the physical environment that they share.

Effector A muscle or gland that responds to a nerve impulse. Effectors make animals respond to stimuli.

Egg The protective capsule that contains a developing baby bird, reptile, or other animal. The word egg can also mean egg cell (a female sex cell).

Egg cell A female sex cell, also called an ovum (plural ova).

Egg tooth A hard lump on the beak or jaw of a baby bird or reptile, used to break the shell when it hatches.

Embryo The earliest stage in the development of an animal or plant.

Emulsify Form an emulsion.

Emulsion A mixture in which one liquid is spread out as tiny droplets in another liquid.

Endocrine gland A gland in the human body that produces and secretes hormones.

Endothermic reaction A chemical reaction that takes in energy, usually in the form of heat. *See also* exothermic reaction.

Enzyme A protein made by living cells that speeds up a chemical reaction.

Epidemic The very rapid spread of an infectious disease through a population, typically in a few weeks.

Epiphyte A plant that grows on another plant as a means of support.

Estrogen A hormone produced by the ovaries of female animals. Estrogen helps control sexual development and fertility.

Ethene A gas produced by plants as a hormone that triggers the ripening of fruit.

Eukaryote An organism whose cells contain a nucleus and membrane-bound organelles. Animals, plants, and fungi are eukaryotes.

Eutrophication Excessive growth of algae in water enriched with nutrients, causing oxygen levels in the water to fall. Eutrophication is often caused by pollution.

Evaporation Change from liquid to gas.

Evolution The gradual change of a population or species as it adapts to its environment by the process of natural selection.

Exchange surface A part of an organism specialized to absorb vital substances or get rid of waste chemicals, often by diffusion. Exchange surfaces have a large surface area.

Exoskeleton A hard outer skeleton, such as that of an insect.

Exothermic reaction A chemical reaction that transfers energy to the surroundings, often in the form of heat.

Extinct Permanently gone. An extinct species no longer has any living members.

Farsightedness A visual defect in which nearby objects appear blurred.

Fertile Able to reproduce.

Fertilization The joining of male and female sex cells to produce a new living thing. Fertilization can also mean to add fertilizer to soil, which helps plants grow.

Fertilizer A nutrient-rich substance added to soil to stimulate the growth of plants.

Fetus The unborn young of an animal.

Flagellum A whiplike growth on a cell that either rotates or lashes back and forth to make the cell move.

Fluid A substance that can flow, such as a gas or liquid.

Follicle-stimulating hormone (FSH) A hormone that stimulates the maturation of egg cells in the ovaries of female mammals.

Food chain A series of organisms, each of which is eaten by the next.

Food security Access to a dependable supply of food that is sufficiently nutritious to keep people healthy.

Food web The interlinked system of food chains in an ecosystem.

Formula A chemical formula shows the proportions of atoms in a chemical compound. A mathematical formula is a rule or relationship written with mathematical symbols.

Fossil The remains or impression of a prehistoric plant or animal, often preserved in rock.

Fossil fuel A fuel derived from the fossilized remains of living things. Coal, crude oil, and natural gas are fossil fuels.

Freezing point The temperature at which a liquid turns into a solid.

Fruit The ripened ovary of a flower, containing one or more seeds. Some fruits are sweet and juicy to attract animals.

Fungus A living thing that absorbs food from living or dead matter around it. Mushrooms and toadstools are fungi.

Gamete A sex cell, such as a sperm or egg cell.

Gene An instruction encoded in the molecule DNA and stored inside a living cell. Genes are passed from parents to their offspring and determine each living thing's inherited characteristics.

Gene pool The complete set of genes in a population, including all the different alleles (variants of genes).

Genetic engineering The use of scientific techniques to alter the genes in a cell or an organism, for instance by transferring genes from one species to another.

Genetically modified (GM) organism An organism whose genome has been altered by genetic engineering. Many GM organisms contain genes transferred from other species.

Genome The complete set of genes in an organism.

Genotype The combination of alleles that determines a particular characteristic (phenotype) of an organism.

Germination The growth of a small plant from a seed.

Gibberellins Plant hormones that trigger the end of dormancy in seeds and flower buds.

Gill An organ used to breathe underwater.

Gland An organ in an animal's body that makes and releases a particular substance. Human sweat glands, for instance, release sweat onto the skin.

Global warming A rise in the average temperature of Earth's atmosphere, caused partly by rising levels of carbon dioxide from burning fossil fuels.

Glomerulus A small cluster of blood vessels at the start of one of the kidney's microscopic filtering units.

Glucagon A hormone that causes the liver to convert stored glycogen into glucose, raising blood glucose levels.

Glycogen A carbohydrate made by the liver from glucose and stored in the liver.

Gravitropism Growth of a plant in response to gravity. Roots, for example, are usually positively gravitropic, making them grow downward.

Guard cells Paired cells on the surface of leaves that can change shape to open and close tiny pores called stomata.

Habitat The place where an organism lives.

Haploid Containing a single set of unpaired chromosomes (half the number of chromosomes found in normal body cells). Sex cells are haploid.

Health The physical condition of an organism. Being healthy means being free of illnesses.

Hemoglobin A compound in red blood cells that carries oxygen around an animal's body.

Herd immunity The protection from disease that individuals benefit from when a large proportion of the population is immune, preventing infections from spreading.

Heart rate The speed of a person's heartbeat in beats per minute.

Herbivore An animal that eats plants.

Heterozygous Having two different alleles (variants) of a gene.

Homeostasis The maintenance of a constant environment inside an organism's body.

Homozygous Having two identical alleles (variants) of a gene.

Hormone A chemical produced by a gland in the body that travels through the blood and changes the way certain target organs work, often with powerful effects.

Host A living organism on which a parasite feeds.

Hybridoma A cell made in a laboratory by fusing an antibody-making cell with a tumor cell. Hybridomas multiply quickly, making them useful for producing large quantities of antibodies.

Hydroponics A method of growing plants in nutrient-rich water instead of soil.

Hypothalamus A small part of the brain that helps control body temperature, water balance, hunger, and sleep, among other functions.

Hypothesis A scientific idea that is tested by an experiment.

Immune system The collection of organs, tissues, and cells that protect the human body from infectious diseases.

Immunity The ability of an organism to resist an infectious disease.

Immunize Make a person immune to a disease, for instance by vaccination.

Inbreeding Breeding between closely related organisms. Inbreeding increases the frequency of homozygous genotypes, making genetic defects caused by recessive genes more likely to occur.

Incubate Keep warm. For example, birds incubate their eggs by sitting on them.

Independent variable The variable in an experiment that is deliberately changed.

Insulation Reduction of heat loss by a body layer such as fur, blubber, or feathers.

Insulin A hormone that lowers the level of glucose in the blood.

Intensive farming A type of farming that attempts to maximize food production and profits, for instance, by using machinery or chemical fertilizers and pesticides.

Interdependence The dependence of different organisms in an ecosystem on each other.

Intestine A tubelike organ through which food passes while it is being digested.

Invertebrate An animal without a backbone, such as an insect or worm.

Iris A colored ring of muscle around the pupil of an animal's eye. The iris controls the size of the pupil and therefore how much light enters the eye.

Keratin The tough protein that fur, hair, feathers, nails, horns, and hooves are made of. The outer layer of an animal's skin is toughened by keratin.

Lactic acid A chemical produced as a waste product in muscles when anaerobic respiration takes place during strenuous exercise.

Larva The early stage in the life cycle of an animal that undergoes metamorphosis when it develops into an adult.

Lens A curved, transparent object that bends light rays to produce a sharp image inside the eye, a camera, a microscope, or a telescope.

Limiting factor (in photosynthesis) Light intensity, carbon dioxide level, and temperature are all described as limiting factors because a drop in any of these can reduce the rate of photosynthesis in a plant.

Line of best fit A line drawn through scattered points on a graph so that about half of the points lie above the line and half lie below it.

Lipase An enzyme that digests fat molecules.

Lipids The scientific name for fats and oils. Lipid molecules are made of three fatty acid units and a glycerol unit.

Luteinizing hormone (LH) A hormone that triggers the release of eggs from the ovaries in a woman's body.

Lymphocyte A type of white blood cell that can make antibodies.

Lysogenic pathway One of the two main ways viruses reproduce. In the lysogenic pathway, the virus's genes become incorporated into the host's DNA, causing copies of the viral genome to be made whenever the host cell divides.

Lytic pathway One of the two main ways in which viruses reproduce. During the lytic cycle, the virus hijacks the cell's enzymes and proteins to make copies of the virus, which then burst out of the cell and destroy it.

Magnification How enlarged an object is when viewed through a microscope.

Mammal A warm-blooded vertebrate (animal with a backbone) that feeds its young on milk and usually has a covering of fur.

Marsupial A mammal that gives birth to very undeveloped young and that usually carries babies in a pouch.

Mass The amount of matter in an object.

Mating Close physical contact between male and female animals that allows their sex cells to fuse and form an embryo.

Matter Anything that has mass and occupies space.

Mean (average) A measure of average found by adding up a set of values and dividing by the number of values.

Median (average) A measure of average found by arranging a set of values in order of size and then selecting the middle one.

Meiosis A type of cell division that produces sex cells, which have half of the usual number of chromosomes.

Membrane A thin lining or barrier. Cells are surrounded by membranes that stop some substances from passing through but allow others to cross.

Memory cell A type of white blood cell that gives the body immunity to disease by "remembering" how to recognize pathogens encountered in the past.

Menstrual cycle A monthly cycle of changes that take place in a woman's body, preparing her for a possible pregnancy.

Menstruation The monthly bleeding that takes place as a woman's uterus sheds its lining as part of the menstrual cycle.

Meristem Tissue found in the growing parts of plants. Meristems contain stem cells, which have the ability to grow and produce many different kinds of plant tissues.

Metabolic rate The rate at which the human body uses energy.

Metamorphosis A dramatic change in the body of an animal as it matures. Caterpillars turn into butterflies by metamorphosis.

Microorganism A tiny organism that can be seen only with the aid of a microscope.

Microscope A scientific instrument that uses lenses to make small objects appear larger.

Migration A long journey undertaken by an animal to reach a new habitat. Many birds migrate every year between their summer and winter homes.

Mineral A naturally occurring inorganic chemical such as salt, often found in rocks or dissolved in water. Some minerals are essential to life.

Mitochondria Structures inside cells that play a key role in respiration by transferring energy from sugar molecules to the cell.

Mitosis A type of cell division that produces two genetically identical cells.

Mode (average) The most common value in a set of numbers.

Model (scientific) A simplified representation of a real object or system that helps scientists understand how the object or system works in the real world.

Molecule A group of two or more atoms joined by strong chemical bonds.

Mollusc A soft-bodied invertebrate that is often protected by a hard shell. Snails, clams, and octopuses are molluscs.

Molt Shed skin, hair, or feathers. Animals with exoskeletons must moult occasionally in order to grow larger.

Monoclonal antibodies Antibodies produced in a laboratory from clones of white blood cells. They target a specific antigen and are used for diagnosis or to treat particular diseases.

Monoculture A method of farming that involves growing a single crop, often over a large area.

Monotreme An egg-laying mammal. Platypuses and echidnas are the only types of monotremes.

Motor neuron A nerve cell that carries signals from the central nervous system to muscles or glands.

Mucus A thick, slippery liquid produced by animals for various purposes. For example, mucus lines the intestines, helping food move through them.

Muscle A type of animal tissue that contracts to cause movement.

Mutualism A type of relationship between two species in which both benefit.

Mycelium The main body of a fungus, consisting of a tangle of threads usually concealed underground or in wood.

Natural selection The process whereby genes that help a particular individual in a species to survive are more likely to be passed on to the next generation, causing the species to evolve.

Nearsightedness A visual defect in which distant objects appear blurred.

Nectar A sugary liquid produced by flowers to attract pollinators. Bees use it to make honey.

Negative feedback A control system in the body that responds to a rise or fall in the level of something by reversing the change. Negative feedback systems help maintain ideal conditions in the body.

Nephron One of the kidney's microscopic filtering units. It filters waste chemicals from blood and gets rid of them as urine.

Nerve A bundle of nerve cells carrying electrical impulses through the body of an animal.

Neuron A nerve cell.

Neurotransmitter A chemical that is released into a synapse by a nerve cell and transmits a signal to the next nerve cell.

Nitrate A chemical compound that includes the elements nitrogen and oxygen. Nitrates are used as fertilizers on crop plants.

Nitrifying bacteria Bacteria that convert ammonia in the soil into nitrates.

Nitrogen-fixing bacteria Bacteria that take nitrogen from the air and convert it into chemical compounds that plants can use.

Nocturnal Active at night.

Noncommunicable disease A disease that cannot spread from one person to another. Also called a nontransmissible disease.

Nucleus The control center of a cell, where the cell's genes are stored in DNA molecules. The word "nucleus" can also refer to the central part of an atom.

Nutrients Substances that animals and plants take in and that are essential for life and growth.

Obesity A medical condition in which excessive body fat can have harmful effects on health.

Omnivore An animal that eats both plants and animals.

Organ A group of tissues working together to perform a function. Organs in the human body include the stomach, brain, and heart.

Organelle A structure inside a cell that performs a specific job, such as making protein molecules or releasing energy from sugar.

Organic Derived from living organisms or a compound based on carbon and hydrogen atoms.

Organic farming Farming that minimizes harm to the natural environment, for instance, by avoiding the use of artificial fertilizers and pesticides.

Organism A living thing.

Osmosis The movement of water through a cell membrane (or other partially permeable membrane) from a weak solution to a strong one.

Ovary An organ in a female animal that produces egg cells, or the part of a flower that contains developing seeds.

Ovulation The release of an unfertilized egg from the ovary of a female animal. The egg is then available to be fertilized by male sperm.

Ovum (plural ova) *See* egg cell.

Oxygen A gas that makes up 21 percent of air. Most living things take in oxygen from the air and use it to transfer energy from food in a process called respiration.

Oxygen debt The amount of oxygen required to remove the lactic acid produced when muscle cells respire anaerobically.

Oxygenated blood Blood that is rich in oxygen.

Palisade cell A type of plant cell found in a layer near the surface of a leaf. Palisade cells are specialized for photosynthesis and contain many chloroplasts.

Pancreas An organ near the stomach that secretes digestive juices and hormones including insulin.

Paralyse Stop from moving.

Parasite An organism that lives on or inside another organism (a host) and feeds on it. Parasites are harmful to their hosts.

Partially permeable Allows some substances to pass through but blocks others. Cell membranes are partially permeable.

Particle A tiny bit of matter, such an atom, molecule, or ion.

Pathogen Any microscopic living thing that causes disease. Also called a germ.

Permafrost Permanently frozen ground below the upper surface of the soil.

Pesticide A substance used to kill pests such as insects.

pH A scale used to measure how acidic or alkaline a solution is.

Phagocyte A cell that swallows and digests bacteria and parts of broken cells.

Phagocytosis The process by which a cell surrounds and engulfs other particles, such as bacteria.

Phenotype A particular characteristic of an organism controlled by genes, such as the color of an animal's fur.

Phloem A type of tissue in plants made up of vessels that carry food from leaves, where food is made, to other parts of the plant.

Photosynthesis The process by which plants use the sun's energy to make food molecules from water and carbon dioxide, producing oxygen as a waste product.

Phototropism Growth of a plant in response to light. Positive phototropism means growing toward the light.

Pituitary gland A hormone-secreting gland (endocrine gland) located at the base of the brain. Also known as the "master gland," it produces various hormones, some of which control other endocrine glands in the body.

Placebo A substance given like a medicine but which has no medical properties and so no physical effects on a patient. Placebos are compared to real drugs in drug trials.

Placenta An organ in mammals that allows substances to pass between the bloodstream of an unborn baby and that of its mother.

Plankton Tiny organisms that live near the surface of oceans and lakes.

Plasma The fluid left after blood cells have been removed from blood.

Plasmid A loop of DNA found in bacteria, separate from their main chromosome.

Platelets Fragments of cells that circulate in the blood and help it clot after injury.

Pollen A powdery substance made by flowers that contains male sex cells. Insects carry pollen from one flower to another, helping plants reproduce.

Pollination The transfer of pollen from the male part of a flower to the female part of a flower. Pollination is essential for sexual reproduction in flowering plants.

Polymer A carbon compound with long, chainlike molecules made of repeating units. Plastics are examples of polymers.

Population A group of individuals of the same species that live in the same area and usually interbreed with each other.

Pore A small opening on the outside of an organism that allows substances such as gases and liquids to pass through it.

Preclinical trial A drug test carried out using animals or cultured cells before the drug is tested on humans.

Predation Capturing and eating other animals.

Predator An animal that hunts other animals for food.

Prey An animal hunted by other animals.

Primary consumer An animal that eats producer organisms such as plants, but not other animals.

Producer An organism such as a green plant that makes its own food by photosynthesis instead of taking it from other living things.

Progesterone A hormone in female mammals that makes the uterus (womb) ready to support pregnancy.

Prokaryote An organism such as a bacterium whose cells are tiny and have no nucleus.

Protease An enzyme that digests proteins.

Protein An organic substance that contains nitrogen and is found in foods such as meat, fish, cheese, and beans. Organisms need proteins for growth and repair.

Protoctists Simple organisms that have eukaryotic cells and are usually single-celled and microscopic. They include many disease-causing organisms as well as algae and amoebas.

Pulmonary artery The artery that carries blood from the heart to the lungs to be replenished with oxygen.

Pulmonary vein The vein that carries newly oxygenated blood from the lungs back to the heart.

Pupa The resting stage in the life cycle of an insect that undergoes metamorphosis.

Pupil The circular opening in the center of the eye's iris through which light enters the eye.

Quadrat A square frame used to count or sample species in their natural habitat.

Radiation An electromagnetic wave or a stream of particles from a source of radioactivity.

Reagent A chemical used to test for the presence of another chemical by making a chemical reaction occur.

Receptor A molecule, cell, or organ that detects a stimulus. Light receptor cells in animals' eyes, for example, detect light and so create the sense of vision.

Recessive An allele (version of a gene) that has an effect on an organism only when there is no dominant allele to suppress it.

Red blood cell A blood cell that carries oxygen.

Reflex An automatic reaction of nerves and muscles to a stimulus, without conscious thought.

Reflex arc The pathway taken through the nerves during a reflex action.

Relay neuron A nerve cell that receives a stimulus from a sensory neuron and passes it on to a motor neuron.

Renewable energy A source of energy that will not run out, such as sunlight or wind power.

Reproduction The production of new offspring.

Reptile A cold-blooded, scaly-skinned vertebrate (animal with a backbone). Reptiles include snakes and lizards.

Respiration The process by which living cells transfer energy from food molecules.

Retina A layer of light-sensitive cells lining the inside of an eye.

Ribosome A tiny structure found inside cells. Ribosomes are the site of protein synthesis.

RNA Ribonucleic acid, a molecule similar to DNA. RNA molecules copy the genetic information in DNA so that it can be used to make protein molecules.

Root The part of a plant that anchors it to the ground and obtains water and nutrients from the soil.

Scavenger An animal that feeds on the remains of dead animals or plants. Vultures are scavengers.

Secondary consumer A predatory animal that eats primary consumers.

Secretion A substance made and released (secreted) by cells.

Seed A reproductive structure containing a plant embryo and a food store.

Selective breeding Selecting individuals within a population that have particular characteristics useful to people, and breeding from them so that later generations are improved.

Sensory neuron A nerve cell that detects stimuli in the environment and passes the information on to the central nervous system in the form of electrical impulses.

Sensory receptor A structure in the body that detects stimuli and responds by generating nerve impulses.

Sex cell A reproductive cell, such as a sperm cell or egg cell. Also called a gamete.

Sex chromosomes A pair of chromosomes that determine the sex of many animals, including humans.

Sex-linked disorder A disorder or disease that is linked to an individual's sex, usually because of genes carried by a sex chromosome.

Sexual reproduction Reproduction that involves the combination of sex cells from two parents.

Sexually transmitted infection An infection that is passed on from one person to another during sexual intercourse.

SI units The standard set of units for measuring in science, including the meter, kilogram, and second.

Skeleton A flexible frame that supports an animal's body.

Solute A substance that dissolves in a solvent to form a solution.

Solution A mixture in which the molecules or ions of a solute are evenly spread out among the molecules of a solvent.

Solvent A substance (usually a liquid) in which a solute dissolves to form a solution.

Species A group of organisms with similar characteristics that can breed with each other to produce fertile offspring.

Sperm cell A male sex cell.

Spore A microscopic package of cells, produced by a fungus or plant, that can grow into a new individual.

Starch A carbohydrate made of chains of glucose molecules. Plants produce starch to store energy.

Statins Drugs that lower the amount of harmful cholesterol in the bloodstream.

Stem cell An unspecialized cell that can divide and create specialized types of cells.

Stimulus Any change in the environment that produces a response from an organism.

Stoma (plural stomata) A tiny hole in the surface of a leaf that can close to regulate the movement of gases into and out of the leaf.

Stroke A dangerous medical condition in which blood flow to part of the brain stops, causing brain cells to die. The symptoms can include paralysis on one side of the body.

Sugar A carbohydrate with a small molecule. Sugars taste sweet.

Symbiosis A close relationship between two different species that live together.

Synapse A gap between two nerve cells where signals are passed from one cell to the next.

Temperature A measure of how hot or cold something is.

Terrestrial Living on the ground.

Testis (plural testes) The organ in male animals that produces sperm cells and the hormone testosterone.

Testosterone The main sex hormone in male animals. Testosterone triggers the development of male characteristics and behavior.

Theory A well-established scientific idea that explains some aspect of the real world and has been tested by experiments.

Thorax The central part of an insect's body or the chest of a vertebrate.

Thyroid gland A hormone-secreting gland in the human throat.

Thyroxine A hormone that helps control the body's metabolic rate.

Tissue A group of similar cells that make up part of an animal or plant. Muscle and fat are types of tissues.

Transcription The copying of DNA to RNA inside a cell. Transcription is the first stage of protein synthesis.

Transect A straight line marked across a habitat to help a scientist survey the species present.

Translation The construction of a protein molecule, using an RNA molecule to determine the order of amino acids in the protein.

Translocation The movement of food molecules and other dissolved substances around a plant.

Transmissible disease *See* communicable disease

Transpiration The loss of water from a plant, mainly due to evaporation from its leaves. It is replaced by water drawn up from the roots.

Transpiration stream The upward movement of water from the roots to all parts of a plant.

Trophic level The position of an organism in a food chain. Examples of trophic levels include producer and secondary consumer.

Tumor An abnormal growth of tissue in the body. Tumors are sometimes cancerous.

Type 1 diabetes A type of diabetes in which the pancreas stops producing insulin. Type 1 diabetes usually starts in childhood.

Type 2 diabetes A type of diabetes in which the body's cells do not respond normally to insulin. Type 2 diabetes usually starts in adulthood.

Umbilical cord A cordlike structure that carries food, oxygen, and other substances between an unborn baby mammal and its mother's body.

Urea A waste product that contains nitrogen and is excreted in urine.

Uterus An organ that contains and nourishes developing babies in female mammals.

Vaccine A substance containing weakened or dead pathogens that stimulates the production of antibodies in a person's body, making the person immune to the pathogens.

Vacuole A fluid-filled structure in a cell surrounded by a membrane. Plant cells typically have a very large vacuole that helps keep the cell plump and soft tissues in the plant upright.

Valve A structure in the heart or in veins that allows blood to flow in one direction.

Variation The differences between individuals in a species. It can be caused by genes, the environment, or both.

Vector An organism that transmits a disease. For example, the mosquito that transmits the malaria parasite to humans is a vector.

Vein A tube that carries blood from body tissues to the heart.

Vena cava Either of the two main veins that bring deoxygenated blood back from the tissues to the heart.

Ventricle Either of the heart's two main pumping chambers. The right ventricle pumps blood to the lungs, and the left ventricle pumps blood to the rest of the body. Fluid-filled structures in the brain are also called ventricles.

Vertebra One of many small bones that form the backbone (vertebral column) of a vertebrate.

Vertebrate An animal with a backbone.

Vibration Rapid to-and-fro movement.

Virus A tiny parasite. Viruses reproduce by infecting cells and making them manufacture copies of the virus.

Volume A measure of the amount of space that something takes up.

Warm-blooded Warm-blooded animals, such as birds and mammals, maintain a constant internal body temperature.

Weight The force with which a mass is pulled toward Earth.

White blood cell Any of several kinds of blood cells that fight disease.

Womb *See* uterus.

x-axis The horizontal axis of a graph.

X-ray A type of electromagnetic radiation used to create images of bones and teeth.

Xylem A type of plant tissue made up of vessels that carry water and minerals from the roots to the leaves and other structures.

y-axis The vertical axis of a graph.

Yield How much of a crop is produced.

Yolk The inner, yellow part of an egg. Yolk is rich in protein and fat to nourish the developing embryo.

Zygote A cell formed from the fusion of two gametes, from which a new individual will grow.

Index

Acknowledgments

The publisher would like to thank the following people for their help with making the book: Shatarupa Chaudhuri, Virien Chopra, Derek Harvey, Cecile Landau, Sai Prasanna, and Shambhavi Thatte for editorial assistance; Victoria Pyke for proofreading; Helen Peters for the index; Gary Ombler for photography; Neetika Malik (Lbk Incorporation), Baibhav Parida, and Arun Pottirayil for illustrations; Mrinmoy Mazumdar and Vikram Singh for CTS assistance; Aditya Katyal for picture research assistance; and Priyanka Bansal, Rakesh Kumar, Priyanka Sharma, and Saloni Singh for the jacket.

Smithsonian Enterprises:
Kealy E. Gordon, Product Development Manager; Ellen Nanney, Senior Manager Licensed Publishing; Jill Corcoran, Director, Licensed Publishing Sales; Brigid Ferraro, Vice President, Education and Consumer Products; Carol LeBlanc, President

The publisher would like to thank the following for their kind permission to reproduce their photographs:
(Key: a-above; b-below/bottom; c-center; f-far; l-left; r-right; t-top)

4 Science Photo Library: Steve Gschmeissner (br). **10 Alamy Stock Photo:** Alan Novelli (cra). **Dreamstime.com:** Kazakovmaksim (br); Standret (cr). **11 Dorling Kindersley:** Andy Crawford / Royal Tyrrell Museum of Palaeontology, Alberta, Canada (br). **Dreamstime.com:** Kazakovmaksim (tc). **Shutterstock:** PolyPloiid (crb). **12 123RF.com:** destinacigdem (fcl). **Dreamstime.com:** Mohammed Anwarul Kabir Choudhury (c). **Shutterstock:** Boxyray (cl). **13 123RF.com:** destinacigdem (cr). **14 NASA:** (crb). **15 Alamy Stock Photo:** Stockr (cr). **16 Science Photo Library:** Francesco Zerilli / Zerillimedia (c). **17 Dreamstime.com:** Tatiana Neelova (plants). **20 Alamy Stock Photo:** Ann Ronan Picture Library / Heritage-Images / The Print Collector (ca); Photo Researchers / Science History Images (cl). **Dorling Kindersley:** Dave King / The Science Museum, London (bl); Dave King / Science Museum, London (bc); Gary Ombler / Whipple Museum of History of Science, Cambridge (cra). **Wellcome Collection** creativecommons.org/licenses/by/4.0: (br). **21 Alamy Stock Photo:** Scott Camazine (bl); Interfoto / Personalities (cr); Steve Gschmeissner & Keith Chambers / Science Photo Library (tr); Science Photo Library / Steve Gschmeissner (tc). **Science Photo Library:** CDC (br). **Wellcome Collection** creativecommons.org/licenses/by/4.0: Wellcome Collection (cl). **23 Alamy Stock Photo:** Dorling Kindersley ltd (bl); sciencephotos (clb). **Dorling Kindersley:** Dave King / Science Museum, London (cl). **Dreamstime.com:** Ggw1962 (cra). **25 Alamy Stock Photo:** Wong Hock weng (c). **Science Photo Library:** Kateryna Kon (br). **26 Alamy Stock Photo:** Science Photo Library (cra); Tom Viggars (fcla). **Dreamstime.com:** Andamanse (cla); Rhamm1 (fcrb); Vasyl Helevachuk (crb); Xunbin Pan / Defun (c); Dragoneye (cb/Antelope). **iStockphoto.com:** micro_photo (ca); PrinPrince (fclb). **27 Alamy Stock Photo:** Niall Benvie (cr); Steve Gschmeissner / Science Photo Library (crb/Bacteria yeast). **iStockphoto.com:** micro_photo (crb/Amoeba). **28 Alamy Stock Photo:** Pixologicstudio / Science Photo Library (crb). **30 Alamy Stock Photo:** Larry Geddis (br/background); Martin Harvey (crb); Chris Mattison (clb). **Dreamstime.com:** Nejron (ca); Carlos Romero Oreja (cb). **31 123RF.com:** Tim Hester / timhester (cl). **Alamy Stock Photo:** blickwinkel / B. Trapp (c); Don Mammoser (br). **Dreamstime.com:** Olga Demchishina / Olgysha (cr). **32 Alamy Stock Photo:** William Brooks (bl); Wildlife Gmbh (clb). **Dreamstime.com:** Alisali (bc). **Getty Images:** Paul Starosta / Corbis (cr). **123RF.com:** Thawat Tanhai (br). **Alamy Stock Photo:** Wildlife Gmbh (bc). **Dorling Kindersley:** Richard Leeney / Whipsnade Zoo (c). **Dreamstime.com:** Adogslifephoto (crb). **iStockphoto.com:** marrio31 (cb). **38 iStockphoto.com:** micro_photo (c). **40 Alamy Stock Photo:** Inga Spence (cr). **Dreamstime.com:** Elena Schweitzer / Egal (c). **Science Photo Library:** Wim Van Egmond (br). **41 Science Photo Library:** Michael Abbey (crb). **42 Alamy Stock Photo:** Kateryna Kon / Science Photo Library. **43 iStockphoto.com:** ELyrae (br). **44 Science Photo Library:** Steve Gschmeissner (c). **46 Science Photo Library:** Tim Vernon (c). **47 Science Photo Library:** CNRI (c). **48 Dreamstime.com:** Ggw1962 (bl). **49 Science Photo Library:** CNRI (c). **52 Science Photo Library**. **53 Alamy Stock Photo:** Nigel Cattlin (l/plant). **56 Science Photo Library:** (c); Microfield Scientific Ltd (br). **58 Science Photo Library:** Eye Of Science (cr). **60 Alamy Stock Photo:** blickwinkel (crb). **Dreamstime.com:** Twildlife (c). **naturepl.com:** Stefan Christmann (clb). **61 123RF.com:** foxterrier2005 (bl). **Dreamstime.com:** Scooperdigital (cr); Darius Strazdas (cl). **SuperStock:** Eye Ubiquitous (tc). **63 Science Photo Library:** National Institute On Aging / NIH (c). **71 Dreamstime.com:** Horiyan (c). **76 iStockphoto.com:** E+ / Andy445 (l). **Science Photo Library:** John Durham (cr). **78 Dreamstime.com:** Threeart (clb). **Science Photo Library:** AMI Images (c). **79 Dreamstime.com:** Ksushsh (cb). **80 Alamy Stock Photo:** Nigel Cattlin (fcra, fcr, fbr). **Dreamstime.com:** Alexan24 (br); Lantapix (cra); Le Thuy Do (cr); Pranee Tiangkate (crb). **Science Photo Library:** Nigel Cattlin (fcrb). **81 Alamy Stock Photo:** Arterra Picture Library / van der Meer Marica (cr). **Dreamstime.com:** Aleksandr Frolov (br). **89 Dreamstime.com:** Dutchscenery (cb). **91 123RF.com:** belchonock (crb). **Alamy Stock Photo:** D. Hurst (ca). **Dreamstime.com:** Ivan Kovbasniuk (clb); Pogonici (c/yoghurt); Splosh (clb/cereal). **iStockphoto.com:** Coprid (cra). **92 Dreamstime.com:** Yulia Davidovich (c). **94 Science Photo Library:** Maximilian Stock Ltd. **105 Science Photo Library:** (br). **106 Alamy Stock Photo:** Scenics & Science (bl). **Getty Images:** DR Jeremy Burgess / Science Photo Library (cl). **Science Photo Library:** Eye Of Science (cr); Steve Gschmeissner (br). **117 Dreamstime.com:** Chernetskaya (br). **120 Science Photo Library:** CNRI (cl). **123 Gross, L., Beals, M., Harrell, S. (2019).:** Lung Capacity and Rhythms in Breathing. Quantitative Biology at Community Colleges, QUBES Educational Resources. doi:10.25334 / Q4DX6N (c). **125 Alamy Stock Photo:** John Gooday (br). **126 Science Photo Library:** Pixologicstudio (r). **132 Science Photo Library:** ZEPHYR (c). **145 Dreamstime.com:** Dml5050 (cl). **153 Science Photo Library:** Maurizio De Angelis (c). **154 Alamy Stock Photo:** Image Source / Herbert Spichtinger (br). **157 Depositphotos Inc:** exopixel (c). **160 Science Photo Library:** Eye Of Science (c). **161 Science Photo Library:** London School Of Hygiene & Tropical Medicine (c). **165 123RF.com:** olegdudko (c). **168 123RF.com:** Noppharat Manakul (cr). **Science Photo Library:** Power And Syred (c). **170 Dreamstime.com:** Rudmer Zwerver / Creativenature1 (clb); Isselee (crb). **171 Dreamstime.com:** Wkruck (clb). **172 Dreamstime.com:** Michael Elliott (br); Евгений Харитонов (cb); Jan Pokorný / Pokec (bc). **178 Science Photo Library:** Eddie Lawrence (c). **182 Alamy Stock Photo:** Cultura Creative (RF) / Rafe Swan (fbl); Kateryna Kon / Science Photo Library (c). **iStockphoto.com:** E+ / alanphillips (bc). **Science Photo Library:** David Parker (bl). **185 Alamy Stock Photo:** Science Photo Library / Laguna Design (crb, cr). **Science Photo Library:** Kallista Images / Custom Medical Stock Photo (crb/Collagen). **186 Alamy Stock Photo:** imageBROKER / Erich Schmidt (c). **187 Ardea:** Agenzia Giornalistica Fotografic (bc). **Dreamstime.com:** Eris Isselee / Isselee (bl); Lauren Pretorius (fcrb). **188-189 Dorling Kindersley:** Wildlife Heritage Foundation, Kent, UK (Leopard). **190-191 Dreamstime.com:** Alfio Scisetti (Four o'clock flower). **191 Alamy Stock Photo:** Peter Cavanagh (bc); Wayne Hutchinson (br). **192-193 Dreamstime.com:** Santia2 (peas). **193 Alamy Stock Photo:** FLHC 52 (br). **194 Getty Images:** Nicholas Eveleigh / Photodisc (blood bag). **196 Alamy Stock Photo:** Juan Gartner / Science Photo Library (c). **197 Alamy Stock Photo:** Sergii Iaremenko / Science Photo Library (c). **198 iStockphoto.com:** Gal_Istvan (br). **199 Dreamstime.com:** Isselee (cl). **202 Science Photo Library:** Rosenfeld Images Ltd (c). **205 Alamy Stock Photo:** Michael Tucker (br). **206 Dreamstime.com:** Judith Dzierzawa (c). **207 Alamy Stock Photo:** FineArt (bl); GL Archive (bc). **Science Photo Library:** (c). **210 Alamy Stock Photo:** Martin Shields (r). **212 Dreamstime.com:** Denira777 (bc). **Science Photo Library:** Geoff Kidd (bl). **213 Alamy Stock Photo:** Karin Duthie (clb); Sue Anderson (clb/Grass); Avalon / Photoshot License / Oceans Image (cr/grass); Minden Pictures / Tui De Roy (cr/Tortoise). **Dorling Kindersley:** Thomas Marent (br). **214 Alamy Stock Photo:** Natural History Museum, London (c). **216 Dreamstime.com:** Luckyphotographer (br); Pniesen (bc). **iStockphoto.com:** bogdanhoria (fbr). **217 Alamy Stock Photo:** blickwinkel / McPHOTO / NBT (c). **Dreamstime.com:** Matthew Irwin (br); Liligraphie (cl). **218 Alamy Stock Photo:** blickwinkel / Fieber (br); David Osborn (bc); Design Pics Inc / Ken Baehr (cr). **iStockphoto.com:** BrianEKushner (cra); E+ / Antagain (cb); superjoseph (cr/Panda); Anup Shah / Stockbyte (c). **219 Dreamstime.com:** Verastuchelova (clb). **Getty Images:** Natthakan Jommanee / EyeEm (bc). **iStockphoto.com:** Antagain (ca). **220 Alamy Stock Photo:** Citizen of the Planet / Peter Bennett (bc). **Dreamstime.com:** Empire331 (cl). **221 Alamy Stock Photo:** John Eccles (cr); Zoonar GmbH / Erwin Wodicka (clb). **Dreamstime.com:** Ronnachai Limpakdee (cl). **Getty Images:** VCG (crb). **222 Alamy Stock Photo:** A & J Visage (clb); Ulrich Doering (cl); Nature Picture Library / Anup Shah (cr); Arterra Picture Library / Clement Philippe (crb). **SuperStock:** Biosphoto (br). **224 Alamy Stock Photo:** Avalon / Photoshot License (clb); Liia Galimzianova (br). **Getty Images:** Paul Starosta (cla). **naturepl.com:** Jim Brandenburg (cra); Stefan Christmann (crb). **225 123RF.com:** Michael Lane (cl). **Dreamstime.com:** Stanislav Duben (cr). **226 123RF.com:** Maggie Molloy / agathabrown (cb/used 25 times). **Dorling Kindersley:** Alan Murphy (ca/Chickadee). **Dreamstime.com:** Henkbogaard (ca/Northern goshawk); Isselee (c/used 10 times). **227 Dreamstime.com:** Thawats (c); Yodke67 (cra). **228 Dorling Kindersley:** Stephen Oliver (cl). **229 123RF.com:** kajornyot (cb). **Dreamstime.com:** Nadezhda Bolotina (c). **231 Alamy Stock Photo:** F1online digitale Bildagentur GmbH / M. Schaef (bc). **Dreamstime.com:** Shao Weiwei / Shaoweiwei (br). **232 123RF.com:** Olexander Usik (cb). **235 ourworldindata.org:** Max Roser. **236 Alamy Stock Photo:** Paulo Oliveira (br). **Getty Images:** Diptendu Dutta / Stringer / AFP (bc). **Shutterstock:** Dogora Sun (c). **237 Alamy Stock Photo:** Francois Gohier / VWPics (clb); Robert Harding / Last Refuge (br); Suzanne Long (ca). **Getty Images:** Oxford Scientific (cr). **238 NASA:** GISS (b/Temperature). **NOAA:** (b/Carbon dioxide). **239 2019 Münchener Rückversicherungs-Gesellschaft, NatCatSERVICE:** (data taken from Munich Re, NatCatSERVICE (2019)) (c). **Alamy Stock Photo:** Galaxiid (br). **iStockphoto.com:** piyaset (bc). **240 123RF.com:** Juan Gil Raga (bc). **Alamy Stock Photo:** Cultura Creative (RF) / Stephen Frink (c); Hemis / LEMAIRE StΘphane / hemis.fr (br). **241 Alamy Stock Photo:** Kit Day (cl). **Dreamstime.com:** Mr.smith Chetanachan / Smuaya (br); Cowboy54 (cr). **naturepl.com:** Sylvain Cordier (bc). **242 Alamy Stock Photo:** National Geographic Image Collection / Jim Richardson (bl); RDW Aerial Imaging (c). **Getty Images:** Ulet Ifansasti (bc). **243 Alamy Stock Photo:** blickwinkel / Teigler (cr); Pat Canova (br); Paulo Oliveira (ca). **Dreamstime.com:** Jezbennett (bl). **ZSL (Zoological Society of London):** (cl). **244 Dreamstime.com:** Ymgerman (br). **245 Dreamstime.com:** Vchalup (b). **246 Alamy Stock Photo:** Tom Stack (crb). **Science Photo Library:** Gary Hincks (c). **Shutterstock:** Nady Ginzburg (br). **247 Alamy Stock Photo:** Dominique Braud / Dembinsky Photo Associates / Alamy (bc). **Getty Images:** Shivang Mehta / Moment Open (c). **248 Alamy Stock Photo:** imageBROKER / Florian Kopp (cb); inga spence (cr); robertharding / Yadid Levy (c). **Getty Images:** Corbis Unreleased / Frans Lemmens (crb). **249 Alamy Stock Photo:** Arterra Picture Library / Voorspoels Kurt (cl/Trawler); Paulo Oliveira (br); Mario Formichi photographer (crb); RGB Ventures / SuperStock / Scubazoo (cr). **Dreamstime.com:** Christian Delbert (cb). **250 Alamy Stock Photo:** Rick Dalton - Ag (cr). **Getty Images:** Universal Images Group (cl). **251 Alamy Stock Photo:** Science Photo Library / Molekuul (cl). **Dreamstime.com:** Stockr (ca); Ken Wolter (crb); Sorachar Tangjitjaroen (cr/Machine). **iStockphoto.com:** DarthArt (clb). **253 Alamy Stock Photo:** Nokuro (c). **Dorling Kindersley:** Arran Lewis (Morula 3D) / gagui (Turbosquid) (br). **254 Alamy Stock Photo:** PCN Photography (c). **Dreamstime.com:** Wavebreakmedia Ltd (cr). **255 Dreamstime.com:** Glolyla (cr). **256 Rex by Shutterstock:** Jeremy Young (br). **Science Photo Library:** AJ Photo (bc); David Leah (cr). **257 Alamy Stock Photo:** Sebastian Kaulitzki (cb). **Dreamstime.com:** Igor Zakharevich (c); Katerynakon (clb). **Forestry Images:** Bruce Watt, University of Maine, Bugwood.org (cr). **258 123RF.com:** Sebastian Kaulitzki (bl). **Alamy Stock Photo:** Custom Medical Stock Photo (bc); Werli Francois (cl). **Dreamstime.com:** Andor Bujdoso (br); Lightfieldstudiosprod (c); Mr.smith Chetanachan / Smuaya (cr). **260 123RF.com:** gl0ck33 (bc); lightwise (bl). **Shutterstock:** Plant Pathology (br). **261 Alamy Stock Photo:** Alexey Kotelnikov (c). **Science Photo Library:** Geoff Kidd (br); Kateryna Kon (bc). **SuperStock:** Science Picture Co (bl). **262 Alamy Stock Photo:** Nigel Cattlin (bc); Yon Marsh Natural History (br). **Science Photo Library:** Dr P. Marazzi (bl). **263 Getty Images:** Science Photo Library / NIBSC (cr). **Science Photo Library:** Nano Creative / Science Source (cl). **264 Science Photo Library:** (c). **265 Alamy Stock Photo:** Science Photo Library / Christoph Burgstedt (c). **267 Getty Images:** AFP / Narinder Nanu (cl). **269 Science Photo Library:** Steve Gschmeissner (cr). **270 Science Photo Library:** Aberration Films Ltd (tr). **271 Dreamstime.com:** Ahmad Firdaus Ismai (clb); Jenifoto40 (cla). **272 Alamy Stock Photo:** Science History Image (br). **naturepl.com:** Stephen Dalto (cl). **Science Photo Library:** Clouds Hill Imaging Lt (cr). **273 Alamy Stock Photo:** Nigel Cattlin (fbr); GKSFlorapics (fbl); Steve Tulley (br). **naturepl.com:** Adrian Davies (cl). **Science Photo Library:** Dennis Kunkel Microscopy (bl)

All other images © Dorling Kindersley
For further information see:
www.dkimages.com